Women Poets
of the Americas

TOWARD

A PAN-AMERICAN

GATHERING

Edited by

JACQUELINE VAUGHT BROGAN

AND CORDELIA CHÁVEZ CANDELARIA

UNIVERSITY OF NOTRE DAME PRESS
Notre Dame, Indiana

Copyright 1999 by
University of Notre Dame Press
Notre Dame, IN 46556
All Rights Reserved
Manufactured in the United States of America

Library of Congress Cataloging-in-Publication Data

Women poets of the Americas : toward a pan-American gathering / edited
by Jacqueline Vaught Brogan and Cordelia Candelaria.

p.   cm.

Papers presented at a conference held Dec. 1995, Cancún, Mexico.

Includes bibliographical references (p.) and index.

ISBN 0-268-01956-8 (cl : alk. paper). — ISBN 0-268-01955-X (pbk.

: alk. paper)

1. Poetry—Women authors—History and criticism—Congresses.

2. America—Literatures—History and criticism—Congresses.

3. Poetry, Modern—20th century—History and criticism—Congresses.

4. Women and literature—America—Congresses.   5. Literature and
society—America—Congresses.   I. Brogan, Jacqueline Vaught, 1952- .

II. Candelaria, Cordelia.

PN1091.W66   1999

98-45417—dc21   —dc21

[809.1'0082]   98-45417

Women Poets of the Americas

CONTENTS

Contents

ACKNOWLEDGMENTS

The coeditors of this volume would like to acknowledge the support and help of several individuals and institutions in helping to bring this volume to completion.

First, we would like to thank the California State University, Los Angeles, for its continued support of the American Literature Association, which directly led to the special symposium, which, in turn, inspired this volume.

For special assistance in supporting that symposium, "Women Poets of the Americas," held in Cancún, December 1995, we would like to thank the Institute for Scholarship in the Liberal Arts and the University of Notre Dame Press at Notre Dame and the Department of English and the Department of Chicana and Chicano Studies at Arizona State University.

We would also like to thank all of the participants in that symposium for collectively creating a spirit that continued to inspire this book. We wish we could have included you all here. To the contributors to this volume, we appreciate your patience in our bringing this volume to completion.

Special thanks go to Margaret Gloster, for her work on the cover design; to Margo Shearman, for her outstanding work as copy editor; and most particularly to Nancy McMahon, who often bore the burden of last-minute detailed work with great patience and good cheer. We would also like to thank Jim Langford, Jeff

Acknowledgments

Gainey, and Ann Rice at the Press for their initial and continued support of this project.

Cordelia wishes to thank her husband, Ronald Beveridge, for his attendance at the symposium and for his everyday support, as well as her son, Clifford Candelaria, for living his commitment to feminist advocacy. Jacque would like to thank her children as well for their attendance at the symposium—for Jessica's clear embodiment of the next phase of womanhood in this world; for Evan's obvious excitement and the spoken wish in front of other women there that his mother's next book be "feministically divined."

The editors gratefully acknowledge permission to use material from the following sources:

Chap. 1: Short quote from "Passage" and "Metamorphosis of the Sorceress," as translated by Maureen Ahern, from *A Rosario Castellanos Reader,* by Rosario Castellanos, edited by Maureen Ahern, translated by Maureen Ahern and others. Copyright (c) 1988. By permission of Maureen Ahern, Fondo de Cultura Economica, and the University of Texas Press.

Chap. 2: Quotation from "Today Is Not the Day," reprinted from *The Marvelous Arithmetics of Distance,* by Audre Lorde. Copyright © 1993. Reprinted by permission of W. W. Norton & Company. Quotation from *Zami: A New Spelling of My Name,* by Audre Lorde. Copyright © 1982. Reprinted by permission of The Crossing Press.

Chap. 3: From *Good Bones and Simple Murders,* by Margaret Atwood. Copyright (c) 1983, 1992, 1994 by O. W. Toad Ltd. A Nan A. Talese Book. Used by permission of Doubleday, a division of Bantam Doubleday Dell Publishing Group, Inc. The lines from "Snapshots of a Daughter-in-Law," the lines from "Diving into the Wreck," from *The Fact of a Doorframe: Poems Selected and New, 1950–1984,* by Adrienne Rich. Copyright © 1984 by Adrienne Rich. Copyright (c) 1975, 1978 by W. W. Norton & Company, Inc.

Copyright (c) 1981 by Adrienne Rich. Reprinted by permission of the author and W. W. Norton & Company, Inc. *Selected Poems, 1965–1975,* by Margaret Atwood, copyright © 1976 by Houghton Mifflin Company. Excerpts from "Circe/Mud Poems," by Margaret Atwood.

Chap. 4: Passages from H.D.'s *Trilogy.* Copyright © 1973 by Norman Holmes Pearson. Passages from Susan Howe's *The Non-conformist's Memorial.* Copyright © 1993 by Susan Howe. Used by permission of New Directions Publishing Corporation. Passages from Kathleen Fraser's *When New Time Folds Up.* Copyright © 1993 by Kathleen Fraser. Used by permission of Chax Press.

Chap. 5: "Pastoral," "After Reading Mickey in the Night Kitchen for the Third Time Before Bed," "Genetic Expedition," from *Grace Notes,* by Rita Dove. Copyright © 1989 by Rita Dove. Reprinted by permission of the author and W. W. Norton & Company, Inc. "Heroes," "Afield," "Rusks," "Lost Brilliance," "Her Island," from *Mother Love,* by Rita Dove. Copyright © 1995 by Rita Dove. Reprinted by permission of W. W. Norton & Company, Inc. (The excerpts from Rita Dove's poems "Magic," "Weathering Out," "Daystar," and "Motherhood," from her book *Thomas and Beulah,* Carnegie-Mellon University Press, Pittsburgh, © 1986 by Rita Dove, are reprinted by permission of the author.

Chap. 6: Reprinted by permission of Farrar, Straus & Giroux, Inc.: Excerpts from *The Complete Poems 1927–1979,* by Elizabeth Bishop. Copyright © 1979, 1983 by Alice Helen Methfessel. Excerpts from *The Collected Prose,* by Elizabeth Bishop. Copyright © 1984 by Alice Helen Methfessel. Excerpts from *One Art,* by Elizabeth Bishop. Copyright © 1994 by Alice Helen Methfessel. Introduction and compilation copyright © 1994 by Robert Giroux.

Chap. 7: Excerpts from: "The Levee: Letter to No One," by Lorna Lee Cervantes. In *Frontiers: A Journal of Women Studies* 11.1. Copyright © 1990. "Bird Ave.," by Lorna Lee Cervantes. In

Acknowledgments

Chicana Creativity and Criticism: Charting New Frontiers in American Literature. Maria Herrera-Sobek and Helena Maria Viramontes, guest eds. for *The Americas Review* 15.3–4. Copyright © 1987. "Visions of Mexico While at a Writing Symposium in P.T., Washington," "Poema para los Californios Muertos," Epigraph. In *Emplumada,* by Lorna Lee Cervantes. University of Pittsburgh Press. Copyright © 1981. Used by permission of Lorna Lee Cervantes.

Chap. 8: Excerpts from *that they were at the beach—aeolotropic series,* by Leslie Scalapino. North Point Press. Copyright © 1985. Used by permission of Leslie Scalapino.

Chap. 9: Selections from *The Cell:* Hejinian, Lyn: *The Cell,* 3 lines from p. 157, 8 lines from p. 214, 9 lines from p. 215, and 4 lines from p. 217 (Los Angeles: Sun & Moon Press, 1992), © 1992 by Sun & Moon Press. Reprinted by permission of the publisher.

Chap. 10: From *A Silence Opens,* by Amy Clampitt. Copyright © 1994 by Amy Clampitt. Reprinted by permission of Alfred A. Knopf, Inc.

Chap. 11: Reprinted by permission of Farrar, Straus & Giroux, Inc.: Excerpts from *The Complete Poems 1927–1979,* by Elizabeth Bishop. Copyright © 1979, 1983 by Alice Helen Methfessel. Excerpts from *One Art: Letters,* by Elizabeth Bishop, selected and edited by Robert Giroux. Copyright © 1994 by Alice Helen Methfessel.

Chap. 12: Excerpts from "Poetry," by Gerald Stern. In *Jewish-American History and Culture,* edited by Jack Fischel and Sanford Pinsker. Copyright © 1992. Used by permission of Garland Publishing, Inc. Excerpts from *PM/AM: New and Selected Poems,* by Linda Pastan. Copyright © 1992. Used by permission of W. W. Norton & Company, Inc. *An Early Afterlife,* by Linda Pastan. Copyright © 1995. Used by permission of W. W. Norton & Company,

Inc. *Heroes in Disguise,* by Linda Pastan. Copyright © 1991. Used by permission of W. W. Norton & Company, Inc.

Chap. 13: Excerpts from "Letter from the End of the Twentieth Century," "Perhaps the World Ends Here," "The Woman Who Fell from the Sky," from *The Woman Who Fell from the Sky,* by Joy Harjo. Copyright © 1994 by Joy Harjo. Reprinted by permission of W. W. Norton & Company, Inc. Excerpts from "Motion," "Skeleton of Winter," "Remember," "New Orleans," from *She Had Some Horses,* by Joy Harjo. Appears by permission of the publisher, Thunder's Mouth Press. Copyright 1983 by Thunder's Mouth Press. Excerpts from Joy Harjo, "Deer Dancer," "Grace," "Deer Ghost," "Crossing Water," "For Anna Mae Pictou Aquash," "We Must Call a Meeting," "Hearshed," "Song for the Deer and Myself to Return On," "Original Memory," "The Real Revolution Is Love," "Legacy," "The Book of Myths," from *In Mad Love and War,* © 1990 by Joy Harjo, Wesleyan University Press by permission of University Press of New England.

Chap. 14: Excerpts from *She Tries Her Tongue . . . Her Silence Softly Breaks,* by M. Nourbese Philip. Copyright © 1989. Used by permission of the author and Ragweed Press.

Chap. 15: Excerpts from *Nappy Edges,* by Ntozake Shange. Copyright © 1972, 1974, 1975, 1976, 1977, 1978 by Ntozake Shange. Reprinted by permission of St. Martin's Press. Reprinted with the permission of Simon & Schuster from *For Colored Girls Who Have Considered Suicide/When the Rainbow Was Enuf,* by Ntozake Shange. Copyright © 1975, 1976, 1977 by Ntozake Shange. "Easter Sunday," "Song for My Father," "Sorcery," from *Danger and Beauty,* by Jessica Hagedorn. Copyright (c) 1993 by Jessica Hagedorn. Used by permission of Viking Penguin, a division of Penguin Books USA, Inc. Excerpts from Bob Kaufman, *The Ancient Rain.* Copyright © 1981 by Bob Kaufman. Reprinted by permission of New Directions Publishing Corp.

INTRODUCTION

"None of the books has ever got it right," states Elizabeth Bishop's colonized version of colonizer Robinson Crusoe, a statement that applies to this book too. Given the obvious and long privileging of male writings, the poetry written by women has been historically undervalued. And although this century has witnessed an explosion of women writers—and recognition of women writers— even here the collective voice(s) of women have been categorized usually according to national origin and sometimes by race and ethnicity. As a result the complex matrix that characterizes much of the poetry written by women in the Western Hemisphere has not usually been considered as transnationally or transracially related, certainly not *pan*-American. While much of it is not explicitly so related—that of Cuban Gertrudis Gomez de Avellaneda or United Statesian Emily Dickinson, for instance—much of it is. In particular, recent contemporary verse seems frequently intent upon breaking boundaries of gender and genre and on crossing borders of geography, race, and ethnicity. But even when the transnational relatedness is implicit, women writers of the so-called New World are, in the words of New Englander Anne Bradstreet, sister "female wits" frequently besieged by "carping tongue[s]" who still insist sewing needles and thread "better fit" their hands.

The purpose of this anthology of essays is to begin bringing together the diverse but not always disparate voices of women poets of the Americas—with the emphasis on the word *begin*—for it is our belief that despite the disparate origins of the poets discussed in this volume, there are nonetheless many cultural experiences and perspectives that the women poets of the Americas share and which their poetry documents, historicizes, criticizes, valorizes, and even helps to create. As "Canto al Parto del Sexto Sol," by Tejana poet Inez Hernandez, describes it, the poem speaks on "behalf of ourselves"—which is not a "self" defined by race, gender, or place, but "humanity" or "all that lives all that is." Similarly, Elizabeth Bishop's poetry gives voice equally to poor and disenfranchised men in Brazil and to her distant white relatives in Nova Scotia. This is not to say that some women poets of the Americas do not affirm their respective individualities and cultural perspectives, often in emphatic particularity. Some of the poets discussed in this volume readily prove otherwise. Yet the concrete specifics of the poets' national, ethnic, or religious identity and economic position do not necessarily negate the interconnectedness of the poetry. In fact, the simultaneous merging and diverging of innumerable "boundaries" prove most characteristic of the realities (whether ethnic, political, or aesthetic) of the literature and life of this hemisphere in the last four centuries, and most certainly so in the last half of this century.

Our emphasis on the *beginning* aspect of this book's purpose in holding an inter-American feminist lens to poetry is a way of acknowledging one obvious fact about this (and any other) finite literary collection: it lacks many viewpoints on verse we would have liked to have included. For example, while the various poets represented here collectively offer a feminist perspective, the multiplicity of "feminisms" flourishing today means that some are not represented here. Furthermore, like all anthologies, this one of necessity leaves out essays on many poets from many countries which we wish we could have included in order to present a more complete look at the diversity and the interconnections of women poets in this hemisphere. It is crucial to note that this volume is a collection of only a small portion of the remarkable papers given at the American Literature Association Symposium entitled "Women Poets of the Americas," held in Cancún, December 14–17, 1995. Limited as even the symposium was by time and space, the representation of individual poets and critics, as well as diverse ethnic and national identities, ideologies, and poetic styles, was similarly constricted. And yet the original symposium from which this volume derives included excellent papers on a remarkable range of poets, including H.D., Mina Loy, Anne Sexton, Inés Hernández, Sandra Cisneros, Bernice Zamora, Gabriela Mistrál, Miriam Moscona, Náomi Quiñonez, Barbara Kingsolver, Linda Hogan, Wendy Rose, Fran Adler, Judy Grahn, and Alejandra Pizarnik, who are not included here. There were as well a host of other panels on particular subjects such as Native American women poets, Tejana poets, Chicana and Latina poets, Jewish poets, and others on "shifting geographies" or "performative myths." We should also mention that since many of the fine male and female critics who attended this symposium are themselves accomplished poets, the symposium concluded with an excellent poetry reading of original work that truly celebrated and gave voice to our collective, as well as individual, efforts in bringing together the women poets of the Americas, as well as our personal voices.

However, due to constraints of space and size that all books inevitably face, our reluctant (or perhaps "resistant" is the preferred feminist metaphor) decision for the published volume here was to select essays focused on contemporary women poets which illuminate specifically the three topics compressed in our title, *Women Poets of the Americas: Toward a Pan-American Gathering*—i.e., gender, genre, and geography/politics. Obviously, the essays collected here overlap in terms of these larger categories. Maria Bolivar's essay, for example, could easily be placed among the essays concerned with politics and geography rather than among the essays primarily concerned with gender. Similarly, Laura Hinton's essay could readily appear among the essays concerned with gender, rather than in the essays devoted to poetics. Yet taken together, the fifteen essays finally chosen for this volume have a coherence that offers a new and compelling look at the fine work being done by women in the Americas. For example, from the opening essay, which discusses the ironies of the naming of the "Americas," the conference itself, as well as Latina poetry, to the concluding two essays, which range from the Caribbean to the complexity of the "Californias," this volume spans a wide range of breaking geographical and political boundaries. In a different way, Charles Altieri's essay, which examines the puns inherent in Lyn Hejinian's "eye/I," dovetails in truly transethnic ways with a similar and even more complicated pun that Cordelia Candelaria finds in the poetry of Lorna Dee Cervantes and other Chicana writers. Along the way, we have new readings of Joy Harjo, Audre Lorde, Rita Dove, Margaret Atwood, Leslie Scalapino, Linda Pastan, Amy Clampitt, Elizabeth Bishop, Jessica Hagedorn, Ntozake Shange, Kathleen Fraser, Susan Howe, and Rosario Castellanos (among others). Nevertheless, despite our enthusiasm for the essays individually and for the volume's collective achievement, we still deeply regret that we are unable to print here more essays devoted to poetry from South or Central America, poetry from Canada or from the Pacific, poetry from other ethnic, religious, or national backgrounds, or poetry from the early part of this century.

We are certain, given current poetic and critical trends, that this step toward a transnational and transracial understanding of women's poetry in this hemisphere will be followed with excellent future work in this area. We are thus pleased in this volume to present essays focusing on gender by María Bolívar, Anna Wilson, Martine Watson Brownley, Cynthia Hogue, and Susan Van Dyne. Critics attending more to the craft or poetics of their various poets include Margaret Dickie, Cordelia Candelaria, Laura Hinton, and Charles Altieri. Those primarily focused on politics or geography include Celeste Goodridge, Susan McCabe, Sanford Pinsker, Janet McAdams, Cristanne Miller, and Maria Damon.

Finally, we gratefully acknowledge that the original symposium from which this volume emerged was financially and spiritually supported by the Departments of English of California State University, Arizona State University, and the University of Notre Dame, as well as by the Institute for Scholarship in the

Introduction

Liberal Arts at Notre Dame. Especially fitting (given the meaning of the institution's name) has been the willingness of the University of Notre Dame Press to support this volume from its inception to its publication. We offer this final product in the spirit of catholicity—i.e., a reaching toward and respecting, if not literally capable of representing, the various constituencies and countries of this hemisphere. In this way we pay tribute to all the chronicles of women's experience of the Americas, whether written or spoken, past or future. And while Crusoe—if not Bishop—might have meant "getting it right" in a narrow monolithic sense, in these *postererías del siglo*—or the closing moments of this century—we are glad at least to get it *write,* or written, and to have had the collective and interactive *rite* of poetry at the symposium that inspired this volume. This volume then is both a celebration of women poets of the Americas and a calling "to" an anticipated and as yet unrealized gathering of voices. In this sense it is not merely entitled, but is genuinely dedicated, to the Women Poets of the Americas.

Jacqueline Vaught Brogan
Cordelia Chávez Candelaria

PART I

Women (Gender)

I

Unappeasable and Arrogant: Women and the Faces of Death (Irreconciliables y soberbias: La mujer y los rostros de la muerte)

MARÍA DOLORES BOLÍVAR

I. OVERTURE

There is not *a* single tradition in Latin America, for the region is anything but a monolithic quantum. *Unappeasable* and *arrogant* are terms brought together here to represent the *pluri*logic sense of discontinuity and challenge women have impressed on their writing. Noncanonical authors have endured discursive death, as sometimes their writing led to their actual physical death, much in the way that pluralogy, limited by the singular *America*, has been repressed in its diversity, through texts and maps. In focusing what I code as "faces of death" in contemporary Latin American women poets, I intend to point to an understanding of *death* represented and constructed as a way of rendering women—evil, loose, untamed . . . —free from patriarchal yoke. My approach to death leans not on its mythical symbolism, though myth and history are unequivocally intertwined. I view death as a means of resistance (one rarely studied as a key element in the construction of postcolonial discourse) and of the repositioning of women in the constitution of their voice.

In the cocktail of current theoretical debate, *pastiche*—representing theoretical disorder—comes forth as a distinctive tag that permits us, the otherwise unheard, invisible, or dead, to be acknowledged as being present. One imposed backdrop to the culture of pastiche is exemplified by the fashionable "virtual."

3

In grasping the realm of the virtual the notion of *the imaginary* crafted by Benedict Anderson becomes a handy reference.[1] The imaginary, *substantiae essentialis* of nations, draws on the well of construction, performance, and writing; the imaginary is ultimately a subdued and complex process of solidity and finitude detaching and, by its own virtue, objectifying. We cannot do away with the imaginary; it is the stuff that makes nations and nationalisms, drawing boundaries and walls with an invisible pen, assuming symbolic realities as shielded and aseptic antipodes or real-realities. Unquestionably a part of that illegitimate bunch of unnamed realities, I praise *pastiche,* in its plurilogic complexity, as a valued artifact to stand for the entelechy that has attracted minds to the plane of poetry and poetics that is *The Americas.*

Should I manage to get away with defining traditions as mere splinters of religions, the poetry I refer to stands for the pervasively antireligious, antipolitical, even antipoetic character of an illegitimate bunch of daughters of modernity: the many Americas, represented in the resisting female voices forged throughout the histor*ies* of our literature*s.* Among the writers I quote in this analysis are the Mexicans Rosario Castellanos (1925–76) and Elena Milán (dates unknown), the Peruvian Blanca Varela (1926–), and the Puerto Rican Lolita Lebrón (dates unknown).

II. *MÁS VALE LA MUERTE QUE EL OLVIDO*
(BETTER DEAD THAN FORGOTTEN)

The tragic end of some Latin American women writers offers testimony of the hardship endured by these authors in their struggle to represent gender difference. In South America, Juana Manuela Gorriti (1818–92) spent practically all her life in exile from the home of her spouse, the Bolivian caudillo Manuel Isidoro Belzú; Delmira Agustini (1886–1914) died at the hands of her husband; Alfonsina Storni (1892–1938) and Alejandra Pizarnik (1936–72) committed suicide. In a chapter devoted to Argentina in David William Foster's *Handbook of Latin American Literature,* Naomi Linstrom points out how Pizarnik was known for her focus upon extremes of experience and how the cult to her came about after her death (51). Other female writers, contemporaries of Pizarnick, have not yet been accorded the attention deserved by the merits of their work and are undergoing that other form of death: discursive death. Olga Orozco (1920–) and Luisa Pasamanik (1930–), both Argentinean poets, fit well this description.

Gabriela Mistral (1889–1957), Nobel laureate in 1945, has been used to symbolize nationalist Chile in a way that narrows our perspective of her image as a successful writer. The world acutely represented in Mistral's "Sonetos de la muerte" (Sonnets of death) is a world where women are forced to hide their emotions and feelings, confined as they are within the desolation of a silent existence. Other Chilean poets, like Teresa Wilms Montt (1893–1921), Winet de Rokha (1896–1951), Maria Tagle (1899–1946), Chela Reyes (1904–), and Mila Oyarzun (1912–), were published in Mistral's time and never granted recognition. Even though some of the best poets in Latin America are women, why is it that the names of Teresa María Rojas (1902–), Clementina Suárez (1903–), Julia De Burgos (1914–53), Claribel Alegría (1926–), Rosario Ferré (1938–), Agüéda Pizarro (1941–), Belkis Cuza Malé (1942–), Nancy Morejón (1944–), Jeanette Miller (1945–), Diana Bellessi (1946–), Gioconda Belli (1948–), Coral Bracho (1956–) or Barbara Delano (1961–) remain virtually unknown to the majority of readers?

Dissenting voices have assumed death as their refuge from a unifying mainstream culture: "Muerte sin fin" (Endless Death) is the title of a poem by José Gorostiza, which represents postrevolutionary Mexico, where cultural diversity and the heterogeneous character of the nation remained critical to a civil society eclipsed by the reconstitution of a centralist state. Death, as stated in the novel by Cuban Alejo Carpentier, *The Kingdom of This World*, was the ultimate liberating path followed by its protagonist Mackendal, to lead Haitians to independence in the early nineteenth century. *Victoria o muerte* was a popular guerrilla slogan of the 1970s. *Primero muerta* (dead first), *ni muerta* (not even dead), *si me han de matar mañana, que me maten de una vez* (if they will kill me tomorrow, let them kill me today)—these are common forms of speech to express pride in Spanish.

During the early phase of the Conquest of Mexico, suicide became a way to avoid contact with Spanish invaders, one of many forms of death that determined the course of history in the "discovered" lands. Examples of how suicide was used in resisting the Spanish colonizer are found consistently in the chronicles of the Spanish Conquest. In the northern Tepehuan region, today the states of Jalisco and Nayarit, when Franciscan and Jesuit missionaries advanced into Indian territories, public immolation by women defying evangelization was frequent. In fact, as early as 1542 the *Leyes Nuevas* (the New Laws instituted by Spain) attempted to stop the native people from taking their lives. Fray Bartolomé de Las Casas called the indigenous way of resisting humiliation and slavery by resorting to death *el desgane vital* (or loss of desire). A shaman, according to the chronicles of the *oidor* Alonso de Zorita (1570), recommended infanticide and instigated mass suicide among Indians in Michoacán.[2] Chontal and Mixe communities actively practiced abstaining from sex as a means to protect their own kind from a life of servitude. In "El siglo de la Conquista" of *Historia general de México,* Alejandra Moreno Toscano tells us how abortion, abstinence, and collective suicide became so common that the Spaniards brought in slaves of other nations to supply themselves with workers for the invaded lands (351–52). For the most part, massive resistance by the victims of Spanish genocide remains undocumented, and historiography seldom represents the defense by death of the native communities in our continent.

Language was very powerful in crafting representations that eluded American realities. *El rescate,* the act of rescuing, is the term used by the Spaniards to refer to actual servitude of American people. To choose to die, in this context, meant to refuse to be rescued. The word *desgane,* lack of will, came to erode the agency of those who saw in death a means to resist invasion and genocide. The Nicaraguan poet and novelist Gioconda Belli reconstructs a fictional account of colonial times in her text "Porque aun lloramos," a fragment of *La mujer habitada.*

> Yo recibí noticias de las mujeres de Teguzigalpa. Habían decidido no acostarse más con sus hombres. No querían parirle esclavos a los españoles. (38)[3]

III. BOUND UP IN RAGE AND READY
TO DIE LIKE JUANA GALLO

In Mexico's popular epic, as captured by *corridos,* Juana Gallo symbolizes a woman whose only reason to live stems from her desire to die. Even the generals were scared of her, as she showed no fear, and her bravery proved to be the very texture of her agency. Her goal was to avenge her dead loved ones, in particular Chon, her man, by offering her own blood to the future of her country. Juana Gallo is nonetheless the male face of a woman fighting for the pride of her kind, and in her nickname, Rooster, there is an implicit downplaying of her femaleness, since *gallina* (chick), is used in Spanish to address, paradoxically, those who lack bravery. Juana Gallo became a legend, for, as Rosario Castellanos wrote in her poem "Passage," from *Materia Memorable* (1969), she transgressed the limits of her own nature and went beyond the average existence reserved to her kind, women: "Beyond the limits . . . " into a place "uninhabitable for my species . . . "[4] In searching to redefine gender roles, women have struggled, often in vain, to break away from those roles, assigned to *her* species, as described in the Peruvian Blanca Varela's poem "Monsieur Monod no sabe cantar," where she codes women as the outsiders of the social order:

> They will not let you in (*No te quieren dejar entrar*). With your little mortal eyes go around the apple. . . .
>
> (*Canto Villano* 24)

Sor Juana Inés de la Cruz (1648–95) and Sor Juana Francisca de Castillo y Guevara (1671–1742) stand as examples of voices forged outside dominant counterreformist thought in the seventeenth and early eighteenth centuries. Although only some Latin American women wrote and published their work in the early modern period, they were emulated by increasing numbers who came to the written word in the following centuries. Notwithstanding the discontinuity and the diachronicity that opposes the coding of women within high tradition, there are also important connections among Criolla women (American-born Spaniards), Mestizo women, and Indian women. Sor Juana Inés de la Cruz, at the start of a *criollista* redefinition of life and death in the Americas, pointed out the shifting borders between church and state and claimed the right to write as a means to express civil unrest.[5] Sor Juana, a member herself of a bastion of censorship—the convent—rebelled against the restricting roles imposed on women by choosing a textual life fashioned precisely by the texture of an alternative discourse.

Women in their communities have shared sentiments about death, as topographies and texts have remained instrumental to dominant power and discourses. Uruguayan critic Angel Rama noted in his posthumous book *Ciudad letrada* how the order imposed by colonialism relied on the written word and on forging a printed discourse, where as the oral word was reduced to the realm of the uncertain and the precarious (9). The rigidity that censorship secured in all textual representations was none other than a vain attempt to subdue reality. Thus, to come in contact with the material real, one has to reinvent, to reimagine all that underwent the vicissitudes of history and death. Another Latin American critic, José Joaquín Blanco, attempted in his book *La literatura en la Nueva España* an ambitious reconfiguration of our perspective on literatures in the Americas, by pointing out how censorship left us with an ever shifting oral culture, one that has as its main trait the mark of forgetfulness and death (34).

Latin American literatures, at the outset of nationalist movements, saw the power of language affirmed in its assignment of representational elements to gender. A Peruvian writer, Catalina Recavarren (birthdate unknown), who wrote between 1925 and 1976, depicted the need for women to struggle against the power structure of memory and the canon. Her book *Memorias de una desmemoriada* (Memories of a memoryless one, 1976) alluded to the painful process of her past as a silenced poet. In Ecuador, Dolores Veintimilla de Galindo (1830–57) stood against discrimination and represented the injustices undergone by women poets like herself. Veintimilla de Galindo committed suicide in 1857 after her text *Necrology* (1857) caused violent reactions against her, because of her defense of Indians.

Romanticism, throughout the second half of the nineteenth century, was openly assigned a character of femininity by virtue of its tendency to focus on those aspects of human life that dealt more with the senses and the spaces we have come to differentiate as domestic spaces. Romantic and Modernista poetry, at the turn of the last century, were imbued with the interpretive mechanisms of male dominant discourse. Postmodernist poetry written by women, for the most part influenced by postwar vanguards (1920s), will show a concern for abandoning the sentimental qualities attributed to female authors. Aralia López González, in her methodological introduction to the book *Sin imágenes falsas, sin falsos espejos,* analyzes how language has omitted the universal character of women by denying them presence of discursive subjectivity, and thus the praxis of their agency (36).

IV. DISCOURSE: THAT OTHER REALM CALLED REALITY

Readings are never innocent. We need to resituate discourses and construct/constitute the voices that represent women. Readings, as Donna Haraway has accurately proposed, often work and function with the logic of technology; they are ways of appropriating realities.[6] Readings in and of themselves produce images, rearticulate modes of apprehension, facilitate the flow of power, propose the topography and the remapping of power, geographies, bodies, and minds (*conciencias*). "A word is a stare," wrote Rosario Castellanos in her poem "Nonentity," in a reiteration whereby she situated women as those who stare and have no voice.[7] Women writers share in this sentiment of frustration of being the staring transgressor, ostracized by their society. Puerto Rican Lolita Lebrón, who spent twenty-five years as a political prisoner in the United States, represented herself as "a wanderer without a home" (*Sándalo en la celda* 12). Women's guilt is passed on to Latin Americans as it is ingrained in Western dominant thought. Elena Milán, a Mexican, wrote poignantly in her poem "Decent Women" to distance herself from the role assigned to her, her mother, and the mother of her mother:

> . . . how many sentences of ostracism did they decree in your town?
> How many burials? How many bodies did they brand with the mark
> of Evil?[8]

Juana de Ibarbourou, an Uruguayan writer of the twenties, brought into her work her concerns for the role played by women in society. De Ibarbourou offered in her poem "Rebelde" an innovative proposal to renew the female spirit in facing death. Charon, the boatman ferrying the souls of the dead across the river, would face her, a passerine lark, daring and seductive:

> Whatever you might wish, whatever leer
> your two eyes might emit,
> masters of fear,
> Charon, I in your boat will be a scandal.[9]

In "Rebelde," Charon, the patriarch, is defeated by the most lively creature one might imagine, a bird, a lark. De Ibarbourou thus enables her female character to turn her ubiquitous presence in the solemn world of Charon into a challenging act of repudiation.

Women's lives, determined by the marginal role reassigned to them by the patriarchal character of the modern nation and the age of mechanical reproduction, depend on their grasping of how the patriarchal system precludes them from life, and exiles them into death. Women poets often share in viewing women as lacking territoriality—in a diasporic search, confined either within or outside the margins, carried on by erring creatures scattered about the peripheral realms of a cultural being (ex)centric, as Jean Franco suggests in *Plotting Women* (Introduction xv). Women poets textualize themselves as eternal migrants in search of their partitioned land, their fragmented voices. Rosario Castellanos resorted to prosopopoeia to transpose the lot of women into a tiny Mayan badger who hops down the ages in an endless search for herself/himself. Reflecting on the Mayan badger, she perceives the minuscule space granted to her/him at the archaeological museum. The badger, *el tejoncito*, takes a diminutive inflection in her/his name and wanders across centuries, unnoticed, belittled, and ultimately forgotten.

> Covering up your laughter
> with your tiny hand
> you come hopping
> down the centuries. . . . [10]

"Who will utter the silences of my dead?" questioned Castellanos in her poem "Elegy", from her book *Rescue from the World,* alluding to the word *rescate* euphemistically employed. "Who will weep the ruin of my house?/Amidst the solitude a bone flute/ spilling austere, sad, piercing music." Castellanos advanced the perspective of a world of multiple voices, though silenced, an important key to reassign words meanings and sounds unheard. The two primary elements, words and silences, are paired by the writer in an effort to represent how they are bound in a reality where territories and expressions are predetermined by rules and codes of power: "There are no words./(This, this is my country./Behold the terreplein for the dance./There are no words.)"[11]

In "Metamorphosis of the Sorceress" (*Materia Memorable* 1969), Castellanos describes abundantly the meanings of silence, a form of absence and death: "Woman, holding her masks, playing at self-deception/and deceiving others,/but when she saw her own true face/it was a flower of pale withered petals: love, absence, and death./On its corolla/a faint scar." There is a hidden protagonistic role played by gendered/degendered voices in their relay of truth: "Because of all she knew she was obedient and sad/and when she departed down that street/—the one she knew so well—of good byes,/beautiful creatures came out to bid her farewell,/the ones she had rescued from chaos, shadow, and/ contradiction and made live/in the magic atmosphere her spirit created."[12]

In another poem, "Presence" (*Lívida Luz* 1960), Castellanos's coding of women gave way to the fantasizing of an uncensored future: "Some day I'll know. This body that has been/my hostel, my prison, my hospital, is my tomb." And a conceptual death reappears in a notion of displacement of a character whose life was wasted in a hopeless search for a life of infertility: "Whatever I have joined in a worry,/a pain, a memory/will desert in search of water, leaf,/original spore, inert matter and stone." A strong image of imprisonment unquestionably alludes to the vows that tie up women in an infinite existence of servitude, "This knot that I have been (bound up in rage, betrayal, hope,/sudden insight, surrender,/hunger, cries of fear and helplessness,/joy flashing in the shadows/and words, and love and love and loves)/the years will cut through." This image relates also to death in a parallel that incorporates irony in the same poem by suggesting even in death women risk a state of nonidentity: "Now one will see the destruction. Nobody/will pick up the unfinished page . . . /And yet, brother, lover, son,/friend, ancestor,/there is no aloneness, there is no death,/although I forget and though I end. . . . "[13]

EPILOGUE

Resistance takes place in the deepest of material worlds; by rearguarding itself, it surpasses the power of the imaginary through the actual experience of distinct and shifting geographies of grounds and bodies, clandestine and, thus, free. Resisting realities are so real that one feels they can be touched, tasted, inhabited in their ubiquitous, yet fragile and temporary, diachronicity. Death occupies a space among these realities, as it remains the ultimate end to the reconstitution of the fragmented mosaic of all resisting communities. The dialectic of subjectivity versus objectivity, though newly and duly old, has collected its toll. Today's struggles take place in the realm of discourse. I refer to struggles for power that focus on interpreting realities, as the main theses of Jean Franco's *Plotting Women* invite us to assume: plots, conspiracies (Introduction xi).

In pasting together these apparently unconnected thoughts

produced by Latin women in the Americas, one encounters their sense of the proximity of death to themselves and to their writing. To write in their context entails a risk often translated into a living death. Perhaps, like Coyolxauhqui, the Mexica goddess butchered by her brothers allied against her in a contest for power, women in the Americas will not be ultimately appeased until their puzzle-like existences are put together again. Women's death is an act of agency, and an *apuesta por el futuro* (a bid to the future), a claim advanced in the name of a hypothetical discursive space where her criminal graffiti, left anonymously all over the place, will suddenly become the legitimate mark of her acknowledged existence.

At the close of our millennium, increased migrations, among which are large numbers of women, and the unprocessed surplus of human resources in a depleted world have turned the texture of reality unpredictable and ubiquitous. The many decades contained in the metaphor "cold war" created a dream oasis that most of us who were born before the sixties grew up craving: a world without walls. Only in our current decade the walls have reappeared regeneratively in a peculiar process of epimorphosis: small walls, stone walls, iron walls, even virtual walls, proliferating to deface the very concept of maps. A process parallel to what we have come to know as postmodernity has triggered the multiplication of nodes of marginality and fragmented identities. It is necessary, in this heterogeneous context, to recodify the signs of women and marginal (subaltern) subjectivities into discourses (languages of power) intelligible to the subaltern classes. Third World women are often represented as imperfect, deterritorialized, marginal constructions (*dejadas de la mano de dios,* left without God's help). The marginal writings of women have endured the type of resistance that communities have resorted to in order to survive the bulldozer of modernity. In mocking Mexico's cynical prayer to modernity—*Pobre México, tan lejos de Dios y tan cerca de los Estados Unidos*—many women seem to exist so far from God, and so close to the edges of canonical constraints imposed from a dominant metropolis. To look at the poetry written by women in Latin America turns us into a world of shattered interlocutions where to come of age, as cleverly stated by Hélène Cixous in her work *Coming to Writing and Other Essays,* might mean

> . . . to make room for the wandering . . . to give it a place and time . . . to give, seek, touch, call, bring into the world a new being who won't restrain me, who won't drive me away, won't perish from very narrowness. (7)

NOTES

1. Benedict Anderson, *Imagined Communities: Reflections on the Origin and Spread of Nationalism* (London: Verso, 1986) 23–24.

2. Gerardo Decorme, "The Tepehuan Revolt, an Historical Review," *Mid-America* 7. 1 (Jan. 1936): 9. *Oidores* (and *veèdores*) were people who had the bureaucratic role of eavesdropping. In colonial times a hypertrophy of bureaucracy existed due to the paranoia that infected what was at that time the largest empire in the memory of western Judeo-Christian humanity. Both bureaucratic positions literally meant serving as the eyes and ears of metropolitan power authorized by the king of Spain. For a more extensive description of cultural and political life in northern Mexico, consult Decorme's complete major work, *La obra de los Jesuitas mexicanos durante la época colonial, 1572–1767,* in his *Misiones,* 2 vols., México, D.F.: Antigua Libreria Robredo de J. Porrúa e Hijos, 1941.

3. In English: "I heard from the women of Teguzigalpa. They had decided to no longer sleep with men. They didn't want to bear any more slaves for the Spanish."

4. Maureen Ahern, *A Rosario Castellanos Reader* (Austin: U of Texas P, 1988) 89.

5. Consistent with a new approach to cultural politics in the seventeenth century, intellectuals and influential politicians born in New Spain began to define a *criollo* identity that intended to free the newer generation from hierarchical/caste submission to *peninsulares,* who were until then the sole tenants of administrative and political power.

6. Donna Haraway, "A Manifesto for Cyborgs: Science, Technology and Socialist Feminism in the 1980s," *Socialist Review* 80 (1985): 84–85.

7. Doris Meyer and Marguerite Fernández Olmos, *Contemporary Woman Authors of Latin America* (Brooklyn, N.Y.: Brooklyn College P, 1983) 21.

8. Meyer and Olmos 41.

9. Meyer and Olmos 19.

10. Meyer and Olmos 31.

11. Meyer and Olmos 19.

12. Ahern 92.

13. Meyer and Olmos 20.

WORKS CITED

Ahern, Maureen. *A Rosario Castellanos Reader.* Austin: U of Texas P, 1988.

Belli, Gioconda. *La mujer habitada.* Managua: Editorial Vanguardia, 1988.

Blanco, José Joaquín. *La literatura en la Nueva España.* México, D.F.: Cal y Arena, 1989.

Carpentier, Alejo. *El reino de este mundo.* Barcelona: Editorial Seix Barral, 1967.

Castellanos, Rosario. *Lívida Luz.* México, D.F.: Universidad Nacional Autónoma de México, 1960.

———. *Materia Memorable.* México, D.F.: Universidad Nacional Autónoma de México, 1969.

Cixous, Hélène. *Coming to Writing and Other Essays.* Cambridge: Harvard UP, 1991.

Decorme, Gerardo. *La obra de los Jesuitas mexicanos durante la época colonial, 1572–1767.* 2 vols. Vol. 2, *Misiones.* México, D.F.: Antigua Lib. Robredo de J. Porrúa e Hijos, 1941.

———. "The Tepehuan Revolt, an Historical Review," *Mid-America* 7.1 (Jan. 1936): 9.

Franco, Jean. *Plotting Women: Gender and Representation in Mexico.* New York: Columbia UP, 1989.

Gorostiza, José. *Muerte sin fin.* México, D.F.: Universidad Nacional Autónoma de México, 1960.

Handbook of Latin American Literature. Comp. David William Foster. New York: Garland, 1987.

Historia general de México. Alejandra Moreno Toscano *et al.* México: El Colegio de México, 1976.

Lebrón, Lolita. *Sándalo en la celda.* Catano, P.R.: Editorial Betances, 1975.

López González, Aralia, ed. *Sin imágenes falsas, sin falsos espejos.* México, D.F.: El Programa de Estudios Interdisciplinarios de la Mujer de el Colegio de México, 1995.

Meyer, Doris, and Marguerite Fernández Olmos, eds. *Contemporary*

Woman Authors of Latin America. Brooklyn, N.Y.: Brooklyn College P, 1983.

Mistral, Gabriela. *Desolación.* New York: Instituto de las españas en los Estados Unidos, 1922.

Rama, Angel. *Ciudad letrada.* Hanover, N.H.: Ediciones del Norte, 1984.

Recavarren, Catalina. *Memorias de una desmemoriada.* Lima: Minerva, 1976.

Varela, Blanca. *Canto Villano.* Lima: Ediciones Arybalo, 1978.

Veintimilla de Galindo, Dolores. *Necrology.* Quito: Producciones literarias, 1908.

2

Rites/Rights of Canonization: Audre Lorde as Icon

ANNA WILSON

"I want the conjure woman," Jane Gallop says in *Around 1981: Academic Feminist Literary Theory* (1992; 169) of her disappointment with the academic tone and apparatus of the African American critical anthology *Conjuring: Black Women, Fiction, and Literary Tradition* (1985), remarking upon, and thus disavowing, her own investment in black folk authenticity, her desire for both the warm approving black mother and a cultural space of incontestable alterity. Unsurprisingly, what she wants is what she knows she won't get: this desire will have to be deferred, redirected into the satisfactions of self-scrutiny. In place of acceptance within blackness, she will have to settle for analyzing why she wants to be there and for the distance from desire that such knowledge brings. Having suspicions as to the political valence of a desire, being elegantly self-reflexive about one's theoretical practice: these are admirable qualities in criticism. But what, ultimately, should be the relation between white feminist critic and black text?

A short, oversimplified history of feminist literary criticism and the treatment of race: there was a time when white women used to write about other white women, unselfconsciously assuming that race could be subsumed within the encompassing embrace of gender. Such absence gave way, in the face of protest by those not figured, to a fitful tokenism, typified by a dozen anthologies in which white women wrote about white women but allowed a woman of color to round out the collection and write about (usually) African American women.[1] At this point, still, both writers and critics of color seemed inevitably and permanently marginal—good for demonstrating depths and complexities of oppression because so very unambiguously nonhegemonically positioned. Then African American writers, in particular, started to occupy a piece of the center ground: Hollywood movies, Nobel Prizes, inauguration poems, and presence of a nonmarginal kind in academia. The writing of white women began to include the texts of women of color not as tokens but as exemplary instances of resistance. These white women were themselves, by now, firmly enmeshed in academic institutions, and when they sought opposition they found it, with remarkable regularity, in the practices of Audre Lorde or Gloria Anzaldua, Toni Morrison, or Cherrie Moraga.[2] The next development, a stage of white feminist criticism still in progress, is one of self-reflexivity: rather than just write about white women writers or black women writers, white critics write about other white critics and their appropriation of texts of color. Jane Gallop examines her own desire for the purity of black otherness. Margaret Homans excoriates Judith Butler and Donna Haraway for their use of the textual strategies of women of colors as alibis for their deconstructive theoretical projects, taking up the analysis made by Morrison and Valerie Smith of a critical and cultural practice whereby blackness figures as embodiment, the ground of experience for the theoretical edifice of the white mind. Elizabeth Abel critiques Barbara Johnson and Homans, and her own reading of Morrison, arguing that both the limitation and the justification for white-on-black reading is the inexorable failure of identification between the two, that they thus work to render whiteness visible.[3] And here I am, one more white feminist adding another layer of refraction to these receding mirrorings. It is not hard to metaphorize this situation—perhaps as a pack of jackals worrying a carcass—but the anxious white feminists' enquiry into our own obsession with the texts of women of colors is not so simply an act of domination and victimization. To present it thus would be to repeat the move that has now been defamiliarized from all angles, presenting the black woman/text as the body upon which/from which others operate, figuring the black text as innocence and purity, the sign of otherness so fervently the object of white desire.

The question of consumption, of who is consumed by whom in the restless reading and rereading that is current feminist critical practice, is complicated. And the relation between critic and text is shifty too. The "conjure woman" is an active agent, one whose ways of knowing may not be so easily pinned down by theoretical practice. It is not necessarily the case that her invocation in white feminists' accounts of difference enacted, otherness articulated, repeats, *tout court,* the cannibal's appropriation of his vanquished foe's courage. Who controls the critical text if its figuration of disruption must be cast in the conjure woman's terms, and what has she to say of this passionate attention?

To address these questions through a reading of "Audre Lorde" as she figures in some recent texts must necessarily repeat the critical process I set out above. But in treating the iconography of Lorde as it occurs in both black and white texts, I seek not only to excavate multiple appropriations and their motivations, but also to emphasize Lorde's implicit and explicit resistance to her canonization.

FIGURING THE MOTHER IN BLACK

Afrekete: An Anthology of Black Lesbian Writing (1995) opens with an editors' introduction in which the title, "Afrekete," is identified as a borrowing from Lorde's *Zami: A New Spelling of My Name* (1982), where Afrekete appears as both Audre's lover and a mythic figure, "a perfect creation of the Black lesbian imagination" (xv): "We chose this title to pay homage to a seminal text . . . it is to Lorde's radical political and artistic legacy that we owe in a significant way the possibility of this book and the possibility of the expanse of the writing included herein" (xiv). In addition to this attribution of creation—the anthology itself born of Lorde's seed—the editors include an extract from *Zami* at the beginning of the selections and conclude the volume with one of Lorde's last poems. Brought forth by Lorde, the writing thus rests within her protective textual arms. "Tar Beach," the chapter from *Zami*, concerns Audre's meeting with Kitty/Afrekete at a Black lesbian party and their subsequent affair. The prose shifts from the precisely observed realistic detail of the party, where Audre categorizes exactly the dress codes of 1950s black butches and femmes and where Kitty wears light-colored, thickly applied makeup, to the visionary, mythic scene of their lovemaking where Kitty is Afrekete and they are one with an Africanized, abundant natural world. The placement of this piece seems to authorize the same journeying on the part of the writers who come after, a play between the mundane and the mythic. But such play is also restrained, end-stopped, by the final poem, "Today Is Not the Day." Dated April 1992, shortly before Lorde's death, it is about anticipating that dying, about leaving the living behind: "Today is not the day./It could be/but it is not."

Lorde's contribution thus moves from her birthing of black lesbian writing, through sex, to death. Within "Tar Beach"—itself, of course, an extract from the "biomythography" *Zami*, a selected-out fragment that stands for and yet does not represent the whole text—Afrekete and Audre's lovemaking is repeatedly described in terms both mythic and mundane. Its placement, and its internal organization, suggest that in the context of *Afrekete* it is produced as a genotype for Black Lesbian writing:

> I took a ripe avocado and rolled it between my hands until the skin became a green case for the soft mashed fruit inside, hard pit at the core. *I rose for a kiss in your mouth to nibble a hole in fruit skin near to the navel stalk, squeezed the pale yellow-green fruit juice in thin ritual lines back and forth over and around your coconut-brown belly.*
>
> *The oil and sweat from our bodies kept the fruit liquid, and I massaged it over your thighs and between your breasts until your brownness shone like a light through the veil of the palest green avocado, a mantle of goddess pear that I slowly licked from your skin.*
>
> Then we would have to get up to gather the pits and fruit skins and bag them to put out later for the garbagemen, because if we left them near the bed for any length of time, they would

call out the hordes of cockroaches that always waited on the side-
lines within the walls of Harlem tenements, particularly in the
smaller older ones under the hill of Morningside Heights. (15)

The abrupt shift between the world in which Afrekete glows di-
vine in her mantled, shining brownness and that profane place
where roaches cluster, barely hidden in the walls' interstices, wait-
ing to emerge, outlines the energy required to construct Lorde's
mythic space and that space's imperiled fragility. But such other-
ness too is made more itself by the proximity and imminence
of decay: the goddess, appareled in pear, is created by the cock-
roach's skittering path toward her throne, in her difference from
that perfection of the mundane.

"Today is not the day./It could be/but it is not." The power
of these simple lines comes, of course, from poet and reader's
awareness of how soon the "not" might be lifted, and from the
fragility of the resistance that the reiterated negation denotes;
the speaking of death as not here yet, not today, reinscribes its
arrival—tomorrow, or the next day. The poem defies and defines
whereof it speaks, both reiterating and holding off, in the double
movement of elegy. The positioning of "Today is not the day" in
Afrekete produces more than its own elegiac endings, of poem,
poet, and volume of writing, begun by Lorde and ending with
her almost-death and almost silence. For we read backward as
well as forward, in the moments before our own dying, turning
back from Lorde's death and our own toward the vibrant cele-
bration of "Tar Beach." And thus the deified Afrekete in her glo-
rious body is rendered mortal too, the waiting roaches the sign
of the flesh's inevitable decay, her divinity revealed as a fictive
act, a momentary balance above the worms of the earth and their
recombinant tendencies.

Afrekete figures Lorde as benevolent God/dess of creation.
She makes an artistic world; she protects the writing she has en-
gendered and enabled; dying, finally, she leaves the tradition she
founded secure. As a reading of Lorde, *Afrekete*'s is not the less
powerful for being incomplete. But that there's more to Lorde
than the maternal emerges from what the editors' selections

include, as well as from what they leave out. "Tar Beach" stands in for *Zami* in the anthology, and in the context of the introduction, it stands in also for Black Lesbian readers' self-discovery and recognition, as well as for Lorde's own arrival at identity. "Tar Beach" tells of the transformation of Audre and Afrekete's relationship into one that can be accommodated within the Harlem community: "It was onto 113th Street that we descended after our meeting under the Midsummer Eve's Moon, but the mothers and fathers smiled at us in greeting as we strolled down to Eighth Avenue, hand in hand" (18). It is the most "homelike" narrative sequence in *Zami* (the one instance of loving connection that is not subsequently betrayed). Kitty's metamorphosis into Afrekete is, however, a *change:* the journey the lovers make together begins at the gay girls' party where the environment is marked by signs not of African purity but rather by the taint of white, hegemonic overlay and infiltration, a layer as palpable in Lorde's narrative as Kitty's makeup. Beyond the boundaries of the extract itself lies the terrain of Audre's various entanglements with whiteness, racism, with black and white homophobia. Taking from Lorde's biomythography, the editors add a layer of myth work, a process intensified by their ordering of and commenting upon Lorde's texts: the Audre of *Afrekete* has transcended the struggle of *Zami*.

SACRED TEXTS AND RELICS

A Litany for Survival: The Life and Work of Audre Lorde (1995), directed by Ada Gay Griffin and Michelle Parkerson, is unequivocally an African American text in terms of its means of production, its funding, and its focus. However, its availability to a white audience, and the awareness of one's racial positioning that watching the film requires, makes it valuable as a means to discuss both white and black appropriations and representations of Lorde.

The film immediately signals its (and Lorde's) self-consciousness about Lorde's position as icon, and the process of appropriation produced by that status; Lorde addresses the camera: "What I leave behind has a life of its own. I've said this about poetry . . . I'm saying it about the artifact of who I have been."[4] The first action that we see Lorde performing in this history of the production of the artifact of herself is her acceptance of the appointment as "New York State Poet." Governor Mario Cuomo, bestowing the honor, confers the "Walt Whitman Citation of Merit for Poets." In the aftermath of this fascinating refiguring of the American literary canon, Lorde goes on to give a speech in the tradition of American dissent. What does it mean, Lorde asks, that she, "Black Lesbian feminist warrior poet mother," should be acquiring this status in a context of the continued and systematic exploitation and oppression practiced in and by the same institution that is honoring her? It means, she answers herself, "that we live in a world full of the most intense contradiction." The speech's position at the beginning of the film might suggest that Lorde has taken up the "master's tools" that she famously repudiated at an earlier moment, the better to dismantle the master's house.[5] But Lorde's jeremiad turns out to be a false trail, for this is the only time in the film that she appears in such a context, resisting appropriation by the offical public sphere, operating within a hegemonic institution as an agent of contestation.

The narrative of herself, and of resistance to appropriation, is centered elsewhere. Many other public events feature in the film, but they are public events in a series of counterpublic spheres: there are long extracts from a conference organized by African American women to honor Lorde, at which we hear Lorde, a South African political activist, and several younger African American poets. There are flashes of Lorde teaching a poetry workshop, of her leading a seminar for Afro-Germans, and stretches of domestic footage, Lorde at home in St. Croix. Lorde's personal history is provided by way of a voice-over that reads extracts from *Zami* against a collage of black-and-white newsclips and photographs from the 1950s and 1960s. The portrait is rounded out by interviews, variously with Lorde and with her friends and fellow poets.

I want to address the film as a series of narratives and to discuss both the internal operation of these discursive layers and the positionings they call out in the white feminist critic watching. That process of engagement itself promotes and constructs other narratives, elaborations based in watching from a distance/ difference. The first narrative is that of Lorde as Mother Poet, inspiration, model, scourge, and resource for a younger genera- tion of African American lesbian writers. In the creative writing class, we hear her exhorting her class to search within for what they have to say; Sapphire, in her interview, locates Lorde as cen- tral to her poetic vocation; even Sonia Sanchez, recounting that she hadn't wanted to read with Lorde because of Lorde's asser- tion of her sexuality, places herself in the relation of one who has learned to listen to Lorde's wisdom. Jewelle Gomez articulates neatly the dialectic around which Lorde's cultural construction turns: "There are some of us who think of Audre—we never say this out loud—but we think of Audre as, um, *mother*" (Gomez's emphasis). The film gives us Lorde as artistic, activist icon in the African American community. When Gloria Joseph, Lorde's lover in the present of the film, protests, "I did not meet Audre as this great big Black goddess to be idealized—I met her, you know, I would say on an equal footing," the deification is almost complete. Joseph's remark is closely followed by Lorde's own re- sistance to her placement. Because the film is edited so that we hear Lorde in voice-over before we see that she is addressing a class of student poets, these words seem directed to a much wider audience: "You have *got* to go on [overriding protests] . . . you *don't* need me, don't you understand, the me that you're talking about you carry around inside *yourselves* . . . you can do it for your- selves . . . Don't mythologize me." At the moment of repudiating her myth, Lorde also reinforces it: she will be the internalized progenitor, the new poets' voices growing out of her presence within.

I must work to position myself in relation to this narrative be- cause it explicitly does not seek to include the white viewer. These are African American women (and a few men) talking to each other about a shared cultural phenomenon; nothing suggests that the appropriate stance here is to identify right along with, cheerfully crossing racial difference to empathize with the im- portance of Lorde to all our artistic and political developments. My stance, then, is one of detachment, the distance that comes from listening to a conversation in which one is interested but does not expect to be included. There are many occasions on which Lorde chose to speak to particular communities, and this aspect of the film recreates that strategy, both enacting it and pointing to it; because the separatism is enfolded within a film that as a whole encompasses a wider audience, it is both more and less itself—more separatist because the gesture is seen by all, and less so because, after all, we are all allowed to listen, whoever we are, even while we cannot effortlessly participate. But it is not so easy to listen to the words of the goddess mother, watching as her legacy is passed down, without wanting to be included, without feeling rejected by this supreme and caring deity. A schematic moment in the film brings my own desire for inclusion to the surface. Lorde speaks of the political work that can and must be done across difference, "I don't have to be you in order to work with you," and I find myself pleased and grateful—emotions that are embarrassingly clarified by the disappointment induced by the next sentence: "I don't have to *be* you to respect your blackness." She has caught me out; I have caught myself out, trying to get within the range of those audiences that Lorde chooses to address.

This narrative declines to speak to a white audience and, largely, to speak of it. The most obvious gap in the film's historical account is the absence of Lorde's (white) ex-husband: a picture of him, wheeling a pushchair, features briefly, but he is not interviewed. This is an absence that repeats the selectivity of the story Lorde chooses to tell in *Zami,* where the narrative closes with the celebratory African sensual encounter with Afrekete, leaving Lorde's interracial, heterosexual interlude quietly in the unspoken future. In the film, Lorde mentions her marriage, and the snapshot of a father in action is sufficient to alert the reader to his suppression from the rich weaving of story, reminiscence, and anecdote; so *A Litany for Survival* repeats *Zami*'s practice of exclusion but with a difference. Respecting Lorde's wish that he not be interviewed, the filmmakers nonetheless gesture toward including and acknowledging him in the history they are constructing, just as they circulate the film to wider audiences.[6]

Meanwhile, my personal and institutional placement calls forth another narrative, one that the film barely addresses but in relation to which it nonetheless operates. This narrative is Lorde as she figures in feminist criticism, specifically in the criticism of white feminists. White feminist engagement with Lorde is represented in the film by Adrienne Rich, who mourns the loss of Lorde particularly as fellow poet, the irreplaceable one with whom her work could be shared, discussed, worked over. Although Rich's meaning for the film's audience encompasses her position as lesbian feminist activist and writer, in other words, her contribution is not from that positionality but from a much more intimate and personal place of poetic connection. Rich's artistic identity can and has outweighed her whiteness: Lorde and the filmmakers speak to the poet. But the tone of Rich's interview is suggestively different from that of many others. While Lorde's disciples and friends are celebratory and upbeat, Rich seems close to tears. She speaks of Lorde in the past tense, as if she were already dead. Literally, the collaborative communication between the two poets presumably ended with Lorde's move to St. Croix, but perhaps the temporal dislocation of Rich's perception also reflects her sense of Lorde's having withdrawn from engagement across racial difference. If Lorde speaks from within the next generation of poets of color, Rich's valediction can imagine no such legacy for white ones.

As I have noted, Lorde's only current and visible act of engagement with whiteness in the film is the clip of her accepting the New York State Poet award, in a speech in which Lorde notes her contradictory position in relation to this public sphere, the cultural arm of the military-industrial complex.[7] Since the granting of the accolade New York State Poet is made to stand for Lorde's fame—and her attitude toward that fame—in the "white world," it is inviting to read its significance in terms of metonomy rather than metaphor: whatever this honor means, so success in dominant culture means. It would be hard to imagine a more meaningless accolade, one more empty of affect or power. It is insultingly obvious that North American states endow their designated poet with about as much political power as is granted the official state bird. Neither is expected to be other than ornamental; the state apparatus functions very efficiently without the engagement of either birds or poems, although occasionally one may wish to paint one on a bomber or engrave something inspiring on a public building in order to arouse a little patriotic sentiment.

The representation of Lorde's institutionalization within the official groves of whiteness in terms of New York State Poet of 1991–93 is, I take it, a statement of where both Lorde's and the film's priorities lie—elsewhere, in other words, primarily in the African American lesbian and women's artistic community. The problem (for me) with this ordering of priorities is that Lorde is so thoroughly and exhaustively and repeatedly read, appropriated, claimed, and honored by white feminists. Are white feminists as alien and politically irrelevant—except insofar as they might provide a platform for a repudiating speech—as New York State? The film—and Lorde as she figures there—ignores white feminism. While indifference does not make Lorde safe from white attention or white desire, it might suggest that one white project should be to curb our urge to appropriate. "I want the conjure woman," Gallop says, and she also suggests, surely correctly, that her search for black comfort and approval, envisaged as maternally inflected, is widespread. Our ceaseless invocation of Lorde's "house of difference" as standard for creative multiplicity, a positionality that allows in identity and nonidentity at once, might, if we take the film's stance seriously, be on a par with poems on bombs. We may claim that there is a difference, a meaningful one as far as white feminists are concerned, but one that vanishes from a different position, where the filmmakers stand; but even this small security of perspective will turn out, I think, a trick of the light.

A final narrative layer, in some ways the most important, at least the most immediate, the one from which no viewer can distance herself: *A Litany for Survival* is made over a period of years, and in it Lorde appears at various stages of relative health and sickness, but while the narrative moves backward and forward chronologically, there is no escaping the overarching teleology of the progress of the liver cancer that Lorde fights and lives with throughout; the final sequences of the film show Lorde skeletal, her voice abruptly altered, effortfully reading "Today Is Not the Day." Then we see her holding a video camera toward the sky, as if to record its image against the time when there is, for her, no sky.[8] Much earlier, in voice-over, Lorde says "We [Black Lesbians] were never meant to survive"; the film records in painful detail the process of Lorde's own failure to survive, at the same time as it presents itself and Lorde's work as a sufficient substitute, another form of survival.

Hardly a new or unexpected move, either the claim that work confers life after death, or the attempt to address and redress death through elegy. The attention to Lorde's disease is authorized both, presumably, by Lorde herself and by *The Cancer Journals* and *A Burst of Light,* where the personal narrative of sickness mediates Lorde's engagement with the politics of disease and its management. Between *The Cancer Journals* and *A Burst of Light* breast cancer metastasizes into liver cancer; a disease that we are encouraged to believe that we can "overcome" re-emerges as one that is figured as inexorably terminal. The reigning discourse in women's health circles inscribes breast cancer as an epidemic, and as an epidemic whose seriousness has been occluded by the patriarchal medical establishment.[9] Lorde's death thus is enacted within another feminist rhetorical frame: she is dying of the disease of which women die because of systemic neglect.

This politicized reading of Lorde's illness requires that the viewer see in Lorde's progress into death not only an anticipation of her own more or less imminent mortality but also of her own specifically female endangerment: having breasts in a masculinist culture is a potentially terminal affliction in itself. But breast cancer is no equal opportunity disease: death rates are higher for African American than for white American women. Identifying with and retreating from this way of death is thus complicated by race: a complication that poses a problem for the healthy white feminist, watching the Black warrior poet die. We must wonder whether we can watch this death and not commodify it as it passes across our othering gaze.

Lorde was, to use an inappropriately Christian metaphor, a

thorn in the flesh of whiteness. She had a way of saying what white listeners in her audience didn't much want to hear. Sometimes she would tell us please to stop listening and leave, because there were black women who needed our seats more.[10] Sometimes, accepting an award, she would use her acceptance speech to remark upon the tokenism that such an honor represented, and to admonish us to come back next year with evidence of having made substantial changes in our practice, rather than empty gestures of which she was the recipient.[11] Yet Lorde's ascerbic voice turns up again and again as the ultimate instance of oppositional strategy—directed not at the white critic who quotes her, but rather at the symbolic order that, we are to infer from this coupling, both would attack. This diversion, redirecting the angle of vitriol so that none shall splash on the white girl's vulnerable toes, and simultaneously taking on the power of that vitriol, allowing it to incorporate into one's own argument, is a hard move to resist. Who wouldn't want Lorde on her side? Who wouldn't want to hide behind the warrior poet? And who wouldn't acknowledge her power and her rightness, conceding her the place of greatest oppression and hence greatest authenticity?[12] These identificatory moves will not save us: as Ray Chow points out, the appropriation of the position of powerlessness is finally another event in the history of colonization.[13]

She will be easier to deal with, now that she's dead: she probably won't be able to talk back when some grossly tokenist use is made of her and her work, her ghost won't be able to make audiences with good intentions squirm in their chairs while she tells them why their lousy award is as relevant to her political struggle as a cup of water to a fire out of control. All of which should make us white feminists still more uncomfortable as we sit before *A Litany for Survival,* weeping. We have already canonized her in the ordinary everyday literary sense; are we going to go on and church her too? Of course, it was important that Lorde could always be relied upon to be angry when appropriated; she could be bothered, most of the time, to tell white women off, and this was reassuring—it showed that we mattered and she still cared. We paid her back by caring about her, by putting her in our books

and granting her the status of Most Epistemically Privileged be-
cause so variously oppressed. She was the one we were careful not
to contradict.

But Lorde recognized the inevitability of living in contradic-
tion—and where does that leave us? Not, surely, guiltily allowing
Lorde the last word, or a privileged position as ultimate exem-
plar of the complex multiplicity of identity. We should by now be
conscious of the mechanisms whereby the half-life of the other
in our own representations serves our own purposes, not hers;
and it is clear that our purposes are not, on any local level on
which we actually operate, the same. We respond to resistance by
incorporation. Are you angry at me? we ask pathetically. How
much better to be angry together at something else. And then
we are safe—safe from contradiction.

Lorde is, both *Afrekete* and *A Litany for Survival* suggest, an icon
for the community that she would recognize as most her own.
She has been translated into the foremother for other black les-
bians that she herself often lamented having had to do without
(while at the same time celebrating the independence and free-
dom of self-creation that such lack forced her to develop).[14] *A
Litany for Survival* celebrates her incorporation into the living
body of an African American women's tradition. Although this
might seem to repeat the myth work of *Afrekete,* its valence is
slightly different. The Audre of *Afrekete* is a deity who has tran-
scended difference and contradiction, but she of *Litany* talks
back, undermining her own sacred texts, letting the gaps show,
rendering visible her fallibility as well as her mortality. Indeed,
the visibility of mortality in *Litany* suggests that visibility itself has
limitations as a political strategy: even visible as she is, Lorde can-
not survive except as the artifact of others.

It is *Litany* that appears to offer a space, and comfort, to the
white viewer. But I suggest that that space is of our imagining and
that we should stay outside and colonize no more. She is no fore-
mother for white feminists, and we need to recognize this even
as we worship at her shrine and touch her relics with reverence.
Weep as we may, we will never gain entrance to Lorde's house of
difference, for our presence there collapses the edifice. When we

invade the gentlemen's club and demand the right to drink at its bar, the old guard laments that things are changed forever and will never be the same again—and they are right. We enter the athenaeum of male hegemony both because we want what they've got, and because we don't want them to have it—we will get it and redistribute it . . . Do we want the black club to stay the same, respecting its exclusion of us—or don't we?

I am not unaware of the apparent difficulty (one might say hypocrisy) of my own position: here I am scolding other white critics, telling them they must not tread the colonizing path, while using that very place myself as the authenticating ground of my critique. But I am not suggesting that white critics should not read, teach, or write about Lorde; rather, that we recognize our inevitable position within another territory. When Lorde looks out from the podium at Albany at a crowd figured as representatives of the state machine, we are part of what she makes it her business to attack. If we take Lorde and her privileging of difference seriously, then it behooves white feminist critics to resist their own desire to belong in Audre's house. *A Litany for Survival* shows Lorde "at home" both domestically and as an active member of both African American and women of color communities. It also shows her in the official public sphere, and she doesn't say the same things there, or act the same way. It is a distinction that white feminists should keep in mind: the conjure woman may mess with us in the street, but she is not about to fold us to her bosom.

NOTES

1. An example of the latter is Elaine Showalter, ed., *The New Feminist Criticism: Essays on Women, Literature and Theory* (New York: Pantheon, 1985), in which Deborah McDowell's essay "New Directions for Black Feminist Criticism" both points to the exclusion of black women writers from white feminist work, and models the critical project for black critics.

2. This move is so general that to pick particular examples seems invidious. But see, for instance, Anna Wilson, "Audre Lorde and the African-American Tradition: When the Family Is Not Enough," in Sally

Munt, ed., *The New Lesbian Criticism* (New York: Columbia UP, 1992); Sidonie Smith, *A Poetics of Women's Autobiography: Marginality and the Fictions of Self-Representation* (Bloomington: Indiana UP, 1987); Thomas Foster, "'The Very House of Difference': Gender as 'Embattled' Standpoint," *Genders* 8 (July 1990): 17–37.

3. See Margaret Homans, "Women of Color and Feminist Theory," *NLH* 25.1 (1994): 73–94; Toni Morrison, *Playing in the Dark: Whiteness and the Literary Imagination* (Cambridge: Harvard UP, 1992); Valerie Smith, "Black Feminist Theory and the Representation of the 'Other,'" in Cheryl A. Wall, ed., *Changing Our Own Words: Essays on Criticism, Theory, and Writing by Black Women* (Brunswick: Rutgers UP, 1989) 38–57; Elizabeth Abel, "Black Writing, White Reading: Race and the Politics of Feminist Interpretation," *Critical Inquiry* 19 (Spring 1993): 470–98.

4. *A Litany for Survival* is currently available in two versions: as a ninety-minute film and as a sixty-minute videotape. My descriptions, except where otherwise noted, refer to the latter. The shorter version has been re-edited, so that in addition to the excision of much material, the order of events has been altered.

5. See "The Master's Tools Will Never Dismantle the Master's House," in *Sister Outsider* (Trumansburg, N.Y.: Crossing Press, 1984) 110–13.

6. The film has not yet been widely distributed, but it has been seen, to great adulation, by selected mixed or white-dominated audiences: at the Sundance film festival, at the 1995 Outwrite conference, and in an edited version on PBS (June 18, 1996). The information that Lorde refused to allow her ex-husband to be interviewed for the film comes from a personal communication with Ada Gay Griffin.

7. The videotape's version of the speech, given at much greater length in the original film, omits Lorde's detailed description of the various evildoings of New York State, including her reference to the military-industrial complex.

8. This is the sequence of the film; in the video the sky-filming episode is cut in at the beginning, where it has the effect of inscribing the inevitability of Lorde's decline and death as a framework for all of what follows.

9. Barbara Smith appears in the film both to make this point and to locate *The Cancer Journals* as a landmark text in the "truth-telling" that enabled this shift of consciousness.

10. The particular incident I have in mind occurred at the first International Feminist Book Fair, London 1984. Lorde was scheduled to speak at a central London theater, and tickets sold out quickly. Lorde came out on stage and told the white women in the audience to give

their seats to black women waiting outside, partly on the grounds that it was to them that she wished to speak, and partly because the location of the theater had made it harder for black women to get there. She then gave an address aimed very specifically at a black lesbian audience. (I hadn't given up my seat—choosing then to believe that there was room for us all, and not anticipating the exclusionary power of Lorde's speech.)

11. See Lorde's acceptance speech on the occasion of her receiving an award from the Triangle Group at the Bill Whitehead Memorial Award Ceremony, 1990, "What Is at Stake in Lesbian and Gay Publishing Today," *Callaloo* 14.1 (Winter 1991): 65–66.

12. Such assertions and appropriations of epistemic privilege have themselves not gone unchallenged; see, for example, Bat-Ami Bar On, "Marginality and Epistemic Privilege," in Linda Alcoff and Elizabeth Potter, eds., *Feminist Epistemologies* (New York: Routledge, 1993) 83–100. As Bar On notes, the authority lent by identity comes with its own reinvestment in the very structures of domination and exclusion it would contest. Nonetheless, Lorde's "house of difference," a conception of home that is always also a disavowal of the possibility of any such space, nestles at the journey's end of many a critical narrative, the resting place where oppositional possibility finds itself at last.

13. See Ray Chow, *Writing Diaspora: Tactics of Intervention in Contemporary Cultural Studies* (Bloomington: Indiana UP, 1993) 12–13.

14. See "A Burst of Light: Living with Cancer," in *A Burst of Light* 49–134.

WORKS CITED

Gallop, Jane. *Around 1981: Academic Feminist Literary Theory.* New York: Routledge, 1992.

Griffin, Ada Gay, and Michelle Parkerson, dir. *A Litany for Survival: The Life and Work of Audre Lorde.* Film, videotape. Third World Newsreel, 1995/1996.

Lorde, Audre. *A Burst of Light.* Ithaca, N.Y.: Firebrand, 1988.

———. *The Cancer Journals.* Argyle, N.Y.: Spinsters, 1980.

———. *Zami: A New Spelling of My Name.* Watertown, Mass.: Persephone, 1982.

McKinley, Catherine E., and L. Joyce Delaney. *Afrekete: An Anthology of Black Lesbian Writing.* New York: Doubleday, 1995.

3

"The Muse as Fluffball": Margaret Atwood and the Poetry of the Intelligent Woman

MARTINE WATSON BROWNLEY

As early as 1971 Adrienne Rich called for women to approach writing as "Re-vision—the act of looking back, of seeing with fresh eyes, of entering an old text from a new critical direction" ("When We Dead Awaken" 18).[1] Among the many critics who have explored this kind of feminist revision, Alicia Ostriker was one of the first to point out that "where women write strongly as women, it is clear that their intention is to subvert and transform the life and literature they inherit" (211). A complex of related terms has emerged for this literary process: *revisionist mythmaking* (Ostriker 11); *revisionary mythopoesis* (DuPlessis 105); *re-visionary mythmaking* (Yorke 13–14); and *revisionist reconstitution* (Friedman 22). One contemporary master of such writing has been Margaret Atwood. In numerous collections of poetry spanning over three decades, she has reworked myth to critique prevailing cultural inscriptions of women.

Critics have focused on Atwood's work mainly in terms of such topics as the female body, metamorphosis and magic, nature, the Gothic, and Canadian nationhood, or recurring images such as those of hands or mirrors. Less direct attention has been paid to another central element in all of Atwood's poetry: women's intelligence. Linda Wagner's comment in connection with one of Atwood's early collections, *Procedures for Underground* (1970), has remained an accurate assessment of her subsequent work:

34

"Knowledge of whatever source is the prize for Atwood's persona . . . " (88). Tough-minded in pursuit of this knowledge, Atwood's poetic personae tend to be marked by thoroughgoing rationality and witty skepticism. Indeed, the coldness that many critics, particularly males, have repeatedly attacked in Atwood's poetry—*bleak* recurs as a favorite critical adjective—derives in large part from the uncompromising intellectual integrity clear in her work.

Although smart, all of Atwood's personae are at the same time inevitably fallible, whether human or nonhuman. Female fallibility is highlighted in her poems about relationships between men and women,[2] which have received the bulk of feminist critical attention given to her poetry. Women's intelligence, in turn, although clear throughout the poetry, appears especially in Atwood's rewritings of classical myth. In such mythic revisions as "Siren Song" and "Circe/Mud Poems," she constantly reworks or supplements her poetic material to foreground female rationality.

In contrast to this pronounced tendency throughout her poetry, one of Atwood's poems offers a counterview of women's intelligence and the myths thereof. In "Let Us Now Praise Stupid Women," Atwood parodies the original ironic reversal of James Agee's title in a wide-ranging critique of contemporary women's literary positions as subjects, readers, and writers.

*   *   *   *

"Let Us Now Praise Stupid Women," which appeared in the collection *Good Bones* in 1992 (in Canada), is a timely piece for the 1990s, given the cult of stupidity rampant in contemporary culture. Gen X of the British royal family romps through the headlines; television offers "Beavis and Butthead"; *Forrest Gump, Dumb and Dumber,* and *The Stupids* fill theaters. One film reviewer terms this rather discouraging cultural development "moron chic" (Young 50).

Atwood's poem plays with other forms of "moron chic" in connection with literature and the stupid woman. The major contention is that everybody loves stupid women, "mostly because with-

35

out them there would be no stories": "No stories! No stories! Imagine a world without stories!/But that's exactly what you would have if all the women were wise" (59). Atwood uses the biblical story of the wise and foolish virgins to illustrate how stupid women produce stories:

> The Wise Virgins keep their lamps trimmed and
> filled with oil, and the bridegroom arrives, in the
> proper way, knocking at the front door, in time
> for his dinner;
> no fuss, no muss, and also no story at all. (59–60)

The persona sums up the wise virgins as finally "insupportable" because they lack "narrative vices" (60). In contrast to these "bloodless paragons" (60),

> The foolish Virgins . . . let their
> lamps go out:
> and when the bridegroom turns up and rings the
> doorbell,
> they are asleep in bed, and he has to climb in
> through the window:
> and people scream and fall over things, and identities
> get mistaken,
> and there's a chase scene, and breakage, and much
> satisfactory uproar:
> none of which would have happened if these girls
> hadn't been several bricks short of a load. (60)

This recasting of biblical parable in terms of Restoration comedy is typical of the literary blends that mark Atwood's already generically blended prosaic poem. She invokes a range of canonical and noncanonical genres dependent on the stupid woman, from *The Waste Land* to "love lyrics" that are "aimed straight at women stupid enough to find them seductive," and from the mass-market Gothic to "sagas of heroes" composed "for the admiration of women thought stupid enough to believe them" (62–63).

Atwood's poem focuses its critique at the discursive level, describing stupid women as "fictions: composed by others, but just as frequently by themselves" (59). The persona reviews the discourses that produce and are produced by the prevailing stereotypes, which, in their turn, create and are created by stupid women. From this perspective female stupidity is shown as performative, reiterated in stories and imitated by actual women. The poem opens with amused condescension in a parodic descriptive roll (role) call of contemporary stupid women in terms of their appearances and activities. Even as early as the beginning of the second stanza, however, the persona shows ambivalence, and as she moves to the representations of such women in literature, the emerging emphasis on female complicity with such fictions begins to implicate the female reader.

Toward the end of the poem Atwood traces an arc of cultural decline and female complicity in it, playing off Oliver Goldsmith's "Song" in *The Vicar of Wakefield* ("When Lovely Woman Stoops to Folly"). For Goldsmith's era cultural expectations dictated that a woman could atone for a mistake in love only by dying. Female complicity in such views is shown by the fact that in the novel the betrayed girl herself sings the "Song."[3] When T. S. Eliot redeploys Goldsmith's line in *The Waste Land,* misdirected love has degenerated into rote lust, and the typist, ignorant of her own significance or any larger meaning, reveals her complicity by simply smoothing her hair and putting on a record. It is arguably stupid to kill yourself for one mistake, and it may also be stupid to reduce potentially intimate human connections to "automatic" responses from boredom and indifference (Eliot 44). However, by the time Atwood invokes the line, female stupidity has emerged as a potential rereading of female intelligence.

In the context of contemporary cultural mores, Atwood shows how the stupid woman has merged with the smart:

> When lovely woman stoops or bungles her way into folly,
> . . . .
> and is taken advantage of, especially by somebody famous,
> if stupid or smart enough, she gets caught, just as in

37

                    classic novels,
    and makes her way into the tabloids, confused and tearful,
    and from there straight into our hearts.
    We forgive you! we cry. *We understand! Now do it some
            more!* (63)

Atwood's lines reflect a series of progressions and regressions: from the sentimental novel through high modernism to the postmodernism that Atwood is often said to represent; from the classic novel to the tabloids, themselves compendia of minor novelistic modes; from love to death, to boredom, and ultimately to commodification and profit. The stupid woman, long produced to fill others' needs and still doing so, learns finally to manipulate the stereotype for commercial gain.

Agee's sharecroppers were not famous men, and Atwood's stupid women turn out not to be so stupid after all. Contemporary intersections of romance and marketplace dissolve the binary between smart and stupid women with which the poem opens.

The persona moves from initial condescension, to an understanding of female readerly complicity, and finally to self-indictment. Recognition of the woman writer's implication in the exploitation of the stupid woman and her share in the responsibility for the myth comes in the next-to-last stanza, which opens with Atwood's description of "the Muse as fluffball" as "our inspiration," and also "the inspiration of men as well!" (62). Thus the theme of collaboration, prominent in a number of Atwood's later poems, is considered here in literary terms.

The poem closes with a more general identification that raises questions about the validity of divisions between women, particularly those accepted or imposed by women themselves. Atwood once again revises, drawing on Baudelaire's famous line echoed by Eliot: "*Hypocrite lecteuse! Ma semblable! Ma soeur!*" (63). More significant for Atwood's regendering of the line than the two canonical male poets is Adrienne Rich's deployment of it in "Snapshots of a Daughter-in-Law," where the line highlights the natural connections between women that become distorted by their oppressed positions. In Rich's poem the abbreviated line ("*ma semblable, ma soeur!"*) occurs in a section describing an "argument *ad feminam,*" where one woman drives "all the old knives/that have rusted" in her own back into the other woman's back—a victim victimizing another in turn. One of the recognitions toward which Atwood works in her poem is foreshadowed in Rich's, where the women know "themselves too well in one another" (*Poetry* 13).

After the regendered line from Baudelaire and Eliot via Rich, Atwood closes with two brief lines: "Let us now praise stupid women,/who have given us Literature" (63). Thus the poem has moved from stupid women as subjects of discourse, through the stupid women who consume and reflect discursive constructions of themselves, to the stupid women who create the discourses. These writers are perhaps the stupidest of all the women in the poem, because they themselves reproduce and retail the conventional derogatory literary stereotypes of their own sex. They play a central role in displacing the original male-drawn binary between intelligent man and stupid woman and redeploying it between women. The resulting artificial boundaries between women only obscure for all women their actual situations as individuals and as a group.

The poem began with stupid women's crucial roles in "stories," but it ends with their importance for "Literature"—with a capital L, to boot. Even before structuralism, stories tended to be treated primarily in terms of their major component, plot, while literature has historically involved, among *many* other elements, more polished formal properties. Appropriately enough, given the emphasis in the poem on the role of the female writer, literature also tends to be connected more directly with individual authors than are stories. "Let Us Now Praise Stupid Women" suggests that literary skill and sophistication cannot necessarily exempt the individual woman writer from the tyranny of traditional plots. "It's the story that counts," Atwood's Circe declares in another context, and "the story is ruthless" (*Selected Poems* 221).

In "Let Us Now Praise Stupid Women," the story that Atwood shows propelling the cultural stereotypes that create and are created by stupid woman is the romance: "even stupid women are not so stupid as they pretend: they pretend for love" (59). Probably the major literary compensation offered to women for their exile from the public sphere, the romance has proved to be an amazingly resilient form. Despite feminist critics' continuing attacks on its ideology and canonical women writers' efforts to delegitimate it throughout this century, the romance survives and thrives in multiple forms in contemporary culture. Although Rachel DuPlessis claims that "couple-based romance remains at the center, and is the privileged resolution of more significant narratives by men than by women" (xi), women still play a substantial role in the contemporary production of romances. The Harlequin "stable" of writers, overwhelmingly female, is only the most obvious example.

Atwood's point about the implication of the female writer in the production of the myth of what she calls the "Eternal Stupid Woman" (61) is interesting enough, but there are some generic problems with it. It doesn't describe Atwood's own poetry. Nor does it fit the poetry of the great majority of the women poets of the twentieth century. From H. D. and Mina Loy, through Gwendolyn Brooks, Muriel Rukeyser, and Sylvia Plath, to Adrienne Rich and many other contemporaries, women poets have been recasting stereotypical stories and myths with continuing and considerable success. Central to both their subject matter and their techniques has been the intelligent woman. They have represented her powerfully. Why, then, does Atwood connect writers of "Literature" and "the Eternal Stupid Woman"?

Atwood, of course, is not only a poet; she's a novelist as well. And any reader seeking stupid women in literature—in droves—can pick up almost any of her novels. At best many of her protagonists are criminally naive; at worst, they are willfully blind. Moreover, most of the minor genres Atwood invokes in "Let Us Now Praise Stupid Women," particularly the sentimental novel and the Gothic romance, have provided many of the conventions for her own novels. For years critics conventionally distinguished Atwood's "bubbleheaded/ladies' magazine fiction" from her "serious poetry" (Thompson 115). Even Atwood herself said in an

interview that her prose evoked an "almost totally different" per-
sonality than her poetry (Ingersoll 71).[4]

It is almost impossible not to read "Let Us Now Praise Stupid
Women" as in part Atwood the poet's critique of Atwood the nov-
elist. Atwood's works have always been extremely self-reflexive,
commenting on themselves as well as on other writings of hers.
Ostriker has pointed out that in contemporary women poets,
standard academic distinctions between the first person pro-
nouns in their works and the poets themselves tend to vanish
(12), and that is often the case with Atwood.

Further indirect corroboration of Atwood's self-critique in
"Let Us Now Praise Stupid Women" comes from one of Atwood's
drawings reproduced with the poem (58). The sketch shows
a figure with a snake in one hand and an apple in the other,
obviously connected with the poem's description of the stupid
woman "as she listens to the con-artist yarns of the plausible
snake,/and ends up eating the free sample of the apple from the
Tree of Knowledge" (61). The figure is a reptilian adaptation of
a mermaid, a woman from the chest up, with a snake's coils and
tail from just above the waist down—literally a phallic woman.
Her hair, which is composed entirely of snakes, is the connection
with Atwood, who from relatively early in her career has been
linked with Medusa by unfriendly critics.[5] Jerome H. Rosenberg
traces this caricature of her to critics' "confusing Atwood and her
Medusa-like personas" (155); Atwood herself dismisses it as "one
of the hazards of naturally curly hair" (Ingersoll 81; see also 40).
However one interprets Atwood's media image, the allusion to it
in the sketch clearly suggests her own implication in the poem
and in the creation of the Stupid Woman.

In her novelistic practice Atwood is not alone. Aside from femi-
nist detective fiction, many of the female characters in contem-
porary women's fiction are not overly bright, and in other ways
these novelists rely on various sexist myths. In general, contem-
porary women poets have been markedly more successful in
breaking mythic stereotypes in their works than have women
novelists. Following Adrienne Rich's formulation in "Diving into
the Wreck," it is the women poets and not the novelists who have

most successfully depicted "the wreck and not the story of the wreck/the thing itself and not the myth" (*Poetry* 67).

As with any generalization, this one of course has significant exceptions. It holds true mainly for canonical and protocanonical women novelists. It does not work for avant-garde women novelists, whose writings usually do not deal with these kinds of identity constructions. Nor is it satisfactory for many ethnic writers. Its binary treatments of poetry and prose ignore ubiquitous contemporary genre hybridization. Finally, there are individual exceptions, both works and writers. Despite these various caveats, however, on the whole the greater success of contemporary women poets in myth breaking as opposed to that of the women novelists is notable. These poets' achievements make the substantially greater attention paid to the novelists and narrative by contemporary critics all the more ironic.

A number of factors account for contemporary women poets' greater success against myth. Adequate consideration of these would require (at least) a separate essay; here I can only briefly suggest a few of them.

Any assessment is complicated in part by the amount of theoretical underbrush that needs clearing away. Questionable binary genderings have long proliferated in discussions of contemporary women writers' relationships to both poetry and prose. From a psychoanalytical perspective, for example, Hélène Cixous contrasts poets with novelists, "who stick with representation": "poetry exists only by taking strength from the unconscious, and the unconscious, the other country without boundaries, is where the repressed survive—women . . . " (98).

Like Cixous, many poststructuralists have drawn gendered binaries between narrative and poetry in order to privilege poetry, especially the lyric. Susan Stanford Friedman points out that for Barthes, Kristeva, and others, "the lyric mode and poetry . . . are tied to the repressed feminine, maternal, and preoedipal, whereas narrative and the novel . . . are linked to the repressive masculine, paternal, and oedipal" (15). A related tendency of some feminist criticism has been to associate any literary imposition of order and any linear thought, even the construction of stories in terms of beginnings, middles, and ends, with masculinity and authoritarianism, analogies that obviously work to the detriment of narrative. The sexism that fuels such binaries is clear in the descriptive language that occurs in references to them. Typical is one critic's comment that "recent theory has focused on the teleological nature of narrative, its propulsion toward mastery and closure, and has sometimes identified it with male desire," while poetry "has been gendered female because of its ahistorical character, its perceived passivity, its emphasis on enchantment and absorption" (Costello 180–181).

In addition to their sexism, these critical exclusions of women from narrative are Eurocentric, disregarding the primary roles of women as storytellers in other cultures. Even within the European context they ignore the many connections of the novel with women from its beginnings. For example, the suppressed history of the emergence of the English novel as a predominantly female form in both production and consumption is only now slowly being written.

Neither poetry nor prose can be adequately theorized in terms of single gender connections. As Susan Gal notes, "A simple category of 'his-and-hers' genres obscures the important insight that women's special verbal skills are often strategic *responses*—more or less successful—to positions of relative powerlessness" (182, italics Gal's). Theoretical equations or analogies between the female and poetry, then, cannot account for contemporary women poets' successes.

Story serves different functions in poems and in novels. A problem for both is the tendency for sexist formulations in myths to be reflected even in works overtly repudiating them. Contemporary poets have been partially successful in containing such implications by strategic fragmentation. Marjorie Perloff notes that in postmodern poetry story "is no longer the full-fledged *mythos* of Aristotle, . . . but a point of reference, a way of alluding, a source . . . of parody." She points out that such deployments of story frustrate readers' desires for closure, because they "foreground the narrative codes themselves and call them into question" ("From Image to Action" 417). In this process gender constructions embedded in the codes are often called into question at the same time.

Similarly, in technique Margaret Dickie has emphasized contemporary American women poets' successful incorporation into their poetry of the heteroglossia that Bakhtin associates with the novel. Beyond Dickie's excellent poetic analyses, however, larger theoretical problems remain with Bakhtin's insistence that neither the epic nor other poetry reflects heteroglossia; his polemical privileging of the novel leaves his treatments of poetry inadequate in important areas. The innovation that Bakhtin connects with the novel is also seen by Dickie in contemporary women poets, whom she presents as "unusually responsive to the multifoliate language of their time and place, unusually resistant to a privileged poetic language, and so ideal language experimenters" (314).

Joan Retallack and other critics have criticized contemporary women poets for not being experimental enough. Nevertheless, throughout this century women poets have developed substantially more experimental forms than have women novelists. Despite claims by critics for the avant-garde novel, in over two centuries the experimental novel is still not as far from Laurence Sterne as one might have expected—or wished. Although a number of theorists have shown that the tendency to associate experimental writing with more radical ideology than realistic works does not necessarily hold for women writers, in the case of contemporary poets formal experimentation seems to have played a role in their success against myth. A good example is their avoidance of traditional poetic genres, a crucial move because, as Sandra Gilbert and Susan Gubar point out, "Verse genres have been even more thoroughly male than fictional ones" (68).

Women novelists' experimentation has been in part constrained by market forces, which have traditionally influenced the novel much more than poetry. More recently, as publishers become subdivisions of multinational conglomerates, the pressure to produce work that will appeal to mass audiences has increased. The tendency of most contemporary novelists to remain primarily within realistic conventions has exacerbated the women novelists' difficulties with myth breaking. The realistic novel with its innumerable details has historically maintained closer ties to everyday life than has poetry. But such conventions also lessen its power against myth, which by definition resists all incursion of the particular. As Barthes points out, myth's path is away from history toward nature. Although noting poetry's vulnerability as "an ideal prey for myth," he ultimately situates it in "a position which is the reverse of that of myth" (134).

A crucial element in this connection is the temporal relationships of poetry and prose. From Aristotle on, poetry, and lyric in particular, has tended to be connected with the universal, as opposed to history and narrative. Ursula LeGuin is typical, writing that narrative, which "does not seek immortality [and] does not seek to triumph over or escape from time (as lyric poetry does)," always locates itself in the past in order to be "free to move towards its future, the present" (38–39). But whatever poetry's universal aspirations, which would move it toward the realm of myth (hence Barthes's concern with its vulnerability), lyric poetry at least is also anchored in the present, and from that position has strong potential for combating mythic formulations. Narrative, which in LeGuin's words "asserts, affirms, participates in directional time" (39), can only with the greatest difficulty avoid replicating historical configurations of the past, including gender constructions.

Locating themselves firmly in the present, women poets have ferociously combated prevailing myths with their individual experiences as women. Perloff writes: "Most contemporary feminist poetry takes as emblematic its author's own experience of power relations, her personal struggle with patriarchy, her sense of marginalization, her view of social justice" (*Poetic License* 310). Thus far women's social and political concerns have been more effectively integrated into poetry than narrative. Diane Middlebrook, for example, comments on "the enormous importance of women's poetry to the political evolution of contemporary women's movements" (3); with two or perhaps three exceptions, the same could not be said about the novelists. From the late 1960s on, the women novelists who have dealt with contemporary issues either directly or by moving to utopic or dystopic plots have in general lacked the technical abilities of the poets.[6]

Thus "Let Us Now Praise Stupid Women" leads to larger questions about the poetic and novelistic achievements of contemporary women revisionists. In its treatment of similarities and differences among women, it also reflects the ongoing concern with gender issues that has marked Atwood's poetry from the beginning, while raising questions about some practical consequences of contemporary theoretical emphases on women's differences.

Critics have long noted the shift in Atwood's poetry over the course of her career from focusing on divisions between men and women to exploring the ties among women. Her recent work has been moving beyond celebrating such female bonds—as Barbara Blakely puts it, poems where "Woman discovers herself in the bloodline of women" (47)—to consider the dynamics of conflict among women. In this instance the trajectory of her literary career has paralleled that of the women's movement and feminist criticism, both of which began over the course of the 1980s to work with female difference.

What "Let Us Now Praise Stupid Women" suggests is certain problems with this emphasis on difference, and its practical limitations. Sherrill Grace has shown that from the beginning Atwood's work has been characterized by what Grace terms "violent duality," a focus not just on Western dichotomies themselves but on the process of overcoming such binaries. Grace sees as one of the dominant polarities in Atwood that between the self and the other, where Atwood "strives to break down the static condition of mutual exclusiveness separating the opposites" (7, 11).[7] "Let Us Now Praise Stupid Women" enacts just this sort of breakdown of differences between women, as it highlights paradoxically the stupidity of intelligent women and the intelligence of stupid women.

Atwood's poem reminds us that women's own valorizations of their differences become insignificant within the context of powerful social and cultural paradigms, attitudes, and stories, which in so many ways reduce all women to the same. In the context of male-dominated culture, all women are in some sense stupid, and under such conditions the only way for a woman to be smart is to behave stupidly. Atwood has always been interested in what she calls in *Survival* "Victor/Victim games" (39), and in "Let Us Now Praise Stupid Women" she shows that the myth of the "Eternal Stupid Woman" (61) can only make all women victims. With this victimhood Atwood's poem also reminds us—yet again—of the power of externally imposed constructions of female similarity that become internalized, those produced by stories and by the social and material constraints that the stories both reflect and create.

The open-ended play of difference crucial for feminist theory and the recognition of differences essential for creating a fair and inclusive feminist politics have rightly dominated feminist criticism for over a decade. But stories, particularly cultural myths, rest on simpler constructions. It may be time to explore whether difference can be rethought in ways that would enable construction of new models, larger and more inclusive models that, to paraphrase Shelley Sunn Wong, would not rationalize or reconcile difference but recognize and then act into difference (49). Such constructions might lead to the kind of stories that would elude, at the very least, the myth of the "Eternal Stupid Woman," and retire Atwood's "Muse as fluffball" at last (61–62).

NOTES

1. Although published in 1972, "When We Dead Awaken: Writing as Re-Vision" was read as an MLA paper in December 1971 (18).

2. See Wagner 90.

3. As early as 1906 Austin Dobson objected to the "impropriety, and even inhumanity" of allotting this kind of song to the seduced girl (quoted in Lonsdale 595).

4. Thompson effectively demolishes "the Atwoodian notion that her poetry and fiction are expressed in two entirely different, stylistically unrelated, philosophically dissimilar voices" (121–22). For other

assessments of Atwood as a poet, as opposed to a novelist, see Klappert 217, Woodcock 252, and McCombs and Palmer 362, 608.

5. *Double Persephone,* Atwood's first book of poetry, opened with a poem featuring a "girl with the gorgon touch" (Davey 134; significantly, in an article entitled "Atwood's Gorgon Touch"); Barbara Hill Rigney writes that the image of Medusa dominates in that collection (67). See also Ingersoll x, 118, Klappert 224.

6. Atwood's *Handmaid's Tale* is a notable exception.

7. See also Grace's book-length study, *Violent Duality: A Study of Margaret Atwood* (Montreal: Véhicule, 1980).

WORKS CITED

Atwood, Margaret. "Let Us Now Praise Stupid Women." *Good Bones and Simple Murders.* New York: Doubleday, 1994. 57–63.

——. *Selected Poems: 1965–1975.* 1976. Boston: Houghton, 1987.

——. *Survival: A Thematic Guide to Canadian Literature.* Toronto: Anansi, 1972.

Barthes, Roland. *Mythologies.* 1957. Trans. Annette Lavers, 1972. New York: Hill, 1986.

Blakely, Barbara. "The Pronunciation of Flesh: A Feminist Reading of Atwood's Poetry." Grace and Weir 33–51.

Cixous, Hélène, and Catherine Clément. *The Newly Born Woman.* 1975. Trans. Betsy Wing. Minneapolis: U of Minnesota P, 1987.

Costello, Bonnie. "Narrative Secrets, Lyric Openings: Stevens and Bishop." *The Wallace Stevens Journal* 19 (1995): 180–200.

Davey, Frank. "Atwood's Gorgon Touch." *Critical Essays on Margaret Atwood.* Ed. Judith McComb, Boston: Hall, 1988. 134–53.

Davidson, Arnold E., and Cathy N. Davidson. *The Art of Margaret Atwood: Essays on Criticism.* Toronto: Anansi, 1981.

Dickie, Margaret. "The Alien in Contemporary American Women's Poetry." *Contemporary Literature* 28 (1987): 301–16.

DuPlessis, Rachel Blau. *Writing beyond the Ending: Narrative Strategies of Twentieth-Century Women Writers.* Bloomington: Indiana UP, 1985.

Eliot, T. S. *The Waste Land. The Complete Poems and Plays: 1909–1950.* New York: Harcourt, 1952. 37–55.

Friedman, Susan Stanford. "Craving Stories: Narrative and Lyric in Contemporary Theory and Women's Long Poems." Keller and Miller 15–42.

Gal, Susan. "Between Speech and Silence: The Problematics of Research on Language and Gender." *Gender at the Crossroads of Knowledge: Feminist Anthropology in the Postmodern Era.* Ed. Micaela di Leonardo. Berkeley: U of California P, 1991. 175–203.

Grace, Sherrill E. "Articulating the 'Space Between': Atwood's Untold Stories and Fresh Beginnings." Grace and Weir 1–16.

Grace, Sherrill E., and Lorraine Weir, eds. *Margaret Atwood: Language, Text, and System.* Vancouver: U of British Columbia P, 1983.

Gilbert, Sandra M., and Susan Gubar. *The Madwoman in the Attic.* New Haven: Yale UP, 1979.

Ingersoll, Earl G., ed. *Margaret Atwood: Conversations.* Princeton: Ontario Review P, 1990.

Keller, Lynn, and Cristanne Miller, eds. *Feminist Measures: Soundings in Poetry and Theory.* Ann Arbor: U of Michigan P, 1994.

Klappert, Peter. "I Want, I Don't Want: The Poetry of Margaret Atwood." *Gettysburg Review* 3 (1990): 217–30.

LeGuin, Ursula. *Dancing at the Edge of the World: Thoughts on Words, Women, Places.* 1989. New York: Harper, 1990.

Lonsdale, Roger, ed. *The Poems of Gray, Collins and Goldsmith.* London: Longman, 1976.

McCombs, Judith, ed. *Critical Essays on Margaret Atwood.* Boston: Hall, 1988.

McCombs, Judith, and Carole L. Palmer. *Margaret Atwood: A Reference Guide.* Boston: Hall, 1991.

Middlebrook, Diane Wood, and Marilyn Yalom. *Coming to Light. American Women Poets in the Twentieth Century.* Ann Arbor: U of Michigan P, 1986.

Ostriker, Alicia Suskin. *Stealing the Language: The Emergence of Women's Poetry in America.* Boston: Beacon, 1986.

Perloff, Marjorie. "From Image to Action: The Return of Story in Postmodern Poetry." *Contemporary Literature* 23 (1982): 411–27.

———. *Poetic License: Essays on Modernist and Postmodernist Lyric.* Evanston: Northwestern UP, 1990.

Retallack, Joan. ":RE:THINKING:LITERARY:FEMINISM: (three essays onto shaky grounds)." Keller and Miller 344–77.

Rich, Adrienne. *Adrienne Rich's Poetry.* Ed. Barbara Charlesworth Gelpi and Albert Gelpi. New York: Norton, 1975.

———. "When We Dead Awaken: Writing as Re-Vision." *College English* 34.1 (1972): 18–25.

Rigney, Barbara Hill. *Margaret Atwood.* Totowa, N.J.: Barnes, 1987.

Rosenberg, Jerome H. *Margaret Atwood.* Boston: Twayne, 1984.

Thompson, Lee Briscoe. "Minuets and Madness: Margaret Atwood's *Dancing Girls.*" Davidson and Davison 107–22, 295.

Wagner, Linda W. "The Making of *Selected Poems,* the Process of Surfacing." Davidson and Davison 81–94.

Wong, Shelley Sunn. "Unnaming the Same: Theresa Hak Kynug Cha's *DICTEE.*" Keller and Miller 43–68.

Woodcock, George. "Canadian Poetry: The Emergent Tradition." *Yearbook of English Studies* 15 (1985): 239–55.

Yorke, Liz. *Impertinent Voices: Subversive Strategies in Contemporary Women's Poetry.* London: Routledge, 1991.

Young, Josh. "Hollywood Humbug." *Esquire* Dec. 1995: 50.

4

Infectious Ecstasy: Toward a Poetics of Performative Transformation

CYNTHIA HOGUE

No poetic fantasy
but a biological reality,

a fact: I am an entity
like bird, insect, plant

or sea-plant cell;
live; I am alive;

. . . .

shun me; for this reality
is infectious—ecstasy.

—H.D., *Trilogy*

Can ecstasy be "caught," passed on like a contagious disease from which we might never recover? So the passage above from H.D.'s *Trilogy* startlingly compels us to consider. H.D. opposes scientific empiricism to the phantasms of poetry. But the text *is* poetry, employing "poetic fantasy" to articulate its claim to "biological reality" (*Trilogy* 125). The contrast is at the least equivocal,[1] slyly disrupting the assertions of science to being factual, uncontaminated by "poetic" figuration or fantasy. At the same time, claiming veracity in language miming "unpoetic," scientific (historically patriarchal)[2] discourse, the passage intends to enact a capacity to convey spiritual truths—"ecstasy"—as poetic facts equivalent to empirical evidence.

H.D.'s spiritual realism provides an approach to feminist poetics that I think of—contemplating the poetry of Kathleen Fraser and Susan Howe—as spiritual activism and term *performative transformation,* following J. L. Austin's discussion of language's performativity (speech-act performance) in *How to Do Things with Words.* Although Austin excludes poetry from his definition of *performative,* as opposed to constative (descriptive) language,[3] I would like in this essay to extend his sense of language's capacity to bring something about, for I am specifically concerned to consider poetry's capacity to produce a change in perception. I suggest an understanding of "performance" not only as theatrical, therefore, but etymologically, as a carrying-through of substance (content, import) via the technical (formal), productive of a per-forming (to and within the) reader. Although ecstasy in the passage from H.D.'s *Trilogy* quoted above is only *figured* as a "disease," for example, in order for the speaker to pass ecstasy on to others, her words must function literally and figuratively. They must produce both an intellectual and a physiological reaction, drawing readers in.[4] Such poetry is, as Susan Stanford Friedman suggested some time ago, potentially "revolutionary" (253).

In turning now to Fraser's and Howe's work, I want to extend Friedman's important insight to how women's postmodern poetry—the "copresence of feminism, experimentalism, and visionary poetics," as Kathleen Crown puts it ("Unsettling" 1)— might be revolutionary as well. I follow Rachel Blau DuPlessis in using the term *revolutionary* to characterize an ethical writing practice that does not require "subjugation" to form and order to write (132). This is the work, DuPlessis asserts in her foundational, feminist essay "For the Etruscans," of "cultural transformation" (17). She suggests that such poetry is exploration, "not in service of reconciling self to world," but rather imagining/ imaging a "nonpatriarchal order, in the symbolic realm and in the realms of productive, personal, and political relations" (19). The hope, to invoke Patrocinio P. Schweickart's theory of a feminist reading practice, "is to *change the world*" (531; Schweickart's emphasis). Such poetry posits ethical subjects that propose a paradigm shift from totalizing unity to "self-division": in a word, "ecstasy." This shift could transform the symbolic order, for acknowledgment of internal difference catalyzes tolerance of external differences.

For Howe, poetry's effect turns on a related etymological resonance: the psychology of the process of conversion. Howe speculates, for example, that significant aspects of Emily Dickinson's poetic methodology are taken from Puritan conversionary sermons. Each recipient of a letter from Emily Dickinson "was forced . . . , through shock and through subtraction of the ordinary, to a new way of perceiving" (*Dickinson* 51). By subtracting the ordinary from words, Dickinson produces a "shock" that "converts" them (etymologically, to turn around, transform) to "a new way of perceiving." The method by which poetic language shocks the reader into new awareness (that combination of physiological and imaginative interaction we call perception) is thus *performative.*

This poetry productive of readerly shock, that "knowledge of rupture" we recognize "as our own," as Fraser observes ("Line" 153–54), gestures toward a poetics to which Fraser and Howe both aspire. Such poetics produce formally innovative poetry with a substantive political purpose that is frankly mysterious and visionary. Located at the juncture of the erased (the "feminine," colonized peoples) and articulation,[5] their work creates dialogic interchange between text and reader. This interaction charges the reader to fill in the textual subject and recharge it with an embodied subjectivity. They "writ[e] over 'the erased,'" in Fraser's pun—not only rewrite and write over a partially erased text, but overwrite (as in an "overwritten" text that, because of that quality of paying attention to artifice, technically draws attention to itself).[6]

Fraser builds on H.D.'s work as model for postmodernist women's writing:

> H.D. introduced the concept of the *palimpsest:* writing "on top
> of" other writing which . . . has been imperfectly erased . . . ; *this*
> moment in history is *re*-inscribed over the faded . . . messages of
> a female collective consciousness, a spiritual and erotic set of

valuings essentially ignored by the dominant culture. ("Line"
155; Fraser's emphasis)

Fraser's "female collective consciousness" engenders linguistic
traces ("messages") that coincide within the palimpsestic frame,
not only creating imaginary interaction where there could be
none in history, but also reinscribing in the present what has
been lost.[7] Such a reinscription can never be precise, however,
and is thus achieved not through projective identification or era-
sure of significant differences (time, culture, race), but by having
established affinities: a shared "spiritual and erotic set of valu-
ings." Linda A. Kinnahan argues that Fraser's work demonstrates
an increasing attentiveness to a formally innovative "retextualiz-
ing of the feminine" (190). Her feminist poetics offers ways to
think through how form interacts with lived experience, to con-
sider "the gendered apprehension of language as it relates to the
material world" (Kinnahan 218).

It offers us as well ways to consider the enactment of form
as (gendered) experience. In rendering responses (emotional/
intellectual/psychic) to a trip to an Etruscan site as multiple lin-
guistic and generic "layers," the poet-subject of Fraser's "Etruscan
Pages," one of four poetic series in the volume *When New Time
Folds Up* (1993), posits "herself" as site of an excavation of socio-
cultural "marks and evidence of events" analogous to an archaeo-
logical dig (*Time* 35). The sight of fragments of Etruscan material
culture—erotic urns hidden away in a museum in Tarquinia, cliff
tombs at Norchia—catalyzed a process for her that eventually
produced the poem, and that the poem's reader-as-archeologist
then reprocesses in reading it. The speaker describes herself in
a letter, included in the series, as first experiencing a state both
out-of-body and beyond language ("I wanted to write about the
trip but I couldn't find words for those places at once so peace-
ful and full of what was & wasn't there" [*Time* 26]). Eventually
she composes a poetic cycle titled "Etruscan Pages" that abjures
formal and thematic completeness, as a way ontologically of ap-
prehending a vanished culture ("Feeling around for something

lost . . . " [*Time* 10]) now inscribed with, and inscribing, her ex-
perience of a preverbal, ecstatic state that unsettled her initially.

"Etruscan Pages" overwrites DuPlessis's "For the Etruscans"[8]—
a symbolically "ruptured," foundational feminist text—as well as
a literally ruptured society—that of the Etruscans ("vanished as
completely as flowers," as D. H. Lawrence, whom Fraser quotes,
images it [*Time* 18]). Like Lawrence and DuPlessis, Fraser associ-
ates the Etruscan civilization with a lost feminine presence, but
Fraser always qualifies the Etruscan " 'Nothing, nothing' " that is
left (12). It has never *simply* disappeared. Presented in quota-
tions, "nothing" covers over an indeterminate "something," re-
vealed in/as linguistic fragments that the poem pieces together
and that thereby *become* the poem. These scraps of language are
analogous to the pottery shards uncovered in an archaeological
excavation which metonymically represent the whole culture that
produced them:

> we know what each mark is equal to
> but not, in retrospect, what was intended
>
> . . . .

(*Time* 11)

Like the Etruscan tombs "where all has been emptied" (*Time* 25),
these marks stand at the boundary of signification, signs emptied
of their original "content" but not their material presence.

Fraser reinscribes the earlier texts, writing "among" the lin-
guistic and material traces of Etruscan culture, because for her
these traces that have survived content are neither wholly sym-
bolic (DuPlessis) nor romantically fetishized (Lawrence). She un-
covers and reconstrues them palimpsestically, finding in them
a spiritualized eroticism and an eroticized spiritualism. On one
of the erotic urns the speaker describes, for example, a woman
lies on the back of a man on all fours as another man "gives it
to her//unreservedly" (*Time* 16). In Fraser's multiple levels of
(ir)reverent punning, art is the *consummating* medium par excel-
lence (pace Keats: "Bold Lover, never, never canst thou kiss"),

coital service construed as a Cixousian gift-that-gives (without conditions, *unreservedly*). The text portrays Etruscan women as feminist ideals, at once sensuous and knowledgeable: "Etruscan women lie languorously/with what they love//. . . .//are equal in all divination/ . . .//Rome sends young men to Etruscan women/for wisdom" (*Time* 17). With its soft alliterations, internal rhymes and assonance, the language of this passage's couplets underscores the balance of sensuous and spiritual wisdom the Etruscan women embody, the passage's theme. The present tense with which the passage opens builds a sense of this em*bodied* presence and timeless lyric present. In rewriting the feminine, Fraser neither relegates it solely to the physical nor etherizes it into pure spirit; she images women as figures for lost wisdom, ideals for restorative change.[9]

But this theme is a level that the next stanza, the central stanza in the entire passage, abruptly covers over: "In war propaganda/ they [the Romans] called her audacious" (*Time* 17). As the Romans grammatically, as well as historically, "occupy" the pronoun previously referring to Etruscan women and the verb tense shifts from present to past tense, women suddenly become a relic—the objectified ideological sign that has come down to us through the ages of patriarchy: *woman.* "She" is survived by the sign of her femininity, "her fringed scarf," the full picture having been expunged by the colonizing forces: "Rome's greed for metals//melting her down" (*Time* 17).

Although Fraser's palimpsestic excavation of Etruscan women poetically reverses this historical meltdown, it does not do so by bodying forth their voices, as in lyric tradition. Rather, the very dissociation of body and voice is highlighted, becoming the new content of the same frame. An excavated tomb, apt figure for a signifying structure emptied of vital substance, is "inscribed with the hidden/particularity of one still alive//I am Larthia//first words/found" (*Time* 13; Fraser's italics). This striking claim to an at once particularized and originary feminine presence is in the form of a free-floating proper name whose context, as well as content, is lost.[10]

In repeating the phrase *I am Larthia,* Fraser revitalizes it, not by imaginatively reinhabiting "her," but by recontextualizing the word *as linguistic sign*. The line break at "hidden" forces us to pause at the word and consider the implications—"inscribed with the hidden" (*the:* definite article; "the hidden": indicating something specific without naming it)—before reading on to complete the predicate. The "particularity of one still alive," isolated on a line by itself, spoken by an unidentified yet authoritative source, yokes the notion itself with the enaction of a particularizing capacity of the "still" living (language memorializing, replacing, and revivifying), the sense of synonymity of body and voice with which individual speakers inhabit their names and the first person pronouns temporarily associated with them: "I am Larthia." Fraser's poem establishes a contiguous affinity of shifting speaking subjects in a discursive space, the "visual field" of the poem itself,[11] which acknowledges both that "something did exist once," and that—opening the field of poetic coincidents "joined at indefinite perimeters" (*Time* 29)—it "may again" (*Time* 33).

Fraser's revitalizing method is characterized by a lexical juxtaposition/recasting and a formal coincidence of history, letters, languages, signs, and normative grammatical and syntactical structures into a new space, or, space for the New. Her refusal of "predetermined order," as Kinnahan observes (194), resonates with Howe's project of distilling, testing, and recreating the traditional lyric in the postmodern (p)age, as described by DuPlessis: Howe "works between abstract thought and precisions of image: a woman . . . rewriting 'masculine' discourses, in the name of a feminist . . . cultural project which wants to transcend gender" (125). Both poets employ a feminized field of linguistic mystery to unsettle our attachments to mastery.

Howe builds on Dickinson's method of poetic conversion. She recounts her attempts to posit textual points she terms "singularities," following mathematical theorist René Thom, where transformation occurs ("plus becomes minus") inside and outside the text. A singularity, Howe explains, "is the point where there is a sudden change to something completely else. . . . It's the point chaos enters cosmos, the instant articulation. *Then there is a leap into something else"* (*Birth-mark* 173; my italics). Howe does not mean a simple reversal here. Rather, the loss of form (chaos) enters a formal system (cosmos) and becomes articulation (form), producing a difference ("something else") that is neither prescriptive nor transient.

"Connections between unconnected things are the unreal reality of Poetry," Howe asserts (*Dickinson* 97). She draws connections in her work that create a paradoxically "unreal reality" consisting of (visual) language-structures (sentences, phrases, words, letters, the spaces between them, and the shapes they form together) that "articulate the inarticulate," as Ming-Qian Ma observes ("Articulating" 469).[12] Howe's poetry, like Fraser's, characterized by its *formal* concern with performative transformations, critically embraces what she terms, in *My Emily Dickinson* to characterize Dickinson's iconoclasm, "contradiction."[13] As Peter Quartermain asserts, Howe brings together "the vision and the real" in her poetry (185): "Her language returns to such cusps . . . , for they mark . . . the nameless edge of mystery where transformations occur" (186).

I want to turn now to Howe's de(con)struction of a quintessentially Western (and white) as well as patriarchal (and male) subject, King Charles I, in her 1993 series "A Bibliography of the King's Book or, Eikon Basilike." Howe situates her long sequence in historical relation to, and in conceptual contradiction of, other bibliographies of *The Eikon Basilike, The Pourtraicture of His Sacred Majestie in His Solitude and Sufferings,* a book of essays, prayers, and debates reputed at the time to have been written by King Charles I as he awaited execution. When the king's book was published after the execution, Howe recounts, its printers were imprisoned. Furthermore, John Milton ("the poet-propagandist-author," as Howe calls him) wrote a revolutionary defense of regicide, which "defended a new rationalism" of individual conscience, entitled *Eikonoklastes.* At the Restoration, *The Eikon Basilike* was claimed to have been written by a bishop who was also a writer, John Gauden, whom Charles II believed (*Memorial* 47–49, passim). "Vexed" by "questions of authorship" through the ensuing years, the book has been the subject of several bibliographical projects intent on verifying authorial authenticity (*Memorial* 49–50).

Like the bibliographical projects, Howe's text begins with questions of origin and authorship. But unlike those projects, it contemplates the nature of a writer's authorizing relationship to a text she or he has produced.[14] Howe's preface to her *Eikon Basilike,* entitled "Making the Ghost Walk About Again and Again," concludes—like a postmodern mirror-image of Fraser's revitalized (but paradoxically unreconstructible) Etruscans—by graphically dematerializing its subject: "Was there ever an original poem?" she asks, and suggests that only "by going back to the pre-scriptive level of thought process can 'authorial intention' finally be located, and then the material object has become immaterial" (*Memorial* 50). Meditating on Charles I's *Eikon Basilike* (Royal image) and on Milton's *Eikonoklastes* (Image smasher), the poem pulverizes the operations of both.

Howe constructs and disperses the king's "Image," the latter operation often replacing the first image with another more appropriate one, a move, as the following passage illustrates, that Howe's poem abjures: "The King kneeling/Old raggs about him/All those apopthegems/Civil and Sacred/torn among fragments/Emblems gold and lead" (*Memorial* 60). As the "ragged," inconsistent, and imperfect rhymes in this passage underscore (him-apopthegems/Sacred-lead), Howe's king is surrounded by the material and discursive "raggs" of his former office. He is a (dis)figured, rather than reified, authorial image, literally de-author(iz)ed, one among other possibilities:

> Real author of The Lie
> "The Lie" itself
> fallible unavailable
> Thin king the Personator
> in his absolute state
> Absolutist identity
> Imago Regis Caroli
> Falconer Madan's copy
> the Truth a truth

Cynthia Hogue

> Dread catchword THE
> the king exactly half-face
>
> (*Memorial* 68)

Like his official royal image, intended to assure readers of an authenticated origin but "exactly" half-faced (partial, or put another way, *two-faced*), the king is always already a "copy," "a truth" contiguous, but clearly not synonymous, with "the Truth." Any attempt to transcribe "THE" truth of the mind's process (thinking) is already a fading reproduction ("Thin king"), reduced to a "Personator"—that is, to an acknowledgment of its status as a mask, as the etymology of personator indicates.

These fragments refuse to cover over the de-imaged (w)hole, the once-dominant figure haunted by an obsolete presence that has been emptied of its former significance. The king in Howe's sequence constitutes a reimagined Symbolic, I suggest, an imperial male term that has lost not only a divinely ordained authority, which a king once embodied and represented historically, as metonym and iconic presence. But, about to lose his head, this king also figures an irrevocable loss of natural (however constructed) as well as cultural and aesthetic authority (the Poundian dictums forbidding abstraction, for example). Linda Reinfeld observes of Howe's radical methodology in an earlier poem, *Defenestration of Prague,* that the "forms and sense of the world, real writing and its images, are played off against one another and detached from every kind of categorical relation" (142). Howe moves not from poetic text to truths outside it, "but always from language to language, an exercise in division" (132).[15] The search for the king's authentic words ends in hearsay, enigma, and obfuscation. His reputed spoken last word, "Remember," is a transitive verb, but as recorded had neither object nor referent: it was "spoken to Bishop Juxon. What Charles meant his chaplain to remember is still a mystery" (*Memorial* 47). The king's writing, moreover, is obscured, confused with the writing of others: "The Sovereign stile/in another stile/Left scattered in disguise" (*Memorial* 64).

The smashed Image is divided from its referent and has lost

its iconic status of immanent presence. Although (or because) another subject has (not) replaced it, it has left a structure the contents of which, done away with like Charles I in British history and the elder Hamlet in literature, render the linguistic framework uncanny: at once familiar and defamiliarized. Howe closes her prose preface to the sequence with the observation that the "absent center is the ghost of a king" (*Memorial* 50). Haunted by the traces of Western patriarchy (instead of maternal castration, as in Freud's "The Uncanny"), Howe's poem spooks us, dislodging our attachments to dominant sociocultural structures that organize and represent thought (*thin king*), to linear coherence, to the illusion of an unmediated relation between thought and word. As she describes the conceptualization of this poem: "I wanted to write something filled with gaps and words tossed, . . . letters mixing and falling away from each other, commands and dreams. . . . If it was impossible to print, that didn't matter" (*Birth-mark* 175). Uninvested in producing reproducible copy, paying attention to the infinite spatial as well as semantic (im)-possibilities of language itself, Howe's text lexically and graphically opposes the king's *Eikon Basilike*. But it also subverts that "First Revolution" (*Memorial* 66), Milton's *Eikonoklastes,* which was—though representative of an epistemological paradigm shift of radical importance—ontologically patriarchal in nature as well: "Fanatical swift moving authority// . . . . /Thirsty after fame/in the very Eikonoklastes" (*Memorial* 72–73). As Howe puts it in an otherwise unattributable statement in the text, we might say that she herself writes "To write against the Ghost" (*Memorial* 61).

Precisely because they are unattributed, such statements as the passage above must be approached in the context of the play of socially constructed hierarchies and frames, the "drift" of "dominant ideologies" (*Memorial* 80),[16] which runs through the text like so many weightless objects in Howe's poetically reimagined Space. Her fusion of history and poetry "functions to reposition the power relations between the two," Ming-Qian Ma argues, "by providing poetry with an entry point into . . . what hitherto has always been the sealed authoritarian discourse of [male] history"

("Poetry" 719). Like Fraser, Howe figures a performative para-
digm shift, a different relation to subjectivity for women poets
(among others).[17] Their category-abolishing project (as Howe
describes Dickinson's poetry) has been to desacralize the Holy
"Ghost" of the dead patriarch, to write against the grain of the
dead father's Law: the defeated monarch, literally losing his
head, exhorting Re-member (*Memorial* 47). As Howe reminds us,
the woman poet will not put him back together again. (The final
form of her refusal is hilariously antipoetic, turning reflexivity
on its head: King Charles's head bobbing on Mr. Dick's kite in
David Copperfield! [*Memorial* 81])

Into the space created by such breaches in and of patriar-
chal authority steps a refracting figure of woman. Howe writes in
her prose preface that there is a telling moment in Charles's
Eikon Basilike that oddly echoes Sidney's *Arcadia:* "A captive
Shepherdess has entered through a gap in ideology. 'Pammela
in the Countesses Arcadia,' confronts the inauthentic literary
work with its beginnings in a breach" (*Memorial* 49). As a multi-
ple figure, a "Heathen woman/out of heathen legend" who is
not only Pammela but also "Archaic Arachne Ariadne," this "dear
She" is, in a line that at once palimpsestically overwrites and in-
vokes H.D.'s famous lines from *Trilogy,* "the blank page/writing
ghost writing" (*Memorial* 67–69, passim). As both writing-surface
and writer, she is a revised feminine figure, at once heathenish
Ariadne and subtly reflexive sign of another "poet's iconoclasm"
(*Memorial* 75)—Howe's own, of course—unraveling any possible
narrative thread graphically as well as thematically by the poem's
end. Emptied (*blank*) of her symbolic significance, whited-out
(*blanc*), in Howe's multilayered corrective of our inherited domi-
nant fictions, "She" is the trace that (dis)colors the patriarchy's
claim to unvarnished Truth.

Thus, recalling the figure of Fraser's Larthia, we can locate
Howe's poem at the juncture of bodies and disembodied speak-
ing subjects, a border between imaginary and symbolic processes
of identity formation, a structuring and destructuring signify-
ing practice that constitutes an ethical feminist poetic practice
(Hogue 22). Howe's "dear She" performatively declares her iden-

tity: "I am a seeker" asserts her into a defining presence (*Memorial* 64). Concomitantly posited in contradiction, however, she disappears but at the same time asserts subjective agency: "She is gone she sends her memory" (*Memorial* 69). She takes up the position of legendary hero but does not assume his overriding claim to "all authority" (*Memorial* 72). Rather, she "inhabits" the coincidence without investing in it.

The poem dissolves in its closing with/into an Ariadnean figure unraveling the symbolic structures through which ideology ensures reproduction within individual identificatory processes:

> She
> was
> winding
> wool
> Cloud
> soft
> threada
> twist
>
> (*Memorial* 82)

Howe ironically reproduces the process by which readers, prepared to identify themselves in the position of a Theseus-like figure, simply cannot, because the text does not fulfill in its "resolution" any narrative or poetic conventions, any more than it did in its "body." Going into and back out of the textual labyrinth, we try assiduously to pick up a narrative thread, but in the end we lose it for good, left with the unraveling image of a woman winding wool, (un)twisting thread.

As sign that cost a king his authorial crown, this figure has exposed by her mere presence that the king's *Eikon* is a "Counterfeit piece" (*Memorial* 67). He has never been the same since, a mere semblance of himself—"Imago Regis Caroli" (*Memorial* 68)—trying to recover from the "aftershock of iconoclasm" (*Memorial* 78). She departs for the edges of nonentity, disassociated from structures of subjugation, gesturing to him so it feels real, but, not sure he follows her, he thinks he's imagining it. He can't read her. Then, her excitement becomes contagious and at last he's able to catch her drift (though he's already splitting for parts unknown): "shun me; for this reality/is infectious—ecstasy" (*Trilogy* 125).

NOTES

My thanks to Kathleen Fraser for her meticulous reading and generous discussion of earlier drafts; her comments were invaluable to my re(en)visioning of this essay.

1. I employ my own revisionary understanding of this term in relation to women's innovative poetry, as "a nonsynthesized, dialectical play between discursive modalities" (Hogue 29). See also Alicia Ostriker's notion of duplicity for Emily Dickinson's poetic strategy, in which "contrary meanings coexist with equal force, because they have equal force within the poet" (40–41).

2. On Susan Howe's wariness of the metaphoric authority Charles Olson's usage of scientific discourse attempts to establish, which prevents him "from addressing . . . the effectively patriarchal authority" of such language, see Peter Middleton (91).

3. Austin excludes poetry, among other theatrical speech, from his "more general account" of speech acts "issued in ordinary circumstances": "a performative utterance will, for example, be in a peculiar way hollow or void if said by an actor on the stage, or if introduced in a poem, or spoken in soliloquy. . . . Language in such circumstances is . . . parasitic upon its normal use[.] . . . All this we are *excluding* from consideration" (22). For a useful overview of the conflicting theoretical definitions of performative speech which uncovers Austin's heterosexism, his homophobic exclusion of otherness as abnormal and decadent (or effete and diseased), see Andrew Parker and Eve Kosofsky Sedgwick (1–8, passim). It is no coincidence that H.D.'s ironic trope for spiritual realism couples disease and vision: "*infectious* ecstasy." Indeed, as Helen Sword contends, H.D. was ambivalent about (Dionysian) ecstasy, for it required the loss of self-control and, as E. R. Dodds puts it, "is highly infectious" (quoted in Sword 140).

4. See Kathleen Crown's fine discussion of H.D.'s visionary feminism: "the goal of the *Notes* [*on Thought and Vision*] is political as well as physical, sexual, and aesthetic; the ecstatic stance proposed by H.D. is a means . . . of accessing with caution the power available in knowing ourselves as Other—standing in the place of an Other . . . This stance is potentially revolutionary" ("Manifesto" 239). Cf. Sword, who tracks

H.D.'s engagement with the notion of ecstasy, in that she "problematizes ... Socrates' four modes of divine madness" (126, 140–72, passim).

5. As Howe observes, "In my poetry, time and again, questions of assigning *the cause* of history dictate the sound of what is thought ... I write to break out into perfect primeval consent. I wish I could tenderly lift from the dark side of history, voices that are anonymous, slighted—inarticulate" (quoted in Middleton 92).

6. Fraser, note to author, 30 Nov. 1995. See also Marjorie Perloff, *Radical Artifice.*

7. On the engendering of subjectivity in relation to history, as well as language, see Teresa de Lauretis, *Alice Doesn't* (158–86).

8. Fraser had read DuPlessis's essay, though she did not have it consciously in mind as she wrote her series. She has described her experience of visiting Norchia as "falling through time" to "a deep, inarticulate place" from which the poem finally began to "well up" (discussion by phone with the author, 8 Nov. 1995).

9. On the feminine in Fraser's work imaged as "a locus for knowledge," see Kinnahan (190).

10. The Etruscan language can be read—sounded out—but not reconstituted. See DuPlessis: "It is as if books were discovered, printed in our own Roman letters, so that one could articulate the words without trouble, but written in an unknown language with no known parallels" (1).

11. Kathleen Fraser, note to the author, 27 Jan. 1996.

12. For a discussion of the visual dimensions of Howe's poetry, see her interview with Lynn Keller (3–7).

13. Ma argues that "the term to describe Howe's critical spectrum more comprehensively [than feminism] is ... 'contradiction,' a term the poet herself emphasizes" ("Articulating" 470). My sense, conversely, is that Howe's perspective, informed as it is by feminist, critical analysis, comprehends "contradiction."

14. On Howe and a Kristevan poetic "shattering" that displays "the productive basis of subjective and ideological signifying formations," see Middleton (90).

15. For related discussions, see also DuPlessis (131–32), Ma ("Poetry" 717–21).

16. See DuPlessis (137–38) and Crown ("'Unsettling'" 18–24) for superb discussions of how Howe in an earlier work, *Articulation of Sound Forms in Time,* marginalizes the center, thereby breaking up dominant structures.

17. See DuPlessis, who observes that an earlier work, *The Liberties,* offers "an astonishing self-portrait of an artist, a woman, trying to inherit herself, to work herself into her own—'patrimony'? 'anarchy'? No, into her own 'liberty'" (138).

WORKS CITED

Austin, J. L. *How to Do Things with Words.* Ed. J. O. Urmson and Marina Sbisa. Cambridge: Harvard UP, 1975. 1–66.

Crown, Kathleen. "H.D.'s Jellyfish Manifesto and the Visible Body of Modernism." *Sagetriebe* 14.1, 2 (Spring/Fall 1995: special H.D. double issue): 216–41.

——. "'Unsettling the Wilderness': The Textual Archaeologies of H.D. and Susan Howe." ALA Symposium on Women Poets of the Americas. Cancún, Mexico. 15 Dec. 1995.

De Lauretis, Teresa. *Alice Doesn't: Feminism, Semiotics, Cinema.* Bloomington: Indiana UP, 1984.

Doolittle, Hilda. *Trilogy.* 1944–46. New York: New Directions, 1973.

DuPlessis, Rachel Blau. *The Pink Guitar: Writing as Feminist Practice.* New York: Routledge, 1990.

Fraser, Kathleen. "Line. On the Line. Lining Up. Lined With. Between the Lines. Bottom Line." *The Line in Postmodern Poetry.* Ed. Robert Frank and Henry Sayre. Urbana: U of Illinois P, 1988. 152–76.

——. *When New Time Folds Up.* Minneapolis: Chax, 1993.

Friedman, Susan Stanford. *Psyche Reborn: The Emergence of H.D.* Bloomington: Indiana UP 1981.

Hogue, Cynthia. *Scheming Women: Poetry, Privilege, and the Politics of Subjectivity.* Albany: State U of New York P, 1995.

Howe, Susan. *The Birth-Mark: Unsettling the Wilderness in American Literary History.* Hanover, NH: UP of New England, 1993.

——. *My Emily Dickinson.* Berkeley, Calif.: North Atlantic Books, 1985.

——. *The Nonconformist's Memorial.* New York: New Directions, 1993.

Keller, Lynn. "An Interview with Susan Howe." *Contemporary Literature* 36.1 (Spring 1995): 1–34.

Kinnahan, Linda A. *Poetics of the Feminine: Authority and Literary Tradition in William Carlos Williams, Mina Loy, Denise Levertov, and Kathleen Fraser.* Cambridge: Cambridge UP, 1994.

Ma, Ming-Qian. "Articulating the Inarticulate: Singularities and the Counter-Method in Susan Howe." *Contemporary Literature* 36.3 (Fall 1995): 466–89.

———. "Poetry As History Revised: Susan Howe's 'Scattering As Behavior toward Risk.'" *American Literary History* 6.4 (Winter 1994): 716–37.

Middleton, Peter. "On Ice: Julia Kristeva, Susan Howe and Avant Garde Poetics." *Contemporary Poetry Meets Modern Theory.* Ed. Antony Easthope and John O. Thompson. Toronto: U of Toronto P, 1991. 81–95.

Ostriker, Alicia Suskin. *Stealing the Language: The Emergence of Women's Poetry in America.* Boston: Beacon, 1986.

Parker, Andrew, and Eve Kosofsky Sedgwick, eds. Introduction. *Performativity and Performance.* New York: Routledge, 1995. 1–11.

Perloff, Marjorie. *Radical Artifice: Writing Poetry in the Age of Media.* Chicago: U of Chicago P, 1991.

Quartermain, Peter. *Disjunctive Poetics: From Gertrude Stein and Louis Zukofsky to Susan Howe.* Cambridge: Cambridge UP, 1992.

Reinfeld, Linda. *Language Poetry: Writing As Rescue.* Baton Rouge: Louisiana State UP, 1992.

Schweickart, Patrocinio P. "Reading Ourselves: Towards a Feminist Theory of Readings." *Gender and Reading: Essays on Readers, Texts, and Contexts.* Ed. Elizabeth A. Flynn and Patrocinio Schweikart. Baltimore: Johns Hopkins UP, 1986. 31–62.

Sword, Helen. *Engendering Inspiration: Visionary Strategies in Rilke, Lawrence, and H.D.* Ann Arbor: U of Michigan P, 1995.

5

Siting the Poet: Rita Dove's Refiguring of Traditions

SUSAN R. VAN DYNE

In our work to recover, reconstruct, or hypothesize specific literary traditions that emerge from the practice of women poets, our practice as feminist and cultural critics depends on our foundational belief that gender and ethnicity will somehow be manifest in the poetry. Whether we see these traditions shaped by literature—the result of reading and revising her poetic foremothers—or by history—the signs of the specific cultural construction of gender, sexuality, and ethnicity that the poet lives as a historical being—or, most likely, by some combination, critics expect gender and race to mark creativity, as if whatever made her, biologically, psychosexually, or historically, must indelibly mark what she makes. These manifestations of the poet as a racialized and gendered creator, we believe, are traceable and specific, always recoverable in the text, even if not always the product of conscious poetic intention.

Given these critical assumptions, how are we to read Rita Dove? The winner of the Pulitzer Prize for *Thomas and Beulah* in 1987 and the first African American woman to be named poet laureate, Dove is both critically acclaimed and highly visible as the most accomplished black voice in contemporary American poetry. Yet in her five volumes of poetry, Dove seems to avoid distinctively racial subjects, attitudes, or idiom more often than she adopts them. I want to propose that Dove serves as a test case whose poetry challenges our expectations of the ethnic poet as a source of distinctive "cultural information" and whose accomplishments force us to reconfigure two literary traditions, an African American lineage of women writers, and the European American tradition of poets. My argument has three threads. First, I want to highlight the question of "blackness" in Dove's critical reception, especially as it has been articulated among those African American and white critics who have been instrumental in making her reputation. Second, I've chosen Dove's poems about motherhood in her last three volumes as the poetic site in which we might expect the intersections of race and gender to be most prominent. Last, I'd like to suggest that Dove's distinctive poetic signature both defies racial and gender categorization and wryly, obliquely acknowledges these as complex subject positions in several literary traditions.

Houston Baker and Arnold Rampersad, who take as their critical charge the definition of an emerging canon of African American literature and the articulation of its enabling literary tradition, have both championed Dove and yet find it difficult to account for the ways that race figures, or seems not to, in her poetry. Rampersad sees Dove's choice of racially unmarked subjects, her poetic preference for formal discipline, elliptical narrative structures, and densely allusive language primarily as a reaction against more polemical and populist practice of African American poets in the decades since the 1960s. While Rampersad is willing to claim, writing in *Callaloo* in 1986 (before the publication of *Thomas and Beulah*) that she is the best poet of her generation and heralds a new direction for black poetry, he rather wistfully ends the essay with a mild racial admonition veiled as esthetic judgment "paradoxically for someone so determined to be a world citizen, she may yet gain her greatest strength by returning to some place closer to her old neighborhood" (60). If Rampersad's praise of Dove's intellectual and poetic gifts also simultaneously confesses his desire that her talent ought to be used to make her particular historical, autobiographical blackness culturally significant for black readers, he is not alone. In order to claim Dove for the African American literary tradition, black critics need to explain what might be misread as her defection or assimilation to a white mainstream style.

Houston Baker, reviewing *Grace Notes* in *Black American Literature Forum,* can bravely begin, "Rita Dove is not a 'Race Poet'" politically, only because he intends to recuperate her stylistically as the direct descendant of Zora Neale Hurston, always for Baker the fountainhead of the black female tradition. While Baker is candid about his motivation "no Afro-American critic . . . would want to exclude Dove from our canonical lists"—the similarities he finds to the unimpeachable Hurston are unconvincingly vague. He cites "Dove's autobiographical lyricism and her astute precision in naming" as the distinctive poetical traits that connect her work with "Afro-American womanist traditions." Oddly, these critics seem to revert to a formula for praising Dove that belongs to a much earlier moment in the history of African American letters, before the emergence of the Black Aesthetic in the 1960s, when "shared humanity" rather than racial distinctiveness was the favored phrase for extolling black achievement. Indeed, Baker's redemptive terms for Dove's "patent sparsity of the sign 'Afro-American' or 'Black'" returns to a deracialized humanism: "Race is poetically transformed into an uncommon commonality . . . that strikes readers as somehow 'archetypically' true" (574, 575). Calvin Hernton, like Baker, must resort to praising Dove's poetry for its "universal" appeal, but he is more wary about the racial erasure that has produced such an appeal. He worries that most of Dove's poems are not only about European landscapes but "reflect what I hazard to call a 'European Sensibility'" (544). What marks each of these influential black critics' responses to what they recognize as Dove's "superb" poetic talent, is their shared anxiety. To fault Dove's choices means reducing the African American literary tradition to a narrow, prescriptive canon of approved subjects and appropriate politics, and yet to endorse the absence of "racial signifying" in her work would undermine the distinctiveness, the racial integrity of the tradition they've spent their careers delineating.

Helen Vendler might be said to have made Dove's career in the mainstream literary world both here and in England. In her early influential reviews, Vendler characteristically found Dove's gender and race irrelevant to her technical mastery, which Vendler compares, already in *Thomas and Beulah,* favorably to Yeats, her personal critical touchstone. Vendler rejoices that Dove's choices of subjects are thematically unfettered, her imagination poetically unaligned: "[Beulah's] domestic confinement offers less to Dove's imagination than the more varied life in the Thomas poems" ("Zoo" 51). Vendler's preference, perhaps more marked than Dove's practice, for male personae has been persistent. She highlights their presence in Dove's earliest book, *The Yellow House on the Corner:* "Such men are closer to her than a female surrogate like Belinda [an eighteenth-century slave], who, though of Dove's gender, is not shown to possess those conceptualizing and linguistic drives that make a poet" ("Blackness" 11). Nonetheless, in her most recent extended discussion, Vendler too must wrestle with the nature of blackness (and, to a lesser extent, gender) in Dove's poetry and with tracing her literary lineage in an African American tradition.

"Identity Markers," the chapter on Dove in Vendler's 1995 book *The Given and the Made,* was originally published in the *Times Literary Supplement* with the title "Blackness and Beyond Blackness." All of Vendler's titles are significant to understand the sense she makes of Dove's artistic career. What's "given" in each of the poets Vendler examines is some unchosen biological or psychological "fact" (Lowell's family history, Berryman's alcoholism, to cite two of her examples); what's "made" is the poet's self-fashioning of identity through art. For Vendler, Dove's blackness is a biological given with a specific historical legacy: "Any black writer in America must confront, as an adult, the enraging truth that the inescapable social accusation of blackness becomes, too early for the child to resist it, a strong element of inner self-definition" ("Identity Markers" 61). Vendler seems to acknowledge here the social construction of blackness, that its negative meanings are external to the child but deeply internalized as a psychic reality, which yet might be resisted as an adult. For Vendler, the task of the adult poet is to leave both rage and resistance behind because, in her account, blackness is also a literary constraint, limiting available subjects, political stances, and finally the poetic imagination of personal possibility: "No black has blackness as sole identity; and in lyric poems, poems of self-definition, one risks serious self-curtailment by adopting only a single identity-marker" (63). Instead, Vendler represents the trajectory of Dove's career as successfully moving "beyond blackness" as her poetry matures. She refuses "poems of victimage," the narcissistic temptation, for Vendler, of writing self-consciously from either a black or a female perspective, or writing poems of protest, and represents blackness as somehow transmuted—"non-autobiographical, mythological, cryptic" (87). Transcended or transmuted into such terms, one might wonder, is this lyric "I" any longer recognizably black?

What is striking to me in these accounts, despite their apparent incompatibility, is how they all ring true to Dove's poetic practice, and represent the challenge she poses to reading "blackness." While the black critics are troubled by the absence of the legible markers of the black literary tradition—the idiom of the folk, or jazz, or blues; a belief in community; an ethic of social protest and collective struggle; a mood of affirmation, pride, or historical continuity—Vendler celebrates Dove's ironic exposure of inner divisions within community and within the racial self as her legacy from Langston Hughes. All want to claim Dove for their tradition as the most prominent and promising individual talent, and each finds the ways she reconfigures that tradition problematic. But what of the poet herself? Certainly Dove identifies herself as a poet for whom "the fact that I am a woman, that I am black, that I am an American, and that I'm living in the time that I'm living in now has an enormous impact on my writing." At the same time, when she names her enabling literary predecessors, Dove cites wide-ranging affinities: "I feel accompanied by earlier generations. Rilke accompanies me. Derek Walcott accompanies me in a funny kind of way, and Toni Morrison does, and Heinrich Heine does" (Vendler, "Interview" 488, 491).

It should be, perhaps, more surprising than it is that Dove's poems about motherhood are among those most frequently praised as universal, since no matter how recurring the situation, what women poets have dared to write about motherhood has often marked watershed moments in poetic history as well as in feminist consciousness. Certainly poets who write as mothers, in the latter half of the twentieth century, have taught us to see that motherhood, as intimate experience and as institution, is permeated by history and politics, and is expressive of cultural expectations as much as individual sensibility. The poems of Sylvia Plath, Adrienne Rich, and Audre Lorde might serve as examples of a few distinctive possibilities in the hypothetical tradition of "poet as mother" which bear the mark of their historical moment, their sexuality, and their race. In the early 1960s, Plath records the tensions between artistic and maternal creativity; she lays bare the rift between the egotistical self-absorption of the poet and the exhausting expenditures of the selfless mother. In the revisionary utopian dreams of the late 1970s, Rich creates a parable of the mother-daughter bond as the most naturally erotic but most culturally estranged relation. In the 1980s Lorde adopts the persona of an outraged, outspoken community mother who takes responsibility for racial survival in an urban landscape littered with the victims of racism. Of course, Lorde's poems belong as well to a specifically African American tradition of female poets. Indeed, poems of black motherhood are a central feature of this tradition, from at least the nineteenth century, and the figure of the mother is much more consistently valorized as the source of racial pride, endurance, and political resistance. She is the symbol of sexual purity and of maternal heroism in the face of crushing loss in the poems dedicated to racial uplift, from Frances Harper to Jessie Fauset. In the twentieth century, that lengthy genealogy continues to affirm the unimpeachable mother love that underlies even apparently unmotherly acts such as abortion, as in Gwendolyn Brooks's much-anthologized "The Mother." The sign of blackness that marks the continuity among these poems may well be that motherhood is emotionally and politically freighted with community responsibility, with the survival of the race.

Dove's poetry is equally revealing in writing motherhood as a cultural phenomenon, although her poems' politics may appear less legible. Each of Dove's three most recent volumes represents a different strategy for exposing her experience as mother to poetic scrutiny, and simultaneously, I would argue, for defining her place in relation to black history and to European culture. In *Thomas and Beulah* (1986) Dove imagines the unrecorded histories of "nobodies" through her grandparents' marriage, which is shaped by the great stories of the twentieth century, the migration of southern blacks to northern industrialization, the depression, a world war, the Civil Rights movement. In the motherhood poems of *Grace Notes* (1989) Dove explores the maternal body more autobiographically, but the intimacies of these poems are counterbalanced by the tone of bemused detachment. Finally, in *Mother Love* (1995), an extended sequence of sonnetlike meditations on the inevitable loss and longing bred by maternity, Dove rewrites classical myth with a sense of its continuing resonance for her own predicament and with an edgy awareness of her historical and racial difference. In each volume, Dove's stylistic signature also becomes more recognizable: she adopts an ironic, reflexive stance that seems to serve as a defense against sentimentality and polemic.

Thomas and Beulah in its outward signs promises authentic, even autobiographical information about blackness. The cover features a pile of snapshots, the topmost one of a black couple in front of a car; that photo is credited to Ray A. Dove and dated 1952, the year of the poet's birth.[1] The closing gesture of the volume, a chronology that intersperses family marriages, births, and deaths with reminders of the public events of economic and social history, also marks these lives as black. Yet within the poems race is never insisted upon. Occasionally we hear snippets of dialogue from the characters that is racially inflected, but the omniscient narrative consciousness that represents these interior monologues isn't. Thematically and stylistically, race is muted; it is present as a given but not as the most important feature of these characters' subjectivity. The ways that this is also true for the poet's consciousness is demonstrated in Dove's creation of

Beulah as the figure of the poet. At first, Beulah's history seems merely the passive backdrop to Thomas's more turbulent emotional life. In the order of the volume, Beulah's narrative is intentionally secondary, and she seems defined by her marriage in ways Thomas is not (indeed, her name in Hebrew means "married" or, more ironically, "promised land"). Although Thomas is the more garrulous storyteller, Dove retrospectively recognized Beulah as her surrogate. In her sleepwalking, daydreaming, her moments of rapt inattention to the details of poverty or domesticity that may constrain her, Beulah embodies the tensions that exist for Dove between gendered and racial identity and her imaginative reach.

A paradigmatic scene occurs in "Magic," the second poem in the Beulah sequence, in which the young Beulah, sent to sharpen knives on a grindstone in the backyard, dreams instead of Paris, heedless that the knives have grown thin and that she's injured by the wheel: "When she stood up,/her brow shorn clean/as a wheat field and/stippled with blood,/she felt nothing, even/when Mama screamed" (lines 11–16). Beulah's vision not only transports her beyond physical pain, it seems to ensure her against psychic damage. In its conclusion, the poem re-inserts Beulah into historical time with a reminder of the racism that could constrain her dreams, but Beulah remains oblivious to this omen:

> One night she awoke
> and on the lawn blazed
> a scaffolding strung in lights.
> Next morning the Sunday paper
> showed the Eiffel Tower
> soaring through clouds.
> It was a sign
>
> she would make it to Paris one day. (23–30)

The magic that this poem works depends on multiple juxtapositions, and emerges from a series of misreadings or reread-

ings that refuse neat political resolution. The sign of racial vio-
lence, a burning cross on the lawn, is both absent and present at
once in the poem. The historical knowledge of the reader fills in
the gap in Beulah's perception, as we retranslate the metaphor
that Dove has provided, and see in the "scaffolding strung in
lights" a more sinister possibility, apprehended almost sublimi-
nally.[2] Beulah is not simply mistaken in transforming the cross
into the Eiffel Tower; she expresses, I think, the poet's insistence
on her own imaginative liberty. Clearly Dove admires Beulah as
a fellow artist who "rehearsed deception" (2) and makes "art/
useless and beautiful" (19–20). And if the dream "that she would
make it to Paris one day" doesn't come true for Beulah, we ap-
preciate that it does for her maternal granddaughter, the poet
who imagines this moment. Dove asks that we pay less attention
to the black body that suffers than to the vision of the dreamer;
she refuses to specify what it is that Beulah awakes to, and insists
that the reader be suspended, for at least a moment, between two
readings, one grounded in history, one that shimmers with pos-
sibility. Beulah's fine distraction here and in other poems, I'm
arguing, is what defines Dove's particular poetic stance; racial
history cannot be escaped, but it need not constrain vision, or
poetic ambition.

Writing the Beulah poems, Dove admits later, gave her unex-
pected access to ways that gender could free her imagination as
well. Dove has always been interested in telling a story from an
unfamiliar angle in order to see what lies "underneath."[3] Intend-
ing to imagine the history of her maternal grandfather, Thomas,
Dove unearthed, on a level she describes as unconscious, her gen-
dered knowledge of the "other side" of the story. She remembers
the gestation of the first poem in the Beulah sequence, written
during her work on the earlier volume *Museum:* "'Dusting' ap-
peared really out of nowhere. I didn't realize this was Thomas'
wife saying, 'I want to talk. And you can't do his side without do-
ing my side'" ("Conversation" 237). "In bringing certain things
to light in *Thomas and Beulah* I discovered other things beneath
them. . . . I realized that I was in fact feeding some of my own

experiences as a young mother into Beulah" (Vendler, "Interview" 489). Dove claims she was reluctant to write poems about motherhood for fear they'd be sentimental, but what the "cover" narrative of Beulah allows her to articulate is, instead, the culturally unspeakable truths, like Plath's, of unmaternal feelings. Perhaps in the 1980s, when feminism had moved to embrace motherhood as every woman's right and had reconstructed an ideology of its emotional satisfactions, Dove needed to displace these emotions to an earlier historical moment (so that they might be attributed to the stress of cultural dislocation, the material deprivation of the depression, or Thomas's failings as a provider) in order to acknowledge them in herself. In "Weathering Out" Beulah resists enculturation as a mother: "He'd lean an ear on her belly/and say: *Little fellow's really talking,*/though to her it was more the *pok-pok-pok/*of a fingernail tapping a thick cream lampshade" (16–19). The title, which refers to the geological process of minerals' being revealed through erosion, suggests Dove's ironic understanding that Beulah's pregnancy serves to define her, yet it also diminishes her. This divided or doubled consciousness that is the hallmark of the poet for Dove, can record even the awareness of its own near extinction, as in "Daystar." Although the mother is sapped by the daughter's emotional needs and invaded by her husband's sexual ones, Beulah withholds something: "Later/that night when Thomas rolled over and/lurched into her, she would open her eyes/and think of the place that was hers/for an hour—where/she was nothing,,/pure nothing in the middle of the day" (16–22). Here consciousness is neither reverie nor daydream but a null state, an evacuation of feeling as well as thought, or maybe a willed obliviousness that could resist interruption and be experienced as self-possession.

In the surreal dream of "Motherhood," Beulah's guilty wishes to be rid of the baby proliferate. She dreams "it disappears/with his shirt in the wash," or she fantasizes that "she drops it and it explodes/like a watermelon, eyes spitting" (3–6). The most disconcerting image of the poem (to its speaker no less than to the reader) is the concluding one, in which the mother's fierce defense of the baby against pursuing wolves bleeds uncannily into her terrifying awareness of irrational aggression, perhaps against the infant:

> tossing the baby behind her
> listening for its cry as she straddles
> the wolf and circles its throat, counting
> until her thumbs push through to the earth.
> White fur seeps red. She is hardly breathing.
> The small wild eyes
> go opaque with confusion and shame, like a child's. (16–22)

Whether she has displaced, in order to act out, her murderous rage, or merely recognized in herself savage instincts, twin to the wolves', that compel destruction as well as protection, Beulah is arrested in that moment of doubled consciousness as mother and murderer. What Dove has exposed in the emotional archaeology of this first group of meditations on maternity, her insistent exploration of the "underneath" of the cultural story, is, I think, the poet's oblique but uncompromising urge for imaginative self-protection against the consuming identity of mother. Beulah's ambivalence about motherhood, while frequently spoken by black women novelists, is relatively rare in the poetic tradition.

Dove looks back on the Beulah poems as signaling a new direction: "Technically that meant that I had to work with poems which were much closer to my present state which was also good for me" (Vendler, "Interview" 490). Critics have unanimously praised the intimate, autobiographical poems of section 3 of *Grace Notes* (published separately as a chapbook, *The Other Side of the House,* in 1988). In the group of seven poems about her three-year-old daughter, Dove witnesses the ways her female identity is perpetuated through her daughter's sexuality and also is irrevocably altered. These are the most comforting of Dove's poems on motherhood; they articulate an essential bond, a blood tie that's celebrated in the mother's first lesson about menstruation, improvised as a revision of Sendak's "Mickey in the Night Kitchen": "How to tell her that it's what makes us—/black mother, cream child. That we're in the pink/and the pink's in us. (22–25). Although Dove's eye knowingly records the eroticism of the mother-daughter bond, her gaze appreciates without appropriating (as Sharon Olds's poems about her children's sexuality seem to threaten). Exposure of the daughter's sexuality in the poem is accompanied by ironic self-disclosure by the mother. Asked by her daughter to compare vaginas, the mother complies: "we're a lopsided star/among the spilled toys,/my prodigious scallops exposed to her neat cameo. (8–11). That these poems have an undeniable sensual appeal, and yet remain healthy, innocent, and unvoyeuristic in their sexual candor, could well be demonstrated by Bill Moyers's blushing insistence that Dove read and talk about whether this poem "really happened" in his PBS interview with the then poet laureate (*Bill Moyers' Journal*, April 1994). Despite the emotional intimacy of this portrait, Dove's distinctive poetic signature remains a certain aloofness, an insistence that consciousness is most pleasurable when unfettered from the physical immediacy of mothering. In one of the most erotic of these poems, Dove links her experience of nursing her infant unexpectedly to a tradition of male poet-lovers in "Pastoral": "I like afterwards best. . . . I felt then/what a young man must feel/with his first love asleep on his breast:/desire, and the freedom to imagine it" (7, 9–12).

Yet the poems also record a discomforting alienation when the daughter's eye reveals what the poet's "I" usually omits, her race. When the mother-poet's racially specific body is shown and ironically owned in these poems, the speaker also responds to these identifications as unfamiliar and estranging. The presence of the biracial daughter mirrors as well as magnifies the mother's difference. Observing her golden hair and thin hips in "Genetic Expedition" produces for the poet a reflection of her own body as racially and culturally marked: "each evening I see my breasts/slacker, black-tipped/like the heavy plugs on hot water bottles;/each day resembling more the spiked fruits/dangling from natives in the *National Geographic*/my father forbade us to read" (1–6). Oddly, this act of intimate uncovering places Dove in a whole history of exotic others, consumed as sexual spectacles by the Western world.

Nothing could be further from the apparently autobiographical disclosures of *Grace Notes* than the poems of Dove's latest volume, *Mother Love* (1995), composed while she was poet laureate. The newest poems force us to re-evaluate the trajectory of her career. Dove may have seemed to be steadily moving "closer to her old neighborhood," as Rampersad wished she would a decade before; we may have been tempted to see a progression in this direction from her earlier explorations of the art and artifacts of European culture in *The Yellow House on the Corner* and *Museum*, in which meditations on the history of slavery played only a small part, to the imaginative reconstruction of family history, two generations removed, in *Thomas and Beulah*, and then in *Grace Notes* to poems that seem recognizably about her own biological family. The introduction to her *Selected Poems* (1993) even includes a previously unpublished poem about her childhood reading habits called "In the Old Neighborhood." In *Mother Love* Dove finds the domain of Europe, both literary and geographical, more fertile ground for her poetry.

The collection, in its themes and its forms, more explicitly than any of her earlier books, challenges the notions of literary authority and racial identification. These contemporary narratives, which retell the Demeter-Persephone myth, are set in Paris, Italy, Greece, or some unspecified allegorical terrain. Dove links her urge toward formal discipline in these poems (mostly erratically rhymed sonnet-length poems) not only to a European literary tradition, but also to the perennial tensions of the mother-daughter relationship, and with the poet's divided or doubled allegiance to these identities, each "struggling to sing in her chains" ("An Intact World" xii). Clearly, the sonnet form and the mythic story are an audacious confirmation of her place as a black woman within the classical tradition, and announce her wish to continue that tradition rather than simply repudiate it. Indeed, Dove acknowledges that her poetic cycles are a self-conscious homage to Rilke, an important influence throughout her career. Perhaps, unannounced, they also represent a tribute to Gwendolyn Brooks's technical mastery of fixed forms and the earlier poet's epic ambitions of the 1940s and 1950s. Brooks's own irregularly rhymed sonnet sequence "Gay Chaps at the Bar" records the "off-rhyme situation" of black soldiers in a white man's war. Brooks also won the Pulitzer Prize in 1950 for *Annie Allen,* whose long central poem "The Anniad" is an epic in alliterative trochaic stanzas. Performing expertly in these forms, for Brooks at midcentury and for Dove now, is itself a political as well as esthetic gesture, and represents, I think, an even more emphatic challenge in the 1990s to the critical expectation that the only or most authentic voice for the black poet is a street-wise or folk-inflected vernacular free verse.[4]

If the myth of Demeter and Persephone promises that death is followed by regeneration, rupture of the mother-daughter bond by its recuperation, Dove's revision in *Mother Love* emphasizes a longing for what is already lost as a permanent feature in the lives of both mother and daughter. The unremittingly elegiac tone of these poems would seem to have no immediate autobiographical source. Although Dove dedicates the volume "FOR my mother, TO my daughter," the sexual betrayal of the mother by the poet, now in her forties, is long past and can only be predicted for her young daughter, Aviva. I'd like to suggest that the ruptures and betrayals that these poems address are as much literary as familial.

"Heroes" is an enigmatic allegory that opens *Mother Love* which I take to be Dove's definition of the antiheroic female poet. The speaker seems to anticipate Persephone in that her desire for a fragile flower sets in motion a train of calamitous events that leaves her an alien and a criminal. The speaker plucks the last poppy in a weedy field only to discover belatedly that the flower was an old woman's only reason for living. Unable to restore the flower, or console the old woman, the speaker strikes her, and when she's fatally injured by falling on a stone, observes, "there's nothing to be done/but break the stone into gravel/to prop up the flower in the stolen jar//you have to take along,/because you're a fugitive now" (16–20). Strangely, the poet's desire for beauty is seen as first robbing and then murdering a mother figure, an intentional betrayal rather than Persephone's unwilling one. The poet's wrenching matricidal act is heroic only in being a stern confrontation with the mortality of all beautiful things: "O why//did you pick that idiot flower?/Because it was the last one/and you knew//it was going to die" (24–28).

The ironies in placing this poem as epigraph to the volume—and Dove's acts of poetic distancing and placing herself in and against several literary traditions—are multiple. The speaker of "Heroes" is shorn of race and gender by Dove's use of the second person "you" and removed from history by the hypothetical framing of the plot and the mostly present tense verbs. Despite these universalizing gestures, "Heroes" suggests an irreverent counterstory to the one we might expect from a black female poet. This poet's raid on her mother's garden violates the genealogy of recovery and indebtedness that, according to Alice Walker's definition of literary tradition, links black womanist artists to their foremothers. At the same time that Dove's poem resists telling Walker's story, its plot has an unsettling similarity to masculine myths, as ancient as Oedipus's and as recent as Harold Bloom's, about the young hero who must kill in order to rule, or to write. What marks this headnote, nonetheless, as indelibly both raced and gendered for me is precisely Dove's representation of her poetic act as both brazen and rueful; even in claiming her place among heroes, and certain literary traditions, she's aware of her inevitable defection, or at least deviance, from other communities, other lineages, other bonds.

In the storytelling of *Mother Love* Demeter and Persephone's experiences are relayed in antiphonal narratives, as in *Thomas and Beulah,* yet the separate sections and the poems within them are even less linear in their sequence, less strictly segregated in their points of view. Although Dove's poetic intelligence travels sympathetically between these two centers of consciousness, neither persona is ever at home or at ease. Instead, displacement is the most pervasive and anguishing emotion of the book. Dove describes her habits while composing as risk-taking through free association of image and language and then "revising incessantly." She works on several poems at once and they exist, often for quite long periods, as fragments (Vendler, "Interview" 487).

The structure of these cycles, each poem a fragment of the story that is revised obsessively by the other point of view, seems the palpable manifestation of these habits. Alternately Persephone speaks, distracted with desire, to be answered by Demeter, beside herself with grief, as in "Afield" (section V). In the octet a repressed Persephone, "hair combed tight/so she won't feel the breeze quickening" (3–4), wanders a meadow and longs to "find the breach in the green/that would let her slip through" (6–7) to return to Hades; in the sestet Demeter recalls a similar sexual obsession. Even though Demeter identifies with perennial female desire, she looks at spring not as the harbinger of fulfillment but of certain decay: "Like these blossoms, white sores/burst upon earth's ignorant flesh, at first sight/everything is innocence—/ then it's itch, scratch, putrescence" (11–14).

The refrain of these poems is a prolonged, chastened articulation of inevitable loss, of having less, and settling for it as the inherited wisdom of female experience: "As my mama always said:/half a happiness is better/than none a goddam all" ("Rusks," section VI, 12–14). Whatever ecstasy or enlightenment is granted to the female body is circumscribed always by suffering. Persephone moves from erotic self-discovery at the hands of Hades to erotic bondage within a few lines: "It was as if/I had been traveling all these years/without a body,/until his hands found me—/and then there was just/the two of us forever:/ one who wounded,/and one who served" ("Lost Brilliance," section V, 26–33). In the disheartening contemporary conversation of "Blue Days" female fecundity is a bad joke on women's uncleanness told between truckers: *"Why/do women have legs?. . . . to keep them from tracking slime/over the floor"* (2–3, 12). The poet as mother must acknowledge that this vulgar tradition is as enduring a myth as any and must be incorporated into her narrative alongside her sensual indulgence in her procreative fruits, the "season's first corn/ . . . /Nothing surpasses these/kernels, taut-to-bursting sweet,/tiny rows translucent as baby teeth" (8–10). Emptied even as they are fulfilled, maligned for the powers they would celebrate, devouring what they have produced, Dove's mothers and daughters alike seem marked by midlife pessimism or a pervasive cynicism about the cultural transmission of anything but pain.

Perhaps the most relevant sequence for placing Dove in her several poetic traditions is the final cycle, "Her Island," which retells of the poet's frustrated pilgrimage to a series of European sacred sites, and her disappointment in Europe's obliviousness to its own cultural legacy. Her hunger to witness, firsthand, these fertile sites that generate narrative because they mark the intersection of human and divine destinies, the interpenetration of a historical world and an eternal one, is never represented as racially marked. Dove might be any late twentieth-century American who finds the sources of her inspiration, the wellspring of her tradition, polluted by the debris of commercialism. She knows herself as gendered and racialized only through the eyes of bit players in this grand quest narrative. Intermittently guides and gatekeepers mirror back to the poet her anomalous identity, as when the gnarled Sicilian guide who promises access to the "chthonic grotto" is both discomfited and patronizing: "The way he stops to smile at me/and pat my arm, I'm surely his first/ Queen of Sheba" (poem 4, 5–7). At the very end of the sequence, the poet seeks the site of Demeter's disappearance as the omphalos of her own mother-daughter cycles, "turning time back/to one infernal story: a girl/pulled into a lake, one perfect oval/ . . . at the center of the physical world" (poem 8, 8–10). But the final circle of hell, the poet discovers, is to be blocked even from visiting the site because a racetrack now surrounds the sacred pool and is ringed in turn with barbed wire. Belated, excluded, peripheral where she longs to be central, Dove recognizes that her appropriation of myth cannot be an escape or even momentary relief from the degradation of history. While the story Dove's poems tell is one of repeated wounding, betrayal, rupture, and loss, the consolation and rejuvenation these poems do offer occurs repeatedly on the level of language. "Her Island" is a sequence of eleven linked poems in which the final line of one becomes the opening of the next so that closure is repeatedly

reseen as a generative beginning, or as the final poem recog-
nizes,

> Only Earth—wild
> mother we can never leave
> . . . .
> —knows no story's ever finished; it just goes
> on, unnoticed in the dark that's all
> around us: blazed stones, the ground closed.
>
> (poem 11, 8–9, 11–14)

Such recognitions, of the multiple stories underneath the
known one, mark Dove's peculiar place as a black woman poet
coming to maturity in the 1980s and 1990s with racial self-
consciousness and an omnivorous poetic appetite. She dares
to perform eloquently in an idiom and a literary tradition that
both includes her and shuts her out, and in the performance
she changes the unfinished story and redefines both the Anglo-
European literary tradition and the African American as well.

NOTES

1. Vendler provides the information about the photo credit in her
review of *Thomas and Beulah,* "In the Zoo of the New," p. 59. In sharp
contrast, Dove has always chosen artwork for the covers of her other
volumes, as if to insist on the artifice of what lies inside: she uses an
abstract Georgia O'Keeffe for *Grace Notes;* for *Mother Love,* a vividly styl-
ized painting of a tropical scene with the silhouette of a naked woman,
perhaps a "native," but one who is represented not as black but as green.
The painting's title "In a Green Shade" further dislocates us with the
echo of Andrew Marvell. Even when her cover art invokes blackness,
Dove insists on the process of mediation through art, as in the original
cover for *Museum,* which featured a German artist's portrait of the cir-
cus freaks "Agosta the Winged Man and Rasha the Black Dove," and
prompted the poem of the same name.

2. Such moments appear in the poems more often as narrative
asides than as the point of the piece: the jeering rednecks who run
Thomas off the road in his new car ("Nothing Down"); Thomas's sub-
versive reading of "playing possum" as racial self-defense ("Roast Pos-
sum"); the busdriver's smirk that deflates Thomas's proud paternity

("The Stroke"). Awareness of white racism is a fact of life for Dove's speakers but not its determining one.

3. See Dove's discussion of her use of history in *Museum* and in *Thomas and Beulah* in "A Conversation with Rita Dove," pp. 230, 236.

4. Dove's admiration for Brooks is evident in her survey "A Black Rainbow: Modern Afro-American Poetry," coauthored with fellow black poet Marilyn Waniek. Their preference for Brooks's early formal poetry is strongly phrased and unusual among black critics, who generally prefer her later, more accessible poetry as more politically effective and more consonant with a black folk tradition: "Her exquisite word-intoxicated poems demonstrate her mastery of craft. . . . While her career took a sudden turn in the Sixties and fell under the detrimental influence of younger, more militant poets, . . . none of Brooks' later work is equal in control or depth to the poems in her first three collections" (pp. 233–34, 236).

WORKS CITED

Baker, Houston A., Jr. Review of *Grace Notes*, by Rita Dove. *Black American Literature Forum* 24 (1990): 574–77.

Dove, Rita. "A Conversation with Rita Dove." Ed. Sanvel Rubin and Earl G. Ingersoll. *Black American Literature Forum* 20 (1986): 227–40.

———. *Grace Notes.* New York: Norton, 1989.

———. *Mother Love.* New York: Norton, 1995.

———. *Selected Poems.* New York: Vintage, 1993.

———. *Thomas and Beulah.* Pittsburgh: Carnegie Mellon UP, 1986.

Dove, Rita, and Marilyn Waniek. "A Black Rainbow: Modern Afro-American Poetry." *Poetry After Modernism.* Ed. Robert McDowell. Brownsville, Ore.: Story Line Press, 1991. 217–75.

Hernton, Calvin. "The Tradition." Review of *Museum*, by Rita Dove. *Parnassus* 13 (1985): 519–50. Rpt. in Hernton. *The Sexual Mountain and the Black Woman Writer: Adventures in Sex, Literature, and Real Life.* New York: Anchor, 1987. 119–55.

Rampersad, Arnold. "The Poems of Rita Dove." *Callaloo* 9 (1986): 52–60.

Vendler, Helen. "Blackness and beyond Blackness: New Icons of the Beautiful in the Poetry of Rita Dove." *Times Literary Supplement* 18 Feb. 1994: 11–13. Rpt. in "Rita Dove: Identity Markers." *The Given and the Made: Recent American Poets.* London: Faber, 1995. 61–88.

———. "An Interview with Rita Dove." *Reading Black, Reading Feminist.* Ed. Henry Louis Gates, Jr. New York: Meridian, 1990. 481–91.

———. "In the Zoo of the New." Review of *Thomas and Beulah,* by Rita Dove. *New York Review of Books* 23 Oct. 1986: 47–52. Rpt. in Vendler. "Louise Gluck, Stephen Dunn, Brad Leithauser, Rita Dove." *The Music of What Happens: Poems, Poets, Critics.* Cambridge: Harvard UP, 1988. 437–54.

PART II

Poets (Genre/Poetics)

6

Elizabeth Bishop:
War, Love, Race, and Class

MARGARET DICKIE

It was 1917 when Elizabeth Bishop was brought from Nova Scotia to the United States and there put into school where she was forced to pledge allegiance to the American flag and sing war songs that made her feel like a traitor, according to her report in "The Country Mouse" (*CPr* 26). But the six-year-old found war itself and the war cartoons with "German helmets and cut-off hands" that her aunt was silenced from discussing in the household no more daunting than her own dislocation in her grandparents' home, she claims. The war was perhaps the only real link with her life in Nova Scotia, where she had seen soldiers who, in contrast to the drab American soldiers, were done up in "beautiful tam-o'-shanters with thistles and other insignia on them" and who "wore kilts and sporrans" (*CPr* 28). Even the war songs were better in Canada, she remembered.

Identifying the style of Canadian patriotism, the military, even war, as stable knowledge to which she could cling in the general upheaval and confusion of her move to the foreign and unfathomable household of her American grandparents, Bishop presents herself as a confused child. This childhood confusion and her interest in different national styles of patriotism were to inform her poetry. In a number of different situations, she was to retain that child's judgmental stance.

Nationality and class rather than war are the alienating issues

of Bishop's early imagination, and they were to figure promi-
nently in the poems she was to write about conflicts of all kinds—
cultural, sexual, ethnic, and racial. She had a keen eye for the dif-
ferent national styles of war memorials, from L'Arc de Triomphe
to the "shabby lot" of statues in Washington, D.C., which served
her well as she surveyed the place of art—even poetry—in pub-
lic life. Selecting the foreign patriotism of her childhood as a fo-
cus of the profound turmoil of her early life, Bishop reveals here
neither fear of war nor sympathy for it, but rather a sense of pa-
triotism as theater which seemed so odd to her even when she
was to experience it again as an adult.

Bishop lived in a century of wars, and war is everywhere in her
poetry. It is almost always intertwined with a private suffering
that appears quite unrelated to the conflict, as her early move
from Canada seems unconnected to World War I, although, as
we shall see, the outer and the inner wars are not so completely
separate. Her attitude toward war may have been conditioned by
her childhood sense of being an outsider, a nonpatriot, a native
of no country. In this, she presents an unusual example of the
woman war poet. Bishop chooses to write about wars distanced
both in time and place from her own experience: for example,
the Civil War in "From Trollope's Journal," the Napoleonic wars
in "Casabianca," the Portuguese wars of conquest in "Brazil, Janu-
ary 1, 1502," or Robert Lowell's conscientious objection to World
War II in "The Armadillo." Even in "Roosters," which attacks
the baseness of the World War II militarism that she witnessed
firsthand in Key West, she uses the distancing device of allegory
and Christian myth. This strategy allowed her to write about war
without being politically current, to parody war poetry without
attacking those poets among her friends like Marianne Moore
and Robert Lowell who were committed to writing it, and even
to examine poetry's complicity in the theatrics of war.

Distanced as her poetry might have been from the wars she
knew, Bishop invariably interjected into the subject of war and
political upheavals some concern of her own—troubled sexual
relations, conflicted love affairs, personal misery. She placed her
love affairs in the context of the wars and the political turmoil

that surrounded them; but often Bishop could not distinguish love from war. She may have railed about American politics in letters from Brazil to Robert Lowell, but she was as wary about expressing her ideas in public forums as she was of political poetry in general, commenting about such work during the depression to an interviewer in 1966, "I was always opposed to political thinking as such for writers. What good writing came out of that period really?" (Brown, "Interview" 293); and in an unpublished review of Denise Levertov's work in 1970, "When has politics made good poetry?" (quoted in Millier 301).

Bishop had great difficulty in coming to terms with the subject of patriotism and in situating herself within countries—both the United States and Brazil—toward which she felt divided loyalties. She was of two minds about political poetry. Writing in an age of politically committed poets, Bishop felt it necessary to apologize to her publisher for the lack of war poems in her first volume, fearing that "the fact that none of these poems deal directly with the war, at a time when so much war poetry is being published, will, I am afraid, leave me open to reproach" (MacMahon 8). It is an odd fear, especially for a poet who wrote one of the most powerful antiwar poems and imagined conflict not just between men as soldiers, but also between lovers, between different classes and races, between servants and mistresses at the center of so many of her poems. In fact, it is so odd that it seems to be one of those strategies behind which she hid so often in presenting herself as an ordinary woman. Her comment seems designed to identify her poems to her publisher as women's work, perhaps open to reproach because they do not deal with the men's subject of war poetry and yet written by a woman savvy enough to know that war poetry was the topic of the day. And war is, despite her disclaimer, often the topic of her poems.

Some of the most puzzling aspects of her first volume of poetry might be attributed to Bishop's ambivalence toward war as a subject that she seemed unable to avoid even if she did not treat it directly often. In her early poetry influenced by surrealism, war or warlike images abound. Since many of these poems are set in Paris, military monuments were everywhere available to her, and she filled her early poems with references to them. In "Sleeping on the Ceiling," the speaker imagines that it is so "peaceful" on the ceiling that it seems to be the "Place de la Concorde," not ironically, despite its name, a site of peace but rather of war, revolution, the guillotine. Yet not sleeping on the ceiling, the insomniac speaker cannot sleep at all, menaced as she is by private warlike horrors:

> We must go under the wallpaper
> to meet the insect-gladiator,
> to battle with a net and trident,
> and leave the fountain and the square.
>
> (*CP* 29)

Leaving the fountain and the square of the Place de la Concorde, the very location of national upheaval, the speaker retreats into an inner world that is equally at war, however dated its weapons and mode of operation. This world returns in "Sleeping Standing Up," with its "armored cars of dreams" and "ugly tanks" that track the wandering children Hansel and Gretel (*CP* 30). Dreams and reality alike are war-ridden in these poems.

It is in "Paris, 7 A.M." that Bishop turns directly, however surrealistically, to the war, beginning, "I make a trip to each clock in the apartment" and identifying the clocks with "Time" itself and "Time" with an "Étoile" (*CP* 26). In Paris, L'Étoile is L'Arc de Triomphe, with the twelve avenues that radiate from it, commemorating Napoleon's victories and evoking imperial glory and the fate of the Unknown Solder whose tomb lies beneath. In Bishop's poem, the hours of this Time/Étoile "diverge/so much that days are journeys round the suburbs,/circles surrounding stars, overlapping circles" (*CP* 26), in a surrealistic meshing of time and space, as imperial power emanates both outward from Napoleon's time to Bishop's own but also outward from the imperial city to the countryside. Locating herself in winter, the actual season of Bishop's Paris stay, the speaker reinforces the reference to military action by noting that "winter lives under a pigeon's wing, a dead wing with damp feathers." Death permeates the landscape of this poem, as the speaker, looking in the courtyard, finds "ornamental urns" on the mansard rooftops where "pigeons" take their walks, although strangely enough "the childish snow-forts" "could not dissolve and die" in this surrealistic picture. She asks, "Where is the ammunition, the piled-up balls/with the star-splintered hearts of ice?" Again taking up the associations of war, the speaker claims, "This sky is no carrier-warrior-pigeon/escaping endless intersecting circles," rather "it is a dead one." She asks, "When did the star dissolve, or was it captured/by the sequence of squares and squares and circles, circles?" The sequence of squares commemorating military victories and civic power has captured the star—both Napoleon and the "star-splintered hearts of ice" that have waged endless war—in timeless memorials that attempt pointlessly to keep alive the war dead.

Opening the poem with the clocks in which "some hands point histrionically one way/and some point others, from the ignorant faces," Bishop goes on to develop the connection between history and histrionics, between actual historical events and the theatrical performance of military commemorations, which end in city street plans or more pathetically simply in urns beside which only pigeons walk. It is as if Bishop, who reports reading Wallace Stevens's *Idea of Order* and *Owl's Clover* at this time, were attempting to rewrite Stevens's statue and even to anticipate the still-to-be-written *Notes toward a Supreme Fiction* with its decaying monuments (*OA* 44, 45–8). She appears so attuned to Stevens's writing that she even sounds like him in her comment to Moore about revisions she had made of "Paris, 7 A.M." in which she apologizes for being so obstinate but insists on "apartments," claiming, "To me the word suggests so strongly the structure of the house, later referred to, and suggests a 'cut-off' mode of existence so well" (*OA* 46), or like the lives Stevens was to describe in *Notes toward a Supreme Fiction* when he writes of "the celestial ennui of apartments."

Inspired by the clock collection in the apartment in which she lived in Paris, "Paris, 7 A.M." draws together various strands of Bishop's early interests. The history and histrionics of time itself dissolve into those vain civic and imperial gestures toward stopping time by creating fixed memorials or mapping space evident in L'Étoile or in squares that commemorate moments in history. What appears to be a poem of surrealistic blending of time and space picks up hints from "The Monument" of how vainglorious memorials are, how perfectly dead the dead warriors remain despite efforts to memorialize them. If it is not exactly a pacifist poem, "Paris, 7 A.M." provides an ironic commentary on the vaunted permanence of military victory.[1]

When Bishop was working on this poem in 1936, she was very much aware of the ravages of the Spanish Civil War, writing to Marianne Moore, "The war in Spain is frightful. I wonder if you saw the amazingly pathetic pictures in the *Times* a few days ago— the wooden and plastic statues and crucifixes, all periods and quantities, dragged out of a church in Barcelona, lying so that at first one thought they were dead soldiers. There was something suspiciously dramatic about the arrangement, which makes it even truer to what I've heard about the Spanish character" (*OA* 45).

Here too she emphasizes the histrionics of war reporting as if the Spanish character were no more trustworthy in this respect than the French had been in "Paris, 7 A.M." And, of course, in her willingness to identify *the* Spanish character, she engages in some histrionics of her own. Even as she was concentrating on this "suspiciously dramatic" treatment of war, Bishop was concerned about her own inadequacy in writing war poetry. Sorting through her work to find a poem that Horace Gregory might want to publish, she wrote in 1937, "I don't know who the other poets you are gathering are, or what the material is likely to be like—but in case it's all 'social consciousness,' etc., and you'd rather keep up a united front, I am sending 'War in Ethiopia.' Of course it is very out-of-date, and I am not sure whether my attempts at this kind of thing are much good, but I should like to have you see it, too, and tell me what you think" (*OA* 55–56). Although "War in Ethiopia" has been lost apparently, this letter suggests that Bishop might have been consciously trying to write war poetry even as she was attacking its histrionics.

The impulse evident in "Paris, 7 A.M." to deflate the significance of war by pointing to the histrionics of its treatment found expression in two quite different early poems, "Wading at Well-fleet" and "Casabianca." They draw on nineteenth-century treatments of the Napoleonic wars—the first on Byron's "Destruction of Sennacherib," the second on Felicia Hemans's poem—but they redirect the imagery from war to personal experience and, in the process, show up its pomposity. "Wading at Wellfleet" opens with Byron's "Assyrian wars" from the Bible which introduced "a chariot" "that bore sharp blades around its wheels"; but, in the modern world, the speaker finds this military image transformed into nature itself: "this morning's glitterings reveal/the sea is 'all a case of knives,'" and "The war rests wholly with the waves" (*CP* 7). The quotation here is not from Byron, but from George Herbert's "Affliction IV" in which "my thoughts" are "all a case of knives," and so the knife imagery moves from the biblical war of Byron's poem through nature into the individual psyche. But, the speaker concludes, the "wheels" of this imagery "will not bear the weight" and they "give way." And so, Bishop's poem undoes the threatening quality of its opening image, rendering it strangely inconsequential. Never tempted, as she was to write in "Santarém," to literary interpretations "such as: life/death, right/wrong, male/female" (*CP* 185), Bishop does not divide her poems into militarism/pacificism, war/peace, but rather indicates how the two bleed into one another as the act of wading at Cape Cod participates in and then retreats from the elaborate analogy of its opening description. She was to repeat this technique in more successful form in "Roosters" where the arrogantly strutting militaristic rooster gives way to the humbling of Saint Peter as if militarism could be pacified by Christian humility.

Another early work, Bishop's "Casabianca," outrageously flouts its predecessor's sentimental celebration of willful military sacrifice. Imaging love as "the obstinate boy," Bishop subverts filial devotion as well as military discipline, making a mockery of Hemans's bombast as well as all war poetry, where "the boy stood on the burning deck/trying to recite 'The boy stood on/the burning deck'" (*CP* 5). Even the sailors who have escaped the burning ship would prefer their regular routine to any heroism or "an excuse to stay/on deck" as much as the "schoolroom platform" in which their patriotic deeds are commemorated. Yet it is only common sense to prefer life to possible death. "Casabianca" seems to be stating the obvious, and yet despite the openness of its reference and declarations, "Casabianca" is a poem that hides its meaning. Its chief interest here is the curiosity of Bishop's reference to the devalued work of that rare figure of the woman war poet. Perhaps, in her efforts to fend off her own sense of inadequacy as a poet, if not of war, at least of "social consciousness," she turned to Hemans as an example of how completely destructive to poetry such an enterprise could be. Reworking these nineteenth-century poems, in Susan Schweik's view, Bishop comments "not only on the language of war but, in exaggerated fashion, on poetry's promotional and disciplinary functions in modern Western war systems" (236). But if Bishop's position appears to criticize such poetic functions, it is curiously empty of any pacifist message, as Willard Spiegelman suggests in noting that she disarms the military apparatus of the poem without filling the void it leaves (160). Although the military floods her imaginative treatment even of topics far from war during this period of her life, Bishop often deflects the full force of its reference.

"Roosters" is the poem that treats the military most directly, and yet, even here, Bishop writes in fables; the roosters' "traditional cries," their "protruding chests/in green-gold medals dressed,/planned to command and terrorize the rest" (*CP* 35), must stand for human cockiness and its attendant military expression as well. Years later, commenting on this poem to an interviewer, Bishop was afraid that it might be read too directly. She reveals, "I suddenly realized it sounded like a feminist tract, which it wasn't meant to sound like at all to begin with" (Starbuck, "'The Work!'" 320). Critics too have commented on its feminist attack on war, reading the turn in the poem's second half to Saint Peter and Christian forgiveness as a transformation from the militarism of the poem's opening.[2] But, arguing that it is a buried aubade as well as the most "fiercely vivid critique of male power and of militarism by an American woman poet dur-

ing the Second World War" (217), Schweik details just how con-
flicted the poem is in an elaborate and brilliant reading of the
poem's dialectic movement. She comments, "Drawing the Peter/
crucifixion analogy *inward*—into the bedroom, that sphere of
the private, the domestic, the feminine, the sexual, the dream—
it implicates the woman speaker in psychic structures of conflict,
violence, and betrayal formerly reserved for specifically male or
vaguely generalized others" (231–32).

Despite the power of "Roosters," Bishop remained of two
minds about writing on such subjects as war. In a letter to Frani
Blough Muser, she notes her excitement over selling "Roosters"
to *The New Republic* (*OA* 87); but, at the same time, she writes,
"The literary highlight of the Key West season at present is
James Farrell, who *looks* tough, maybe, but is just like a lamb that
can swear—no, a sheep would be more accurate. I am utterly
disgusted with 'social-conscious' conversation—by people who
always seem to be completely unconscious of their surroundings,
other people's personalities, etc. etc." (*OA* 87).

Nor did she feel any more comfortable with "social-conscious"
poetry, it would seem. Writing about "Roosters" to May Swenson
almost twenty years later, she was anxious to domesticate it and
remove it from public reference, claiming that she had worked
on the poem over four or five years but had started it in the back-
yard at Key West at 4:00 or 5:00 A.M. "with the roosters carrying
on just as I said" (*OA* 316). But, closer to the composition of the
poem in her infamous argument with Marianne Moore about its
details, Bishop reveals her fascination with and her insistence on
its socially conscious and military details. Admitting that in the
first part she was thinking about Key West, Bishop adds that
she also had in mind "those aerial views of dismal little towns
in Finland and Norway, when the Germans took over, and their
atmosphere of poverty" (*OA* 96). Claiming too that she wanted
"Roosters" and not Moore's suggested "The Cock" as a title, she
admits that she wanted to repeat "gun-metal" and "had in mind
the violent roosters Picasso did in connection with his *Guernica*
picture." She explained, "About the 'glass-headed pins': I felt the
roosters to be placed here and there (by their various crowings)

like the pins that point out war projects on a map" (*OA* 96). Thus, wanting to "emphasize the essential baseness of militarism," as she wrote to Moore, she wanted also to tie her poem to particularities of reference. Although she writes a fable, she writes also from an alert attention to the details of an ongoing war.

Oddly enough, the military that seemed everywhere evident in *North & South* disappears almost entirely from Bishop's next volume. Even writing from Washington, D.C., she does not respond to its monumental architecture as she had responded earlier to Paris. Her year as consultant in the Library of Congress was a difficult one for her personally, and it provided few subjects for poems (Millier 219–27). Only "View of the Capitol from the Library of Congress" treats Washington as her surrealistic poems had Paris, and it is not a view but sounds of the air force band that provide her with a perspective on the nation's military life (Millier 223). Writing from the unusual experience of listening to band music that faded in and out of hearing, Bishop provides a sardonic commentary on the efforts of the "Air Force Band" insistently dressed in "uniforms of Air Force blue" "playing hard and loud, but—queer—/the music doesn't quite come through" (*CP* 69). This ceremonial city is obscured by a nature more gigantic, somewhat like the threatening waves in "Wading at Wellfleet," as Bishop notes that "giant trees" silence the band (*CP* 69). Again, as in the earlier Paris poems, the past—both natural and civic—overshadows the present, and the "*boom-boom*" of the air force band seems a feeble attempt to declare its own glory or even assert its military presence.

It took Bishop some years to write two other poems about war and politics which her year in Washington, D.C., must have inspired. "Visits to St. Elizabeths" and "From Trollope's Journal" reflect a much later stage in her development and in her political awareness which was to be ripened by her long stay in Brazil. Still, even in her Washington year, the public role of poetry in time of war could not have escaped Bishop's consideration since part of her duties in the Library of Congress involved visits to Ezra Pound, then incarcerated at Saint Elizabeth's Hospital for the

Criminally Insane. The visits were trying for Bishop, as Millier reports (220–22), not just because Pound was a difficult patient, but also because Bishop, herself succumbing to bouts of alcoholism during this difficult year, could see in Pound's madness a frightening version of what might have been her own fate. Thus, her visits to Saint Elizabeths were also a confrontation with her own weakness and guilt, "the house of Bedlam" that both she and Pound seemed to inhabit and even to have built themselves.

Writing from the model of the nursery rhyme, "This is the house that Jack built," Bishop calls Pound "tragic," "talkative," "honored," "old, brave man," "cranky," "cruel," "busy," "tedious"— running the full range of his qualities; but in the end she judges him as "the wretched man/that lies in the house of Bedlam" (*CP* 135). This indictment of Pound's self-deception and lies (and her own self-mockery) is Bishop's most sympathetic statement of the sufferings of war and concomitantly her most serious expression of doubts about the value of serious poetry. "This is a world of books gone flat," she writes (134), as if "the poet" in Pound could not be separated from "the man" and his inadequacy. Time may have proved Bishop accurate in her judgment; but, when this poem was written only a few years after the controversy over Pound's Bollingen Award and the poetic establishment's defense of art against political judgments, its criticism of Pound had a particular political charge, taking the unpopular side of the whole debate over the poet and the value of his poetry apart from his politics. Perhaps Bishop's sense of her own failures in the unhappy year she spent in Washington forced her to reflect on the civic duties of the poet. And certainly part of the impulse for this poem was her personal reaction to Pound as a difficult and irascible man. Still, the poem presents Pound as tragically irresponsible, not saved by his art and not just cranky but cruel as well. Written long after her year in Washington, the poem reflects too the political awareness of her years in Brazil where the artist was never safe from political involvement or protected from his own rash acts as Pound had been.

Some time later still, Bishop returned to Washington, D.C., as a scene and to war as a subject in "From Trollope's Journal," which she told Robert Lowell was almost all a complete quotation from Trollope himself (*OA* 387), even if it was, as she claimed later on, "actually an anti-Eisenhower poem" (*OA* 439). Although she may have used Trollope's commentary on the monuments, the sentiments are familiar again from Bishop's own early treatment of national monuments, although here they interject into the equation the whole question of race that might have come out of her experience in Brazil:

> As far as statues go, so far there's not
> much choice: they're either Washington
> or Indians, a whitewashed, stubby lot,
> His country's Father or His foster sons.

> (*CP* 132)

The "sad, unhealthy spot" of the White House on Potomac's "swampy brim" is matched by Trollope's own throbbing "anthrax," and even the surgeon who attends him comes "with a sore throat himself" and "croaked out," " 'Sir, I do declare/everyone's sick! The soldiers poison the air' " (*CP* 132).

As a commentary on war, "From Trollope's Journal" is almost as treasonous as Pound's World War II broadcasts. An attack on the sickness of the defenseless soldiers recuperating in Washington, D.C., from the ravages of the Civil War, the poem voices a pitiless indictment of the sickness of war. Even phrased in Trollope's English xenophobic reaction to America, the sentiments are repellently self-centered and callously unconcerned with the larger human sacrifices of war. Published in 1961, the poem expressed the antiwar sentiment of the time, although only a few years earlier it would have come under suspicion as radically anti-American.

Bishop's return to war as a subject and to Washington, D.C., as a location in these two late poems brings with it some of the concerns of her life in Brazil which turned her toward politics and the military as a subject. In her early poetry from Brazil, she took on the cast of that country's history and politics, revealing her talent for caricature. From the Portuguese conquerors in "Brazil, January 1, 1502" to the hysterical military police in pursuit of a killer in "The Burglar of Babylon," Bishop treats the conquering army as well as the Brazilian military as objects of contempt. Comparing them to lizards, she belittles them further in "Brazil, January 1, 1502." These "tiny" lustful conquerors are no match, however, for the native women. Nor are the soldiers tracking Micuçú in "The Burglar of Babylon" of any finer quality. They remain completely unequal to this so-called enemy of society (*CP* 112) who seems nonetheless at home among the poor of his own social class. Even with tommy guns in hand, they are nervous, shooting the officer in command in a panic, and Micuçú eludes them successfully, until, shooting a soldier at close range and missing, he is finally killed. These scenes are cartoonlike in their exaggerated parody of South American incompetence in its lust for military power. And yet, like the exaggerated concern for the dog with scabies in "Pink Dog," the sentiments of these poems cover a severe indictment of the repressive political regimes that first colonized and then came to rule the country.

But Bishop did not have to go to Brazil to see such conflicts. The racial conflicts between the white colonizers and the maddening Indian women and the class conflicts between Micuçú and his captors may have come out of Bishop's Brazilian experience, but they are not new to her poetry. Despite her disgust with "social-conscious conversation," she was fascinated by that other war between race and class that characterized so much of the internal politics of her time. Her early poems from Key West often take as subjects such conflicts. Although she was a member of the dominant culture in the United States, a country that, despite its ethnic variety, has regarded ethnic groups as outsiders, Bishop had occasion from earliest childhood to consider herself an outsider, witnessing conflicts of class and race quite unusual in American life—for example, between the impoverished, if homogeneous, rural community of her maternal grandparents in Nova Scotia and the richer society of her paternal grandparents in Worcester, Massachusetts, where she was moved as a child, or between servants and mistresses in her early adult life in Key West.

If she thought of herself as "a New Englander herring choker bluenoser" in Brazil, as she told Lowell (*OA* 384), she also had an interest in other classes and races, as if she could study in their conflicts something of her own conflicted identity. Adrienne Rich has claimed that her poems about servants and mistresses take the place of poems examining intimate relationships (130). But, in fact, these poems about mistress and servant, landowner and tenant, white woman and black woman, indicate a strange interest in the intimacy in which these racial conflicts play out. Commenting on "Songs for a Colored Singer," the poem Bishop wrote in the 1940s with Billie Holiday in mind, Rich again questions this choice:

> This is a white woman's attempt—respectful, I believe—to speak through a Black woman's voice. A risky undertaking, and it betrays the failures and clumsiness of such a position. . . . What I value is her attempt to acknowledge other outsiders, lives marginal in ways that hers is not, long before the Civil Rights movement made such awareness temporarily fashionable for some white writers. (*BBP* 131)

Rich wants to claim Bishop for a female and lesbian tradition that has tried critically and consciously to "explore marginality, power and powerlessness, often in poetry of great beauty and sensuousness" (*BBP* 135), and, at the same time, to acknowledge the problems inherent in an establishment poet's taking on such a task.

Although other critics have judged Bishop less severely, Rich is correct in acknowledging the outsider perspective from which Bishop views these figures and the subservient situations in which they find themselves.[3] And yet, of course, they were very much a part of her life and circumstances. In some sense, they held her interest over a lifetime and in varying environments because she identified with them. So she writes too as an insider, knowledgeable about the marginal, the exiled, and the dispossessed in society because she was one herself. She knew the bonds, even chains, of attraction and repulsion between classes and races which linked lives that would be solitary and lonely without them. In taking up such subjects, Bishop was acknowledging a range of experience that she, as a solitary women, even a lonely tourist, knew intimately; but, like Sylvia Plath's appropriation of the Jew in a Fascist society as a metaphor for her own condition as a woman, Bishop's poetic possession of the dispossessed is a problematic choice. She does not evince any of Rich's open-hearted political sentiment about class exploitation. At the same time, she writes from a deep sensitivity to ties that blur the boundaries of race and class.

Violence is often at the heart of the lives of the Key West African Americans she treats. For example, "Cootchie," Miss Lula's maid, appears to be a person known only by the erasure of her identity; in life as in death, "black into white she went," first as a maid and then as a suicide "below the surface of the coral reef" (*CP* 46). According to Thomas Travisano, Miss Lula ran the boardinghouse in Naples, Florida, where Bishop stayed on her first trip, and her black servant Cootchie told Bishop, "That's why I like coloured folks—they never commit suicide" (83–84). But, of course, Cootchie does commit suicide in the poem and causes both the poet and Miss Lula to commemorate her. Like the war monuments in Paris, Miss Lula's memorial is only a way of covering up experience, a very stylized way of holding in abeyance baffling circumstances. But the poem is titled "Cootchie" not "Miss Lula," and the maid dominates the poet's sense of how artificial most art is, how little even the most elaborate artifice can rescue. "Black into white she went" is a powerful reminder of racial dominance against which art cannot defend its subject.

How little the outsider can understand racial conflicts is evident in "Faustina, or Rock Roses," where the speaker observes Faustina tending the white woman in "a crazy house" (*CP* 72). Another subject drawn from real life in Key West, she too is both victim and victimizer in a conflict of intimacy.[4] Bishop writes, "Her sinister kind face/presents a cruel black/coincident conundrum.//Oh, is it/freedom at last" (*CP* 73) "Or is it the very worst,/the unimaginable nightmare" (*CP* 73).

The question of "freedom at last" turns first to death and then to release from servitude; but whose death and whose release are the conundrum. Is death of the mistress freedom for the maid or freedom from the maid's sinister kindness for the mistress herself? And what is the "unimaginable nightmare"? The visitor is as intertwined in the scene as those she surveys; she is "embarrassed" not for intruding into this privacy, but for being part of the disguise, for betraying her own stupefaction within which she may discover, if not concern, at least that she should be concerned. And, taking this in, the reader too can see herself drawn into the poem, understand how her own view of what is going on may betray a voyeuristic curiosity rather than concern, a desire to know what the poem means rather than what death signifies in the lives of these two women.

This is not a poem of rich and poor so much as it is a poem of trust and protection spelled out in racial terms where trust has always rested on exploitation. The white woman whom Faustina tends lives in a decaying house where the floorboards sag and the bedroom is cluttered with ragged garments. She is not rich, nor is Faustina, complaining of the terms of her employment, either without resources or all-suffering. "She bends above the other," the speaker says of Faustina, noting both her superior and her subservient position. The racial component of the situation suggests that exploitation works both ways.

What the visitor sees, if she sees at all, is the solidarity of mistress and maid, their interdependence, as a "dream of protection and rest" that may turn into a "nightmare" at any moment.[5] The fragility of such a relationship is all the more frightening because the women depend utterly upon it. The speaker of the poem too manipulates this fear by the mixing of such opposites as stupefaction and concern, sinister and kind, dream and nightmare. And this speaker, like the visitor, is no transparent observer; she is a kind of voyeur gasping for breath in the linguistically excessive "yes" in the opening lines and "oh" in the final lines (*CP* 72, 74). In the "crazy house" of this poem, everyone is threatened. "Oh" turns easily into "O," into blankness and a cipher. "There is no way of telling," the poet concludes of this conflict.

Violence of a quite different kind is evident in an early poem written in Brazil, "The Armadillo," which also expresses ambivalence toward the natives who honor Saint John's Day each year by sending up dangerous fire balloons. But it introduces into what seems a purely descriptive scene the completely extraneous presence of Robert Lowell to whom the poem is dedicated, and he turns the poem in the direction of political commentary. The poem starts casually as one of Bishop's accounts of local Brazilian customs; but its tone changes in the final stanza:

> *Too pretty, dreamlike mimicry!*
> *O falling fire and piercing cry*
> *and panic, and a weak mailed fist*
> *clenched ignorant against the sky!*

(CP 104)

This outburst, so long delayed, seems completely detached in its protest from the scene on which it comments. What is *"Too pretty"*—the fire balloons, the devotion to the saint, the speaker's own descriptive powers, the potential danger of the fire? Is this firebombing reminiscent of the firebombing of World War II? The poem's particularities seem to draw it away from any general reference, and yet the ending in italics has the power to unsettle the details. It is clear that, whatever is too pretty, the clenched fist will not overcome it. Physical force and "pretty" art that mimics the world are alike ineffectual, both inadequate to the panic that the falling fire brings.

Because this poem is dedicated to Lowell and titled "The Armadillo" instead of "The Owl's Nest," an earlier alternate title, the fist clenched against the sky calls up not just the armadillo's retreat from the fire, but all forms of retreat, "head down, tail down," such as Lowell's status as a conscientious objector during World War II, as well as bouts of madness through which he retreated, "weak" and "ignorant." Violence, the speaker seems to suggest, can never be countered by violence, folly by folly. In a world where fire balloons attract and appall us, where piety itself is pretty and dangerous, and—in a surprising turn toward the military—where clenched fists are weak and ignorant, the impulses to self-protection and self-destruction are fatally intertwined. Bishop keeps free from the confessional "I" that Lowell uses, suggesting that that will is everywhere threatened not just in the modern world but in its history where saints were honored and fists "mailed."

Bishop's wars may have been internal but she figured them in ancient terms— the "insect-gladiator" of her nightmares in "Sleeping on the Ceiling," the "creaking armor" of the Christian conquerors of "Brazil, January 1, 1502," and the "mailed fist" clenched against the sky of "The Armadillo"—as if the quaintness of the reference might suggest something of her criticism of war itself. The images bear a certain burden of ridicule as the tiny insect diminishes the grandeur of the gladiator and the "tiny" Christians are further miniaturized by their "creaking armor," the fist rendered impotent by its ignorance. It is as if Bishop were engaging in her own "pretty" "mimicry" by capturing war in such literary and old-fashioned terms.

The relation between art and war, between efforts at commemoration and the acts of war, between poetry and politics— a recurring interest from her surrealistic Paris poems to her realistic Brazilian writing—finds its summary statement in "12 O'Clock News," a prose-poem that juxtaposes the objects on the writer's desktop with an account of a reconnaissance flight in what might be the Vietnam War. According to Millier, this poem had been with Bishop in fragments of verse since her Vassar days (474); but, as it was completed, it depends on details of a war against an unknown "small, backward country, one of the most backward left in the world today," a "tiny principality" where " 'industrialization' and its products" are "almost nonexistent" (*CP* 174), which sounds like Vietnam.

As the poem plays details from the writer's desk against details of the war, an eerie connection between writing and war emerges. The writer's "gooseneck lamp" is matched against the full moon half the world over where "Visibility is poor"; the "typewriter" with the "elaborate terraces" of the enemy landscape; "pile of mss." and a "slight landslide"; "typed sheet" and a "field" that may be either "airstrip" or "cemetery"; "ink-bottle" and "some powerful and terrifying 'secret weapon'"; typewriter eraser and a dead native; and finally, in the most gruesome connection, "ashtray" and:

> From our superior vantage point, we can clearly see into a sort of dugout, possibly a shell crater, a "nest" of soldiers. They lie heaped together, wearing the camouflage "battle dress" intended for "winter warfare." They are in hideously contorted positions, all dead. We can make out at least eight bodies. These uniforms were designed to be used in guerrilla warfare on the country's one snow-covered mountain peak. The fact that these poor soldiers are wearing them *here*, on the plain, gives further proof, if proof were necessary, either of the childishness and hopeless impracticality of this inscrutable people, our opponents, or of the sad corruption of their leaders.
>
> (CP 175)

All that destabilizes the clear connection between the writer's effort at her desk and war activity is the tone of the reporter on the twelve o'clock news, at every point exclaiming his/her "superior vantage point" while revealing his/her naivete. As the news goes on, it becomes increasingly clear that the reporter can tell us very little about the other country and even less about the war itself; all she or he can really report is death and destruction. If the equation between writing and war is complete in this poem, then writing is destructive, not a memorializing of war but rather its apotheosis.

For a poet who had spent a lifetime writing about war, witnessing the conflicts not just of nations but of races and classes within the United States and Brazil, this final acknowledgment of the close collaboration between writing and war is, as James Merrill said, her "saddest poem" (quoted in Millier 474). She had never liked "social-conscious conversation" or socially conscious poetry, and yet she returned again and again in her poetry to those points at which the world in which she lived and the world that she created could not avoid collision. The news reporter's language in "12 O'Clock News" is as inflated as the rhetoric of Felicia

Hemans's poem of the Napoleonic wars which the young Bishop had parodied, and the poet's deflation of it is as extreme; but, in the course of a long life of thinking about such matters, Bishop had come to fear that the poet's desk was not free from the world's corruption, her own creativity not unconnected to the subject of war from which she so often had recoiled.

On the dust jacket of *Geography III,* where "12 O'Clock News" was published, John Ashbery is quoted as writing: "The extraordinary thing about Miss Bishop is that she is both a public and a private poet, or perhaps it is that her poetry by its very existence renders obsolete these two after all artificial distinctions (artificial insofar as poetry is concerned)" (MacMahon 105). Strangely enough, in connecting the private and the public in her late poetry, Bishop came to understand the value of both, as she had learned their hazards. Perhaps the person who taught her most in this respect was Lowell, and especially in his scandalous use of private letters from Elizabeth Hardwick in *The Dolphin.* In a long and tormented letter to Lowell, Bishop writes, "One can use one's life as material—one does, anyway—but these letters— aren't you violating a trust? IF you were given permission— IF you hadn't changed them . . . etc. But *art just isn't worth that much.* I keep remembering Hopkins's marvelous letter to Bridges about the idea of a 'gentleman' being the highest thing ever conceived—higher than a 'Christian,' even, certainly than a poet. It is not being 'gentle' to use personal, tragic, anguished letters that way—it's cruel" (*OA* 562).

And, given these views and Lowell's own willingness to make the most intimate details of his private life a matter of public record, it is certainly ironic that, when Bishop came to write an elegy for him, she memorializes his private moments—when he told her he had discovered "girls" one summer in Maine and "learned to kiss" (*CP* 188)—but she concludes by noting— somewhat gratefully—that he can no longer change his art:

> You left North Haven, anchored in its rock,
> afloat in mystic blue . . . And now—you've left
> for good. You can't derange, or re-arrange,

your poems again. (But the Sparrows can their song.)
The words won't change again. Sad friend, you cannot change.

(*CP* 189)

The poet who had started by considering the deadness of those unchanging monuments that surrounded her in Paris as a young woman, had come finally to rely on that permanence of public memorial, on words that will not change, on permanence as a stay against the folly of public derangement, even that of her good friend Lowell. Bishop came to appreciate that moment of stasis. She desired, at least for her troubled friend, the permanence of art.

NOTES

1. The military was even closer than the Paris war memorials, she notes, writing from Paris to Frani Blough: "Some of the French Army lives in this house, and I am always squeezing into the elevator with a dashing young thing all spurs, swords, epaulets, and a headdress of red, white and blue feathers (honestly) about 18 inches high" (*OA* 37–38).

2. See, for example, Ostriker 54, and Spiegelman 156–58.

3. Willard Spiegelman compares Bishop's treatment of Manuelzhino and his mistress to Wordsworth (167). Bonnie Costello acknowledges that class differences remain in place in "Manuelzhino," although their stability is shaken. She claims that "the landowner remains within her own world, ambivalently open to new potentialities and freed from cliche" (83).

4. Lorrie Goldensohn comments on the "sinister potential of our bonds to the maternal or surrogate maternal presence" here as she identifies Bishop's acquaintance with this woman who sold lottery tickets in Key West (74–75).

5. Lorrie Goldensohn notes the "historically corrupted" terms of the exchange between a needy white in the care of a powerful black servant in an interesting discussion of the problems of trust within love in Bishop's work (75).

WORKS CITED

Bishop, Elizabeth. *Elizabeth Bishop: The Complete Poems, 1927–1979*. New York: Farrar, 1983.

———. *Elizabeth Bishop: The Complete Prose*. New York: Farrar, 1984.

———. *One Art*. Selected and edited by Robert Giroux. New York: Farrar, 1995.

Brown, Ashley. "An Interview with Elizabeth Bishop." *Elizabeth Bishop and Her Art*. Ed. Lloyd Schwartz and Sybil P. Estess. Ann Arbor: U of Michigan P, 1983. 289–302.

Costello, Bonnie. *Elizabeth Bishop: Questions of Mastery*. Cambridge: Harvard UP, 1991.

Goldensohn, Lorrie. *Elizabeth Bishop: The Biography of a Poetry*. New York: Columbia UP, 1992.

MacMahon, Candace W. *Elizabeth Bishop: A Bibliography, 1927–1979*. Charlottesville: UP of Virginia, 1980.

Millier, Brett. *Elizabeth Bishop: Life and the Memory of It*. Berkeley: U of California P, 1993.

Ostriker, Alicia. *Stealing the Language: The Emergence of Women's Poetry in America*. Boston: Beacon, 1986.

Rich, Adrienne. *Blood, Bread, and Poetry: Selected Prose, 1979–1985*. New York: Norton, 1986.

Schweik, Susan. *A Gulf So Deeply Cut: American Women Poets and the Second World War*. Madison: U of Wisconsin P, 1991.

Spiegelman, Willard. "Elizabeth Bishop's 'Natural Heroism.'" *Elizabeth Bishop and Her Art*. Ed. Lloyd Schwartz and Sybil P. Estess. Ann Arbor: U of Michigan P, 1983. 154–71.

Starbuck, George. "'The Work!': A Conversation with Elizabeth Bishop." *Elizabeth Bishop and Her Art*. Ed. Lloyd Schwartz and Sybil P. Estess. Ann Arbor: U of Michigan P, 1983. 312–30.

Travisano, Thomas. *Elizabeth Bishop: Her Artistic Development*. Charlottesville: UP of Virginia, 1988.

7

Rethinking the "Eyes" of Chicano Poetry, or, Reading the Multiple Centers of Chicana Poetics

CORDELIA CHÁVEZ CANDELARIA

This essay and its title emerge from a specific material context. In the 1970s and early 1980s when I was re-searching literary texts and criticism on Chicana and Chicano literature—then usually labeled Mexican American and/or Chicano literature—I encountered what others did: limited library resources, mostly inaccessible new work, and a small number of by then familiar titles.[1] Like previous searches, the experience was simultaneously frustrating and inspiring, its outcome encouraging and disappointing. To find published work by writers heard or talked about at conferences and to discover others for the first time buoyed my interest in the growth of our fledgling field, especially when facing the difficulty of locating sources in new periodicals, alternative presses, and ill-equipped repositories. Like others working (at the time often in mutual isolation) on the larger project of redefining the canons of knowledge, I believed that the construction of Chicana/o literary discourse required the intervention and authority of *our own minds, experiences, and voices* in the national and global literary production.[2] Since I was an untenured college professor, however, my needs were decidedly mundane: finding available classroom material to supplement course syllabi in my field of passion if not of formal preparation. I also was pressed to locate published scholarship on marginality and subaltern discourses to help conceptualize and then argue the case with the patriarchs who were obstructing the gates of the academy in my specific neighborhood.

This context of practical need motivated my original book proposal to edit a general anthology of Mexican American literature which I eventually sent out to over a dozen publishers in the early 1980s. None of the publishers I contacted affirmed my sense of this need, but several invited me instead to do a critical study, which they indicated would build interest and knowledge in the field. As with all scholarship but especially first-generation research tools, the book, *Chicano Poetry, A Critical Introduction,* that resulted from my initial proposal was conceived as a work-in-progress.[3] In the context of the academy's vigorous polemics about knowledge construction and canonicity, it was clear that the vitality of literary publishing of that time would substantially expand and reframe the book. The proliferation of postmodern/ist critical frameworks in the classrooms, academic journals, and general public discourse confirmed that realization with even greater emphasis. Well under way, the revision changes *CP* to account for the growth and transformation of the poetry, of Chicana/o literary criticism, and of my own critical skills. The present essay, then, revises for *Women Poets of the Americas: Toward a Pan-American Gathering* the last chapter of *CP,* "Epilogue: the 'Eyes' of Chicano Poetry," by focusing on the poetics of Chicana-identified verse.

Before explicating the revisions referred to in the second part of this essay's title, I begin with a gloss of the first part, "The 'Eyes' of Chicano Poetry," which I originally chose to convey the meaning-making multiplicities of my subject. In writing the conclusion to *CP* I revisited the tradition of *corrido* (folk ballad) and popular song, one crucial source of the poetic, which I discussed in the book's introduction. I used "Cielito Lindo," a familiar song embedded in border culture and western American folklore (like "Home on the Range"), as a rhetorical trope to call attention to how the poetry's rich bilingual texture reflects through synecdoche its historical *mestizaje* (i.e., its cultural syncretism). Its well-known refrain, "*ay ay ay ay,*" served my purpose as a summative metaphor of the poetry because it originally emerged from the material source of the culture, the people, *el pueblo*. As well, the refrain permitted the homophonic pun "eye/I/ay/allí" of the poetry to rhyme representationally with the "ay ay ay ay" of the refrain (*CP* 203–4). This rhetorical device, I suggested, under-scores how Chicano poetry fuses its poetic and political functions "to show the strange residing in the ordinary" and "to recognize the ramifications of both the strangeness and the ordinariness as visionary insight" (*CP* 203). Through self-reflecting emphasis on language and semiotic representation, the homophonic trope contributes as well to the project of memorializing the bilingual, multicultural experience and related myth-making reconstruc-tions of self, society, space, culture, and memory. I sought in this way to offer an alternative to the deficit models of Mexican American ethnicity by affirming Chicana/o intellectual, artistic, and political achievements over historical and sociocultural vic-timization, unless, of course, that was the theme of the specific poem's representation(s).[4]

The epilogue was written out of the creative space of my own poem-writing as I tried to mesh the imaginative and experimen-tal qualities of poetry with its requirements of logic, form, and generic conventions. I wrote that Chicano poetry discloses (1) "the *eye* of the poetic observer and seer" who "offers a per-sonal lamp to illuminate experience of the world"; (2) "the *I* of the poet's self, the artistic persona" in conversation with the *I* of the hearer/reader, an *I* shaped into symbols and parables "that transcend the writer's ego"; (3) "the *¡ay!* of pain and suffering evoked by the poet's depiction of *tristezas* from Chicano history and [everyday] experience"; and (4) "the *allí*[5] (i.e., the 'there') representing the poet's locus of interest whether barrio, campo, llano, or any other space [including cyberspace] in or relating to Aztlán," both the *there* that the eye perceives and the *where* in which the action occurs" or is "imagined" (*CP* 203–4). The rhe-torical device of rhyming the "eye/I/ay/hay/allí" of the poetry with the "ay ay ay ay" of "Cielito Lindo's" refrain was my way of underscoring how these poets deployed language and poetics to represent the amazing bi- and multilingualism, sociohistorical di-versity, intertextuality, and thematic multiplicity of *chicanismo*.

But with the turn-of-the-century clock ticking ever louder and, in digitalized bleeps and blinks, more self-consciously, and as I have thickened and revised my own understanding in recent decades, I have rewritten "The 'Eyes' of Chicano Poetry" to address its critical limitations and omissions. Hence, the first word of the present essay's title: "*re*thinking." Despite serving its purpose as a research tool offering the first comprehensive introduction to the field, *CP* was researched, written, and published when the crucial impact of Chicana-identified voices was beginning to alter the dialogue in Chicano studies and in feminist discourse. Furthermore, *CP* labors within a formalist critical framework whose intended Chicana feminist and culture studies viewpoints remained largely unabsorbed inclinations of ideological desire rather than fully enabled theorizations negotiating elements of postcolonialist discourse. The second half of this essay's title, then, summarizes my continued and I hope more textured conversation with *Chicano Poetry,* the book, as well as with the poets, poetics, material histories, social effects, and intellectual and political practices that produced it. Not the least of these has been the thousands of readers who bought or borrowed the book and the hundreds of them who communicated with me about it over the years.

This essay's subtitle, "Reading the Multiple Centers of Chicana Poetics," differentiates itself from the "Eyes" *qua* "Ays" of the title's first half by drawing a relationship between the process of reception and understanding (i.e., reading), and the manifold creative practices that produce manifold representations (i.e., multiple centers) of Chicana-identified poetry and poetic principles (i.e., Chicana poetics). I mean the term *reading* to be understood, in its fullest sense of decoding and meaning-making, to refer to the activity, or transaction, that requires the reader's (or hearer's) active participation in the process of decoding the sign and signifier put forward by, in this case, Chicana poets. By *multiple centers* I seek to convey the plural varieties and wide-ranging diversities of Mexican American female experiences, histories, intertextualities, and identities—referred to elsewhere as the subjectivities of the "*wild zone.*"[6] The intersecting subjectivities of

Chicana identity comprise many centers of consciousness—for example, inner, outer, personal, public, and private dimensions—cutting across permeable borders of linguistic signification in dynamic transaction. Because Chicanas come from many varied economic, educational, geographic, marital, and occupational backgrounds and statuses, their discourses result in shifting representations that merge, diverge, converge, and emerge in a multiplicity of signs and signifiers of identity.[7] These include, for example, inscriptions of identity known as urban, *campesina,* small town; bisexual, lesbian, heterosexual; poor to affluent; highly educated or moderately so, illiterate, self-taught; mono- bi- or multilingual; recent immigrant, first or later generational, native born without memory of diaspora, and many other roles and images.

It follows, therefore, that out of this plural and extensive variety the idea of *a Chicana*-identified referent in any discourse and certainly in poetry *depends on* and *cannot be separated* from the context, subject position, and related factors of what or who is being described or defined. Likewise, to define *Chicana poetics* requires similar contextualization and attention to subject positionality and to contingencies relating to poet, poem, and intertextual fields. Consequently, one of the most notable changes of the larger *CP* revision is that it departs from attempting inclusive coverage or proposing comprehensive formalist frameworks and instead offers readings of poetry focusing on the poets' mediation *between* and *among* the identity effects and cultural practices dynamically crisscrossing the language(s) and image(s) of their poems. I focus on how their figurative encodings of idea and concrete image often elide and sometimes collide interactively with the poetic form and literary patterns relevant to their subjects.[8] To stay within the space limits of *Women Poets of the Americas* I present only a small section from the revised *CP* chapter on the work of Lorna Dee Cervantes.

A post–World War II California native, Cervantes (b. 1954) is a tenured professor at the University of Colorado at Boulder where she teaches creative writing and literature. Her first published volume, *Emplumada* (1981), continues as one of the most critically acclaimed, late Chicano Renaissance titles, and her *From the Cables of Genocide: Poems on Love and Hunger* (1991) has received similar notice.[9] Her work was included in volume two of the prestigious fourth and fifth editions of *The Norton Anthology of American Literature* (1994 and 1998), making her one of only three Mexican Americans among the one hundred-plus authors. Her consistent participation in alternative publishing (for example, the Flor y Canto anthologies, *Mango, Quarry West,* and recently *Red Dirt*) also contributes to her established place in Chicana/o letters, a niche enhanced by her visiting writer invitations to the University of Houston, the Naropa Institute, Antioch's Latin American Writers Workshop, and others.

The poems in Cervantes's *From the Cables of Genocide: Poems on Love and Hunger* extend her inscription of the gendered, ethnic, and subjective persona heralded in her first published volume, *Emplumada.* The book's startling title positions its constitutive elements on perilous, unstable tightropes (cables) linking the cruelties of mass murder (genocide) to the promise of love, thereby immediately setting up a dialectic of poetic argument. Within this equation, hunger, which can be both physiological appetite and psychosocial desire, functions as a compelling force driving the dialectic from within. But cables are also lines of communication—i.e., letters or wired messages—as well as lengths of tensile strength, a meaning that allows Cervantes to exploit even further the colliding possibilities of her title-signifier. Through an interplay of poetic transactions that bridge her multiple subjectivities as a teenage *pachuca,* commited scribe, teacher/scholar, and Bay Area urban transplant to the front range of the Rocky Mountains, the book illuminates the process of the poet's interrogation of memory, experience, and desire. This process thus discloses the multiple centers of her particular journey toward discovery of personal agency and writerly authority through the manipulation of language and literary discourse.

The poem "The Levee: Letter to No One," first published in *Frontiers: A Journal of Women Studies* (1990), articulates this interrogation and manipulation especially effectively. Through a series of concrete bird images and maternal motifs, the poem recalls the mood and theme of Cervantes's early masterpiece, "Beneath the Shadow of the Freeway" (in *Emplumada*). "The Levee" opens with a scene of the speaker on a solitary walk along a river embankment during which she sees another solitary woman walking and, later, observes her crying. This scene of movement and observation functions as a threshold conceit for the work of the poet—that is, the introspection and observation from which poetry emerges—which begins with the poet's internal monologue but succeeds only when it enters into an external dialogue with the reader. Describing her observations as she walks leads the speaker to give a close description of the other woman, who "looked like my mother" (5).[10] From this opening conceit the poem develops as a series of musings produced by the speaker's impressions of the woman stranger and her place in the world of "sewer spew" and "blue herons" (5). Dramatic and concrete, "The Levee's" opening lines immediately engage interest by inserting the reader/hearer into the emotional suspense of its compressed plot. Why is the woman in "red stretch pants" crying? Why is the speaker/poet even interested in the stranger? Whose mood does the language reflect, the speaker's or the other woman's? The reader's immediate and intimate engagement in the speaker's *seeing*, heightened by the other woman's *feeling*, derives as well from the poet's skillful, meticulous attention to scenic detail: the "sewer spew," the "blue herons, collapsing and unfolding," the "silt and salt [of] this reservoir" (5). We are told that the woman "was there a long, long time,/sitting on the levee, her legs swinging," thus forcing awareness that the speaker too was preoccupied on the same spot for a long time, further stimulating interest in the real or projected connection between the two.

Having secured reader/hearer engagement, the poem then presents another intricately developed conceit—a series of rhyming tropes—presented to forefront "The Levee's" negotiation of past and present, especially how experience and perception in the present emerge unavoidably from past practices. The cumulative result of these rhyming tropes is to evoke the psychosocial effects of memory on present outlooks, experiences, and choices. She links, for example, the "water," "tears," and "piss" to the "salt" and "silt" of "sewer spew." She rhymes as well the bird images of "hair in a middle-aged nest egg" and "egret's tail" to "herons" and "swallows" (5–65). This matching of images echoes and reifies the title's dialectic argument of love versus hunger by bridging disparate ideas and figures as a means of interrogating the speaker's subliminal bond with the stranger who "look[s] like [her] mother." Moreover, the poem's two characters, the solitary women, balance each other's subjectivities, at first colliding in difference while occupying the levee as they sit like mute observers deep in their private thoughts, but, in the end, eliding into a yoked pair, walking "back" to the shared sounds of the "slice" of water "to imitate the movement/of hunger through wind or waves."

The speaker's bond to the woman thus carefully etched through imagistic rhyme, Cervantes's technique unavoidably sets up intertextual linkages to female figures, especially maternal ones, in her other writings, and those of others. Through parallel allusions to the mothers and grandmothers in her other poems, for instance, the poet forces a reading process that pushes beyond the boundaries of the "Levee" poem's theme of "hunger" and "loss" to the "hunger" of *mother loss* operating in "Beneath the Shadow of the Freeway" and "Oaxaca," to cite two poems. Cervantes embeds the theme in her word choice, which underscores the traumatic effects of material squalor, pain, and absence— "leftover piss," "knife of their throats," "hunger," "wrenched," "denial," and others consistent with the pain represented by the homophonic "¡ay! = I" proposed in the original *CP* epilogue. Along with the intertextuality and matched tropes, they produce a paradoxical poetic tension that evokes a poignant longing for mother bonding, even between strangers.

This quintessential longing lies at the core of the tragic La Llorona legend and its incredibly lasting iconic, ultimately affirming resonance among Mexican Americans. La Llorona, a Medea-like Mexican figure, is viewed by many scholars as the mythic folk construction that developed from the fame and infamy of the historical La Malinche (a.k.a. Doña Marina, Malinálli, Malíntzin). Associated with wanderings around rivers, La Llorona appears in countless local variants of the folktale, but they all share a kernel plot of a mother's infanticide or abandonment of her children and the punishment she suffers as a consequence.[11]

If mother loss, then, girds both "The Levee's" thematic center of Chicana consciousness and its technical poetics (including the embedded Llorona allusion), it also builds to the complex affirmation associated with the Chicana feminist recuperation of the Llorona myth. As in "Beneath the Shadow of the Freeway," a poem memorializing her mother and grandmother by representing the harsh experiential realities of poverty and woman battering in a way that nonetheless concludes on a hopeful note, Cervantes ends "The Levee" with an explicit phrase of hope: "The river is a good place/for . . . beauty's flush." The word *good* and the cleansing sense of *flush* cast an affirming rinse over the poem's meditation and reinforce the tacit affirmation residing in the speaker's authenticity of voice and achieved author/ity. In this way, the poet mediates a connection between the centers of identity of the strangers on opposite sides of the levee and, in the closing phrase, hints at a measure of psychic and spiritual resolution in the poet's feelings of loss and hunger.

Added intertextual nuance in this melancholy lyric about a solitary poet-singer lurks in its intertextual summoning to consciousness of a similar ode in American literature, Walt Whitman's "Out of the Cradle Endlessly Rocking." Out of the primal waters (ocean, tears, rain, and so forth) that mark both poems, each speaker sings of reconciliation with past (childhood) loss through anticipation of poetic futures. In each the poet/speaker discovers the eternal tension underlying the universe's "symmetry"—the fused, the wrenched apart—and each apprehends the "good" in the decidedly lowercase nouns of mundane experience (for example, a waterbank as a place to piss) and creative construction (for instance, poetry, song, walking, noticing, and remembering). Cervantes's subtlety in "The Levee: Letter to No One" characterizes most of the poetry in *From the Cables of Genocide: Poems on Love and Hunger* (notably "Pleiades from the Cables of Genocide," "On Finding the Slide of John in the Garden 1973," "Colorado Blvd.," and "Macho"). The volume not only secures her work on my shelf of poetry of the Americas, but I think it simultaneously challenges and enhances as well the discourse by and about women in general and the multiple centers of Chicana consiousness in specific.

Cervantes's use of the bird motif in "The Levee: Letter to No One" echoes and thickens its deployment in her first volume, *Emplumada* (1981), which yokes "the fragility and transitoriness" of "experience" in order to achieve what Cervantes calls "distanc[e] from history" (*CP* 183). The volume's epigraph states that *emplumado* means "feathered; in plumage, as in after molting," while *plumada* denotes "pen flourish," the conflation providing an encoding of the act and process of writing. The poet thereby unites her inscription of life's fleeting temporality with the idea of literature's permanence, an effect captured in the title poem's elision of the molting plumage of birds with the instability of words and the constantly shifting act(ion)s of writing. This effect stands out in "Bird Ave.," a poem published in a special Chicana issue of *The Americas Review* (1987)[12]. In "Bird Ave." Cervantes continues the deepened, more problematized configurations of birds—flying, caged, fragile as feathers, powerful as flight, expressive as *plumas* writing the world's multitudinous stories. Inspired by a San José street sign, the poem's title reveals the poet's incisive creativity as she teases out of the ordinariness of the abbreviation for "avenue" of city street markers an allusion to the Latin "*Ave!*" (hail), which calls up sacred hosannas to the Virgin Mary, as well as to the Latin word for bird.

Filled with syncopating tropes that play off one another, "Bird Ave." presents the multiple Chicana urban voices of pachucas[13] who are typically left out of poetic idioms. The poem's contrapuntally arranged tropes add texture to the *testimonio* (personal narrative) of the poem's pachuca speaker, Cat-eyes. As Cat-eyes remembers her tough youthful encounters on the streets, she is reminded of another pachuca, Mousie, and of "teased tough hair [and] teased tight skirts," which constituted the pachuca dress code of the time. These memories glide casually into the speaker's memory of "my head [banging]/on the blacktop for effect," an elision that maintains her barrio-tough exterior despite the fact of being violently beaten up in a street fight. The technique's subtle syncopations of language and metrical line level the fight to the same plane as all the other recollected images, resulting in a contestation of ideas and a reversal of rhythms that capture the material experience in its fluid vitality and instability. The poem's muscular urban tone (for example, " *'Don't Fuck With Us'* our motto" [43]), dense figuration (for example, "ganga de camellias y rosales" [42]), and aural syncopation (for example, "you flacafeaface" [42]) develop incrementally to suggest multiple centers of Cervantes's experience—from the barrio world(s) of emulated male violence and urban Chicana *pachuquisma* to flashes of bittersweet self-discovery. The forefronted voice(s) of pachuca experience and complex Chicana sensibility(ies) represented in *words* through *poetry*—i.e., the scribe's *plumas*—ultimately suggest a "spreading" of the poet's "wings" of personal agency and poetic authority, a resonance that returns to the compressed significations of *emplumada* and "bird ave[s]."

Thus, "Bird Ave.," like "Emplumada," the title poem in Cervantes's first volume," dialogizes (in the Bakhtinian sense of a discourse of polyphonic voices)[14] the flashback of Cat-eyes's *testimonio* and simultaneously pluralizes the literary idiom of American poetry. This dialogic idiom threads through Cervantes's most evocative poems, mediating *between* and *among* the identity effects and cultural practices of a formally educated, urban Chicana reflecting on her adolescent experience. For example, in *Emplumada*'s "Uncle's First Rabbit" and "For Virginia Chavez," Cervantes, the *reflecting* (in both senses) poet, converses with the constructed persona of her youth to memorialize two important presences of her girlhood, the shell-shocked "uncle" and the battered friend, respectively. Two other pieces in *Emplumada,* "The Anthill" and the famous "Beneath the Shadow of the Freeway," similarly mediate dialogically *between* and *among* the identity markers of the speaker's reminiscences about struggling with bilinguality in a monolingual society, about feelings of psychocultu-

ral inferiority, and about longing for cultural clarity when politi-
cal empowerment appears elusive. Through dynamic mediation
across the multiple subject positions of for example, pachuca,
scribe, scholar, Bay Area transplant, and so forth, Cervantes dem-
onstrates the empowering agency and authority derived from the
writing process itself and from its construction of an interactive
poetics of *testimonio,* which, for meaning-making, requires critical
gender, ethnoracial, and class-inflected responses from the reader/
hearer. Literary scholar Marta Sanchez describes dimensions of
this process as the poet's "harmonizing [of] gender and culture"
through her vocation as "scribe."[15]

Two other poems (also in *Emplumada*) that exemplify how
the multiple centers of Cervantes's particular identity and cul-
tural experience as a formally educated, urban Chicana mediate
within the texts and intertexts of her poetics are "Visions of Mex-
ico While at a Writing Symposium in Port Townsend, Washing-
ton" (45–46) and "Poema para los Californios muertos" (Poem
to dead Californios 42–43). The poems enunciate a theme de-
scribed in *Chicano Poetry, A Critical Introduction* as concerned with
the *allí* (or *there*)[16] "of geographical space in terms suggesting
both personal and cultural identity" (*CP* 217), and both are em-
phatically positioned in the border regions between chasms
of difference: the distant past and the immediate present, be-
tween the *aquí* of the contemporary United States and the *allá*
of Mexico.

In "Visions of Mexico" she laments that Mexico "can only rip-
ple through my veins/like the chant of an epic corrido" and that
too often it exists only as disparaged popular caricature: "Mexico
is stumbling comedy." In addition, Cervantes uses a contrasting
allí as a backdrop for "that far south" in order to place Mexico
in topographical and cultural perspective, much as she used
the "freeway" in "Beneath the Shadow of the Freeway" and the
"levee" in "Letter to No One." In this poem, Port Townsend,
Washington, functions as the dissimilar locus, a place too "far
north" from her soul, where she doesn't "belong," and which suf-
fers from the lack of "pueblos green on the low hills" and of "all

those meadows: Michoacán/Vera Cruz, Ténochtítlan, Oaxáca"
(45). Despite the distance and lacunae of things "Mexican,"
when she's "that far south" she feels better, and her "own words
somersault naturally as my name," signifying her ease *allí/allá*
(over there). But feeling at ease does not bar her awareness that
"this far south we are governed by the law/of the next whole
meal" (45). Nor does she exaggerate her understanding of Mex-
ico as her ancestral *patria* by "pretend[ing]" she "can speak all
the names" for she "can't" because she comes "from a long line
of eloquent illiterates" whose "gesture[s]" are "utterance[s] more
pure than word" (45). This line leads her to introduce the
poem's twofold thematic center: that life experience, however
abject, harsh, and *un*poetic or outside the *doxa* of the moment,
in fact constitutes the marrow and tissue of poetic language, and
that self-inscription is a crucial act toward political empower-
ment. Asserting that the "senses" of Chicanas and Chicanos
are "keen" and "our reflexes" provide "accurate punctuation,"
Cervantes writes that the very "gunnings" and "knifings" of "a
single night" cause the "poet within us" to "bay . . . " (46). The
poet thus transmutes into the genera of dialogic *testimonio* her
experience of places, her recollection of them from a distance,
and her sense of self feeling the total *allí* of her surroundings.

Markedly different in tone, the treatment of place in "Poèma
para los Californios muertos" (Poem for the dead Californios)
opens with elegiac feeling in recalling "*los antepasados muertos*"
(dead ancestors) whose "refuge" in the "*tierra*" (land) can only
be imagined in the contemporary reality of California's "older
towns" where the "high scaffolding cuts" of freeways and sky-
scrapers rupture the "belly valleys and fertile dust" like a "ce-
sarean" (42). Her wonderment is stirred by a "brass plaque" she
sees "outside a restaurant in Los Altos, California, 1974." Tactile
and concretely visualized, the historical marker for the site bears
the inscription "Once a refuge for Mexican Californios" (42), an
image that operates as a mnemonic stimulus to the primal "mem-
ory" of "*la sangre fertil*" (fertile blood). Spanning time, space, his-
tories, and cultures—just as the poet's code-switching spans lan-
guages—the plaque brings to mind her dead ancestors and

provokes her resentment about the political and cultural effects of conquest, figured in the poem as *"fantasmas blancas"* (white apparitions) representing the new "high-class" of material affluence and conspicuous consumption (42). With the same anger that fueled the earliest Chicano protest poets, "Poema" concludes on a note of alienation far removed from the elegiac lyricism of the opening lines because at the end the speaker "see[s] nothing but strangers" and "bitter antiques,/yanqui remnants" (43). The bitterness and "rage" permeate all her senses, and these altered perceptions transform even nature into "shriek[ing]" blue jays and "crushed eucalyptus" (43). Underscoring the physical sensory impressions—that is, of the *body* seeing and touching the brass plaque—Cervantes adds the power of feelings—the *body's* force—to signify the creative and cognitive power of the writing process and of the concomitant process of interactive reading.

The plural range and variability of Lorna Dee Cervantes's poetry in *Emplumada*, in *From the Cables of Genocide: Poems on Love and Hunger,* and in recent anthologies and journals represents a microcosmic *and* metonymic example of how Chicana-identified poetics are shaped by the shifting contexts and subject positions of the poet and her constructed speaker(s) and persona(e). Cervantes is, of course, only one example, and exemplar, of Chicana poetics from the wild zone of intersecting subjectivities and intertextual fields which constitutes *feminista*/womanist/feminist discourse. Other talented Chicana poets whose writings complement the germinal work discussed in *Women Poets of the Americas* include Lucha Corpi, Alicia Gaspar de Alba, Yolanda Lúera, Demétria Martinez, Cherrie Moraga, Naomi Quiñonez, Marina Rivera, Gina Váldez, Bernice Zámora, and others.[17] While such a list cannot convey the compelling texture of their individual voices and the specific details of the multiple centers inscribed in their particular poetics, I am nonetheless motivated to express at least this measure of respect for their singular achievements until the revised second edition of *Chicana/o Poetry, A Critical Introduction* is published.

NOTES

1. For example, the list of readings for my classes in the late 1970s and early 1980s included Fabiola Cabeza de Vaca (*We Fed Them Cactus* 1952), José Antonio Villareal (*Pocho* 1955), Rodolfo Gonzales (*I Am Joaquín* 1967), Luis Valdez and El Teatro Campesino (*Actos* 1978), Alurista (*Floricanto en Aztlán* 1978), and so forth. It also included writings by Premio Quinto Sol recipients like Rudolfo Anaya and Estela Portillo Trambley, and Casa de las Americas Award winner Rolando Hinojosa Smith, along with a few staples of *literatura chicanesca* for thematic coverage (for example, Helen Hunt Jackson's *Ramona*, Mary Austin's *Land of Little Rain* and *Isidro*, J. Frank Dobie's *Coronado's Children*, John Steinbeck's *Tortilla Flats*, and so on.) The works of criticism on my early reading lists included Américo Paredes's *With his Pistol in his Hand* (1958), Philip Ortego's 1971 dissertation, F. Chris Garcia's *Chicano Politics* (1973), Francisco Lomelí and Donaldo Urioste's *Perspectives in Literature: A Critical and Annotated Bibliography* (1976), and my own "Ethnic Minority Literature Teaching Module" (Idaho State University, 1976); "La Malinche . . . A Model for the Present," *Agenda: A Journal of Hispanic Issues* (1977), and chap. 20, *A History of the Mexican American People* (1977).

2. Among the earliest examples were Jesús Maldonado, *Poesía chicana: Alurista el méro chingón* (Seattle: UW Centro de Estudios Chicanos Monograph, 1971); Luis Valdez, "Introduction," *Aztlán: Anthology of Mexican American Literature* (New York: Knopf, 1972); Joel Hancock, "The Emergence of Chicano Poetry," *Arizona Quarterly* 29.1 (1973); Francisco Jiménez, "Chicano Literature Sources and Themes," *Bilingual Review* 1.1 (1974); and Carlota Cárdenas de Dwyer, *Chicano Voices Instructor's Guide* (Boston: Houghton, 1975).

3. Candelaria, *Chicano Poetry, A Critical Introduction* (Westport, Conn.: Greenwood, 1986); hereafter cited as *CP.*

4. Early affirmative viewpoints can be found in Marta Cotera's *Diosa y Hembra: History and Heritage of Chicanas in the U.S.* (Austin: Information Systems Development, 1977); in some of the essays in Rosaura Sánchez and Rosa Mártinez Cruz, eds., *Essays on La Mujer* (UCLA Chicano Studies Center, 1977), and in my *Agenda: Journal of Hispanic Issues* articles between 1977 and 1979, and in my "Reflections on Women in the Academy," *Rendezvous: Journal of Arts and Letters* 13.1 (Spring 1978): 9–18.

5. Here changed from the spelling *hay* of the original *CP* chapter in an attempt to convey dialectally the *there* of my native New Mexican patois.

6. Candelaria, "The 'Wild Zone' Thesis as Gloss in Chicana Literary Study" (1989; rpt. 1993) revised for reprinting in Robyn R. Warhol and Diane Price Herndl, eds., *Feminisms: An Anthology of Literary Theory and Criticism*, rev. ed. (New Brunswick, N.J.: Rutgers UP, 1997): 248–56.

7. Not only is the variability of backgrounds and statuses true *among* Chicanas, it applies as well to the experience of individual women. For example, my Mexican American heritage *merges* with my New Mexican geographical and cultural roots, but the Roman Catholicism of my received heritage *diverges* from my evolved spirituality, just as my cultural sense of *familia* often *converges* with my intellectual self-identity, but they are not synthetically *merged*.

8. An approach indebted to the models proposed by, for example, Mikhail Bakhtin in *Rabelais and His World*, trans. Helene Iswolsky (Cambridge, Mass.: MIT P, 1968); Paul Ricoeur in *Interpretation Theory: Discourse and the Surplus of Meaning* (Fort Worth: Texas Christian UP, 1976); Linda Hutcheon in *A Poetics of Postmodernism: History, Theory, Fiction* (New York: Routledge, 1988); and the essays in Alfred Arteaga, ed., *An Other Tongue: Nation and Ethnicity in the Linguistic Borderlands* (Durham, N.C.: Duke UP, 1994).

9. Lisa Radinovsky, "Lorna Dee Cervantes," *The Oxford Companion to Women's Writing in the United States* (New York: Oxford UP, 1995), 160; Tey Diana Rebolledo, *Women Singing in the Snow: A Cultural Analysis of Chicana Literature* (Tucson: U of Arizona P, 1995), 131, 210; Cordelia Candelaria, "Latina Women Writers: Chicanas, Cuban American and Puerto Rican Voices," *Handbook of Hispanic Cultures in the United States: Literature and Art*, ed. Francisco Lomeli (Houston: Arte Publico, 1993), 153–55.

10. *From the Cables of Genocide: Poems of Love and Hunger* (Houston: Arte Publico, 1991), 5.

11. See José E. Limón, "La Llorona, the Third Legend of Greater Mexico: Cultural Symbols, Women, and the Political Unconscious," in *Between Borders: Essays on Mexicana/Chicana History*, Adelaida R. Del Castillo, et al., eds. (Encino: Floricanto, 1990), 399–432; and Cordelia Candelaria, "La Llorona" in *The Oxford Companion to Women's Writing in the United States*, Cathy N. Davidson and Linda Wagner-Martin, eds. (New York: Oxford, 1995), 468, for recent discussions of La Llorona.

12. Cervantes, "Bird Ave." in *Chicana Creativity and Criticism: Charting New Frontiers in American Literature*, Maria Herrera-Sobek and Helena María Viramontes, guest eds. for *The Americas Review*, 15.3–4 (1987): 41–43. Cervantes notes that *Bird Ave.* is book two of her new collection, *Drive* (letter to author, 11 March 1998).

13. Or "female zoot suit gang members," more commonly known in contemporary street patois (called *cálo*) as "cholas." There is no perfect translation for this in-group designation of a youth counterculture phenomenon, but "punk skinhead bird" connotes a cognate social form of youth rebellion and working-class ethnic identity.

14. Mikhail Bakhtin, *The Dialogic Imagination: Four Essays,* Michael Holmquist, ed., Caryl Emerson, trans. (Austin: U of Texas P, 1981).

15. Sanchez, *Chicana Poetry . . . Emerging Literature* (1985), 85–86.

16. See note 5 above on the dialectal homophone *allí/hay/*eye.

17. Like the early writings of Ana Castillo and Sandra Cisneros, who have recently emphasized fiction, and the exciting new work of Carmen Tafolla, Alma Luz Villanueva, and Helena Viramontes.

18. I gratefully acknowledge B. J. Segura Manriquez's reading and suggestions in the revision of this essay.

8

Formalism, Feminism, and Genre Slipping in the Poetic Writings of Leslie Scalapino[1]

LAURA HINTON

If we imagine mimetic literary narratives to operate like Henry James's House of Fiction, with its "million windows" full of perceptual glass, we might imagine the nonmimetic narratives of the contemporary Language School to focus upon, and even to rearrange, the elements *composing* glass.[2] True to the school's postmodern impulses, its texts revel in the texture and shape of language's constructional parts. Like the sand grains integral to a pane of glass, compositional irregularities reveal a bending and refracting—rather than a conveying—of light.

"Language [for these writers] is not something that *explains* or *translates* experience but is the source of experience," Douglas Messerli explains in his introduction to *"Language" Poetries: An Anthology* (2). Most critics agree that the glass does not promote vision. It *becomes* the vision itself. But how this occurs has been the source of much critical speculation. Following Roland Barthes's discussion of "zero-degree writing," for instance, Marjorie Perloff has suggested that postmodern texts are those that internally challenge traditional subject-object referentiality.[3] Ron Silliman has shifted the binary paradigm to that of the signifier-signified: while traditional realism "was that dream within the arts of a completely transparent form," in which "the realist art object" is "a sign . . . subordinated to the signified," avant-garde texts render the signifier visible.[4] Messerli emphasizes that Language Poets in particular generate "a political action" in their emphasis on signification (3). But he perceives the "action" to involve the reader, "asked to participate *with* the poet/poem in bringing meaning to the community at large" (Messerli 3).

One of the most experimental writers to emerge from out of the Language group is Leslie Scalapino, whose writings are extremely fragmented and challenging to any reading community, unusually devoid of traditional narrative conventions. In spite of her work's intense level of experimentation, affecting referentiality and political signification alike, Scalapino's writing, I argue, generates another kind of "political action": by calling attention to the political status of the *woman* writer. Barrett Watten has noted that Scalapino's work sustains a "disciplined avoidance of totality"; it "traces a network of contingent relations in which subject and object have no fixed positions." So indeterminate are these positions that "things seem to happen because they are not propositionally tied to an assertion of fact through a stable identity of the narrator" (Watten 51). Radically dismantling the subject-object or signifier-signified binarisms in subjectivity and signification, such work would seem to eradicate the binarism implied by *gendered* subjectivities. Nevertheless, through the poetics of the avant-garde, Scalapino sustains a critique of gender while insisting upon this "disciplined avoidance of totality." Analyzing gendered genres from the past as well as from postmodernity, she renders a subtle feminist critique inside the general avant-garde problem of subjectivity and representation. Her writings suggest that it is possible to blend a formalist aesthetic with feminist insight.

Efforts to gender avant-garde writing as a practice emerged from the French feminism informed by psychoanalysis of the 1970s and 1980s. Hélène Cixous, after Barthes's theory of *écriture,* proclaimed an *écriture féminine,* or "woman's writing," to exist. Although it is perceived by some Anglo-American feminists as an essentialist theory, confusing body with social text, I would argue that Cixous's gendered *l'écriture* is symbolic, that "woman's writing" performs a textual effect potentially explosive and erotic.[5] But Cixous's examples of *l'écriture féminine* are drawn primarily from writings by men, like George Bataille and Jean Genet. While she has made claims about women's speech in general, her canon of *l'écriture féminine* authors does not bear her generalizations out.[6] Likewise, Julia Kristeva's parallel theory of "revolution in poetic language"—which describes a female-identified mode of signification, the semiotic chora—does not discuss women writers as a class at all.[7]

These theories have left much terrain uncultivated. Little *recent* feminist theory has devoted itself to the avant-garde, and little avant-garde criticism has devoted itself to the subject of women. Yet to ignore the gendered politics of writing in the acutely "political" discourses of the Language School would seem to acquiesce in a socialized silence too reminiscent of prefeminist critical discourses. One notable effort to break this silence on the topic of women and the avant-garde is Craig Owens's "The Discourse of Others: Feminists and Postmodernism." Owens's essay argues forcefully that women artists are particularly well positioned to focus upon the unstable subject of postmodernism, since "woman" has functioned as a sign alternatively denigrated and denied by the Western subject.

"Excluded from representation by its very structure, they [women] return within it as a figure for—a representation of—the unrepresentable (Nature, Truth, the Sublime, etc.)," Owens writes.[8] Accordingly, women are best positioned to render their own "exclusion." In line with Owens's argument but modifying his notion of "exclusion," I examine the method by which Scalapino's writing is bound up with female "exclusion." The figure of "exclusion" is presented within Scalapino's intense, mobile plays upon narrative positionality. Such plays are embedded within language contexts that retain some referentiality to patriarchal constructions of the female "subject," as *non*subject.

In an earlier book by Scalapino, entitled *that they were at the beach—aeolotropic series* (1985), and in her more recent *The Return of Painting, the Pearl, Orion/A Trilogy* (1991), as well as in the epic novel *Defoe* (1994), a symbolically female "subject" passes through what seem slightly familiar generic frames. These frames are never wholly convincing or intact textual genres. The Scalapino "subject" slips in and out of the frames, or textual modes, but never really possesses them, or stays within them very long—just long enough to call their structuring into question.

True to Language School poetry practices, in general, Scalapino's writing is insistently analytical, that is, it analyzes phenomena through the perceptual apparatus available within language itself—it focuses upon the makeup of the window, not the view through or "beyond." Scalapino's use of formal genre devices enhances this analytical quality in her work. She uses and disposes of patriarchal literary forms, treating them as empty. Such "forms" often refer to states of being female in male-signified discourses. Scalapino's uses of various forms and genres, like the sentimental novel, for example—the popular form associated with both female writers and consumers—or the comic book, provide a kind of empty antistructure for her "exclusion" within and through female subjectivity. She avoids totality in this subject by "resting" only in a series of analytical "separations"—to borrow two terms often used by Scalapino in her fiction and essays.

The female subject, for Scalapino, does not exist as a unified or even a deconstructed set of binarisms. Instead, it is built upon "separational" categories. The concept of "separation" is a subtle one running throughout her work, indicating her particular view of this subject's a-positionality. Many avant-garde writers have attempted to create an a-positional subject, one without location or form. Scalapino, however, achieves this effect through a gendered edge of "separation," expressing the paradoxical relationship between inside and outside that politically informs the subject.

In a collection of philosophical essays, entitled *How Phenomena Appear to Unfold,* Scalapino writes that "the attention of the mind . . . is neither in nor outside that experience" (114). Here she describes the a-positionality of the subject. But her description might challenge some avant-garde theories, such as that of Kristeva's "revolution" based in a "negativity" (Kristeva 28). It also might challenge Owens's concept of "exclusion," since

Owens bases his paradigm for the female artist and her subject in an alterity formulation of the "other." Scalapino's "separation" between self and "other" absorbs any distinction between the two. It therefore modifies separational categories like "inside and outside . . . perceiver and perceived," as Bruce Campbell notes (53). Campbell employs a female-body metaphor to describe Scalapino's particular "attention of the mind," not only inner-directed (as directed toward the self-awareness of attention), but outer-directed (as attention directed to an object): "the 'experience' of the mind is invaginated, the outer limit folded back into the interior" (55). Such a metaphor might suggest essentialist notions of the female body-writer. I reread this metaphor through Owens's term *exclusion*. Through this term, we view "woman" not as a negative "other" but rather as a signifier that operates both inside and outside at once. "She" is a constructed subject that illustrates the irony of both positions.

Inside-outside phenomenal plays are the structural bases of Scalapino's (non)subject. She hints at the phenomenon of genre, from both classic literatures and popular culture. These include the sentimental novel, associated with female heroines, readers, and writers; and the comic book, associated with male action heros or villains. They also include textual modes that refer to genres, like surrealism or stream-of-consciousness techniques from the Modernist tradition. Such modes bear a generic suggestiveness. In Scalapino's scattered use of generic frames and textual modes, multiple, mobile narrative fields open up through which the writerly female (non)subject can pass. If there *is* a "subject" in Scalapino's writing, it is one that is reproduced only momentarily, in between the folds of all these forms—folds that embrace a wit that proclaims these to be *just* forms, always on the rise and fall in the woman writer's path.

Forms are accommodated, but quickly used and given up, disposable building materials of patriarchal literatures. Scalapino's formal references to frames of time flatten form but also sweep form into a continuous, fluid, irreverent, and feminist writing path. The framing, specifically, of *gender* occurs subtly. In "Note on My Writing," from *How Phenomena Appear to Unfold,* Scalapino reflects upon her use of the cartoon genre. About *The Pearl,* she writes:

> Cartoons are a self-revealing surface as the comic strip is continu-
> ous, multiple, and within it have simultaneous future and past di-
> mensions.
>
> Being inside each frame, is the present moment. But at the
> same time the writing (the frame) is really behind, in the rear of
> "what is really occurring." (22–23)

In *The Return of Painting* (also from *Trilogy*), Scalapino pre-
sents an "Appendix" she calls "The Comic Book," announcing it
"is simply vision. It is not part of the novel. (since there is not a
novel)" (*The Return of Painting* 63). The exaggerated use of de-
scriptive surfaces and frames of time from the cartoon genre is
one of her methods toward constructing a gendered subject. In
the appendix, we read about "a sort of tight sweater version of
Lana Turner unconscious spoiled . . . A little high school girl, in
her thirties, smoldering who could cry and be hurt. She looks
down waiting for the other to submissively yield her seat" (63).
Less interested in the action-figure masculinity of comic-book
content and more interested in the activity of gendered forms,
Scalapino's commentary rejects the active-passive, male-female
dichotomy that has been attributed to traditional narratives.[9] In-
stead, "simultaneous" constructions and the visibility of the
frames-in-time that dominate the comic-book genre fascinate
Scalapino. She rejects a perception of motion based on linear or
chronological time; rather, she creates an image of back-and-
forth motion, conveying a sense of simultaneity, just as narrative
frames are viewed simultaneously, before and after, in the comic-
book form.

The skewing of the conventions of narrative time through al-
lusions to the comic book sustains the subject's a-positional ef-
fects. In "Buildings are at the far end," from *that they were at
the beach—aeolotropic series,* positionality of place is asserted but
immediately abandoned, made facadelike, a strange fabrication.
Relatedly, the subject plays the simultaneous roles of perceiver/
perceived in lines such as: "I'm in the background in the sense

that I came out of a train station and taxis are in the foreground";
or, "I watched people come inside a restaurant, the waitress
bored. Her bored before they'd come in" (6). The latter state-
ment (which actually precedes the former by a paragraph in the
original) stakes out the duality of positionality for the subject—
who is both perceiver (inside the restaurant, but outside the wait-
ress) and the perceived (by the people coming into the restau-
rant, the waitress in her boredom). The use of the waitress is a
brief, if empty, appeal to the female-worker stereotype provid-
ing service, food, and wit. But what is emphasized is that there
is no relationship between the interior state of the waitress
(her boredom) and the fact that the people had "come in." To
"come in" is not to enter, change, or redistribute any facts about
the waitress's interior life, itself a kind of falsity of interiority, a
surface.

The use of the waitress and her "surface" in this passage sug-
gests that women have represented interiority all too readily in
the novel. The inside/outside tropes that "separate" simultane-
ous spaces refer to a subject that is feminized by the sentimen-
tal novel tradition, in particular. In this tradition, interiority
is identified with women: from Pamela to Clarissa to Isabel
Archer. Speaking of the work of another Language poet, Mei Mei
Berssenbrugge, Scalapino suggests that a reworking occurs in
"the interior relation of experience," which we see Scalapino her-
self attribute to female stereotypes of consciousness:

> Berssenbrugge posits the reconstituting of location (and/by ob-
> servation of it), in which the human is only a part of the whole
> structure so that observation is occurring from phenomena and
> from the structure itself (so that we can see that).[10]

This comment might describe Scalapino's own structuring of the
"excluded" female subject. Because of the history of feminized
interiority, Scalapino shows "that observation is occurring from
phenomena and from the structure itself."

Since the subject is contingent upon the "phenomena" of lan-
guage to begin with, descriptions of those phenomena, their
form and directionality, are studied in her fiction. These descrip-

tive features of narrative, however, are dismantled or rearranged. In *The Return of Painting,* for example, Scalapino reflects upon the issue of description. The section entitled "A Novel" begins: "People going to small shops, on a street one over that runs parallel, so that it is not facing them" (5). The description of directionality is actually the description of its lack, pointing to a void in the subject: "They go down the street. Are out. He does not know she has come that way" (8).

Description's lack is conjoined with the failure of the writerly subject's ontology in the following passage:

> An otter ran across the sand, it was the size of a large dog sleek dark—feeling is nothing, it is not feeling . . . Actions are nothing—this is impossible. Have used them up—and writing isn't anything. . . . (14)

In *The Return of Painting,* Scalapino creates the *appearance* of the descriptive novel. But she does not perform its traditional narrative function of visualizing space. The rendering of any description in *The Return of Painting* always resolves into a commentary on the problem of vision. Description comically fails, because the controlling gaze of directionality, like the linear form of narrative-in-time, lacks control, or is purposely misguided, through fragmented syntax and grammatical breakdowns.

Traditional representations of visual space attempt to create what Messerli describes as a "narrative snapshot of experience"; in this context, the writer "digs" for ideas, bringing them to the surface and presenting them as the "real."[11] Scalapino comments upon Messerli's statement in the text of a recent interview:

> One can use in the writing a sense of an old genre, not simply referring to it, as if imitating the interior movements of that form (as it arises out of a way of seeing in a time); then one's creating the illusion of seeing, and the work being, interior movements in reality by imitating—then even seeing the illusion itself becomes "a narrative snapshot of experience" of perception as it's being an act.[12]

This comment concerning "seeing" might be applied to the experience of reading *The Return of Painting*. The following line from *The Return of Painting* suggests that "seeing" and describing are related to the female subject: "One breast was missing but it did not matter in regard to her being beautiful. Dressing her, she wore a wide hat and my gloves and a silk dress which is blue" (*The Return of Painting* 6). "She" is "missing" more than a "breast," however. She is missing the distinction between inside and outside that contributes to the sense that there is a perceiver watching an object. The subject is "separated" or dissected: according to the color and fabric of a dress, not yet draped upon this (disembodied) figure. At least a portion of "her" being is excluded from representation. The fact that what we might like to view as the novel's heroine is missing a bodily intactness—that she is missing an intact subject—marks the "exclusion" that is the female *subject's* quasi presence. Here the "old genre" of the sentimental novel and its "narrative snapshot" of the classic figure of the heroine vies against "the interior movements of that form"—quoting Scalapino.

The Return of Painting reminds us that "interiority" itself *is* the subject of many eighteenth- and nineteenth-century novels. The genesis of interiority is combined with the "illusion of seeing" that the novel, as a form, traditionally provides. Scalapino's more recent novel *Defoe* also probes the problem of seeing and representation, especially for the female subject *Defoe* partially mocks. In *Defoe,* the reader constructs but then dispels sentimental archetypes about female subjectivity. The analytical charge to keep subjectivity from coalescing into form, gendered or otherwise, is sustained throughout *Defoe*'s epic length, a length ironically associated with traditional sentimental genres, from the eighteenth-century novel to classic cinema.

The problem of the subject in *Defoe* is rendered again as a problem of visual description. Some description seems the product of an omniscient narrator. In the following passage, this narrator sustains a passionate sentimental energy through the imagery of a Modernist-surrealist style:

> A surge of people out on the narrow streets and in the squares.
> They're out talking and admiring each other's clothes. There's a
> movement of flying up inside as if in one's chest there's constric-
> tion of joy . . . Men leaning on their motorbikes or along build-
> ings. A thin blue evening sky with rippled clouds at the ends of
> the intersecting streets. (*Defoe* 55)

Soon, however, the female "subject" (who does not really exist in
any objectified form) is inserted as a kind of accomplice to de-
scription: "Moving then slouched sideways-smile to *her*" (55; em-
phasis added). We are told that "perception occurs before the
context—it is not in a setting" (68). A following set of descrip-
tions establishes an objectified setting while also erasing it: "She's
running in the wet alley. Coming out into a street motorbike in
the dark many of them around her . . . Empty-handed running
one of them is on her . . . There's blurring. She slips" (69). "She
slips" in the *up*-setting of the partial, incomplete context. An-
other series of statements clinches the problem of seeing/the
subject: "She's looking at nothing in particular her eyes already
open. Watching but so that it is not the retina which is seeing"
(69). These passages are followed by another series of passages
emphasizing the problem of "seeing" as one of "being":

> Whatever's there is not appearing whole. She feels curious, as
> restlessness having spent too long lying down. That the feeling
> which seems to be within her . . .
>
> Being happy or more than that which is really out there has
> no "inner reality." (69)

There is no "inner reality" because there is no inside or outside
stance for this subject to adopt. In *Objects in the Terrifying Tense
Longing from Taking Place* (1993), another collection of essays,
Scalapino discusses a concept she calls the "rim," described as a
field for the "concentration" her writing embodies or contains.
The "rim" is a concept distinct from the typical binarism of in-
side/outside guiding novelist vision. In *Objects,* Scalapino specifi-
cally comments upon the impetus of *Defoe* in the politics and

memory of war (Vietnam merged with the more recent American war against Iraq). These memories serve as "rim"-like constructions of events that inform the fiction. The novel emerged as if a reproduction

> then from all periods of one's/my subjective field—as if that is a
> visual field that is opened and at the same time narrowed to its
> sky horizon (as the entire rim of the actual sky) as concentration.
> So that the night and all actual dreams, whatever were occur-
> ring then, abut the day, are in it—and the rim of that (form) ac-
> tual horizon is held and eliminated, as concentration. (*Objects* 72)

By putting forth intensely "held," highly constructed observations and perceptions, Scalapino suggests that "the text eliminates subjective grounds" (*Objects* 73). Likewise, in *Defoe*'s handling of visual description emerging from the "rim" or form of subjective perception, "sheets of images of action" appear to "float up" (*Objects* 74), disembodied, "real," but always questionably so.

Defoe is perhaps Scalapino's most ambitious attempt to create an alternative novel as a series of perceptual rimlike "separations." In a chapter entitled "The Harp," we are offered a mediation upon "the object" of perception that involves "separation" as a series of acts of loss:

> Where the object loses, or begins, its connotative existence is to
> be just then non-connotative . . . photographing one piece in fast
> contrast of very black with the black pieces floating in its black
> wind, or blue wind, with the phrases on it, would place the piece
> at the point of dissolving. forming as an object and socially.
> which is nothing. An object's form isn't anything as that. So it's
> the point of the form and the conceptual meaning separating.
> (or rather, being the same) (*Defoe* 37–38)

It is in the paradox of sameness, as well as in "separating" or difference, that form takes its conceptual ordering principle. Scalapino goes on to apply the conceptual statement about "separating" the object to a description that would, in a more representational novel, resemble a sentimentalized (and representationally intact) world: "Sensation of hanging clothes on a line in the intense heat of day./very warm night and the clothes still on the line" (*Defoe* 38). The following line to this sequence returns us to the concept of separating, and the dislocation of any resting place for the female subject: "the place of separation" (38).

Through such "separation," the female subject—once "whole" in the sentimental or domestic novel through objectification in works by the author Daniel Defoe himself, as well as Samuel Richardson and Henry James—is ironically, partially, intact. The partial intactness of the subject reveals Scalapino's insistence neither fully to reject nor embrace the subjectivity within traditional novels. Scalapino exploits that subjectivity, allowing it to remain as a kind of shell, a temporary abode marked for the "feminine."

The comic book formalizes the irony of this witty, wry subject with which we are teased. The author notes in *Objects:* "Inner life is the same as epic, as fantasy, super-real . . . Their separation has been eliminated" (75). The fantasy genre of the comic book acknowledges, through stiff "action" frames viewed sequentially, that interiors and exteriors, like stasis and motion-in-time, operate as monadlike inseparable categories of representation. The comic-book genre, a self-reflexively empty form, at least as Scalapino uses it, grants the "excluded" female subjectivity a temporarily interior form. The comic book can do so, because space is always melodramatically artificial, allowing its subject a certain mobility or flight.

"One takes refuge in the comic book as one has no confidence," Scalapino writes in *Defoe.* "So it's utterly empty, and really so. That's the same" (47). In this reference to the "empty" comic-book form, Scalapino alludes to the irony of the feminist/avant-garde subject she continually explores in this long work. We are told that "she," the "heroine" of *Defoe,* is feeling "very depressed." The existence of the subject is found in a series of depressed feelings "she" reproduces: "The blues is not holding onto any thought, and not construct a narrative in it, when a narrative gets started . . . It's an overlay rather than a tautology in which time is felt only by individuals" (*Defoe* 48). Scalapino comments in *Objects* that "images arise as the way of undercutting the image in one" (75); she speaks of the images, specifically, in *Defoe.* We might apply this concept more broadly to all of her works.

An "undercutting" of the image of *self,* for Scalapino, is the work of fiction. For this author there is no self. Rather, there is only the activity of fiction. Again, in the interview, she suggests that "the postmodern" is that which displaces totalized forms like the self, traditionally gendered male. Scalapino comments upon the way in which time and movement in writing create the sense not of a self but of a "mind" as series of "events":

> I've become aware that the form of my present and past writing is "the mind as literally action of events"; movement that is actually events outside which are the mind's inside (of the writing). The form is collapsing the mind as being action. This is driving the mind, like beating the bushes, finally to where it would have nowhere to go except to take a leap that would then be also resting. ("Interview" 58)

As "one takes refuge in the comic book" or other fantasy-epic genres offered in *Defoe,* as well as in other works like *The Return of Painting,* form, indeed, "is collapsing the mind as being action." Repeated comments in *Defoe* note that "the mind," like action, has little to do with female or other interiors: "It isn't interior value . . . There isn't interior to it as it's filled with animosity sporadically or continually" (*Defoe* 4). Interiors, for Scalapino, are like genres: false frames of form. These false frames serve as humorous repositories for the female subject. Female "depression," for instance, is treated as an empty literary state in *Defoe.* For this subject, there is "nowhere to go except to take a leap that would then be also resting."

1. Earlier thoughts on Scalapino's feminist poetics appear in my essay "Postmodernism, Narrative, Women: An Introduction to the Writings of Lyn Hejinian and Leslie Scalapino," *Private Arts* 10 (1996): 47–56. The present essay is an elaboration of ideas originally sketched there.

2. James presents his famous House of Fiction extended metaphor in the 1908 preface to *The Portrait of a Lady*.

3. In discussing the effects of what she calls "indeterminacy," Perloff distinguishes between those texts that maintain a subject-object referential hinge and those that do not. Wallace Stevens's poetry exemplifies the former category; Perloff quotes J. Hillis Miller when she writes, " 'The dialogue between subject and object . . . is Stevens's central theme.' " While Stevens rejected "one form of Romantic dualism"— that of "natural and supernatural, the 'real' and the transcendent worlds" — he remained "committed to the other, perhaps more central Romantic and Symbolist dualism between the 'I' and the other, self and world, because his lyrical form posits a unified, coherent world view throughout its subjective speaker" (20). Perloff quotes Barthes's *Writing Degree Zero* to suggest what occurs when the subject-object hinge is undermined: "modern poetry . . . destroyed relationships in language and reduced discourse to words as static things" (Barthes, quoted in Perloff 3).

4. Silliman reframes the pioneering work of Ferdinand de Saussure, who analyzed the arbitrary relationship between the linguistic signifier and its signifed object.

5. See "The Laugh of the Medusa," or Cixous's longer work in collaboration with Clément, *The Newly Born Woman*. Jones is one of Cixous's most articulate challengers, writing that Cixous and other French feminists are "idealist and essentialist, bound up in the very system [of biological sexual difference] they claim to undermine" (367). I follow the more symbolic reading of Cixous's theories suggested by Stanton, who writes that "the world is the word"—Stanton paraphrases Cixous herself—and this "world" is one that "is experienced phenomenologically as a vast text" (41); see Cixous, "Le Sexe ou la tête," *Les Cahiers du GRIF* 13 (Oct. 1976): 7.

6. One exception to this tendency is her reference to the twentieth-century Brazilian woman writer Clarice Lispector.

7. See *Revolution in Poetic Language*. Kristeva's examples of "revolution" are drawn from Symbolist and Modernist male writers like Stéphane Mallarmé and James Joyce. Jardin's theory of "gynesis," developed from Kristevan theory, likewise hypothesizes the presence of a "woman in the text," but this "woman" has little to do with real women writing.

8. See Owens (59). This essay focuses upon several women avant-garde visual artists but says little about literary artists. See also Flax, who maps out some of the intersections between postmodern artistic

practice and feminist political interest, but does not address the topic of the literary avant-garde.

9. Mulvey famously critiques the visual power that dominates traditional narratives through their "active" male agency, and the male gaze that objectifies "passive" cultural femininity. See also de Lauretis, who elaborates Mulvey's thesis, and discusses its literary implications, as well.

10. See *Objects in the Terrifying Tense Longing from Taking Place* (64). This quotation comes in the context of a discussion of Berssenbrugge's effect of a "continual removal," which Scalapino — paraphrasing another writer, Barrett Watten—says is "delineated as a modern condition."

11. Messerli makes this statement in his introduction to *"Language" Poetries*. He cites poet Louis Simpson's analogy of the poet as coal miner, whose "primary product . . . brought to surface represents 'real' experience" (Messerli 9).

12. I quote my published text, "An Interview with Lyn Hejinian and Leslie Scalapino" (66). The original interview took place with both writers in Oakland, California, during June 1993. The oral text has subsequently been revised as a written text by Scalapino, Hejinian, and myself.

WORKS CITED

Campbell, Bruce. "Neither in nor Out: The Poetry of Leslie Scalapino." *Talisman: A Journal of Contemporary Poetry and Poetics* 8 (1992): 53–60.

Cixous, Hélène, and Catherine Clément. *The Newly Born Woman*. Trans. Betsy Wing. Minneapolis: U of Minnesota P, 1986.

de Lauretis, Teresa. *Alice Doesn't: Feminism, Semiotics, Cinema*. Bloomington: Indiana UP, 1984.

Flax, Jane. "Postmodernism and Gender Relations." *Feminism/Postmodernism*. Ed. Linda J. Nicholson. New York: Routledge, 1991. 39–62.

Hinton, Laura. "An Interview with Lyn Hejinian and Leslie Scalapino." *Private Arts* 10 (1996): 58–77.

Jardin, Alice. *Gynesis: Configurations of Woman and Modernity*. Ithaca, N.Y.: Cornell UP, 1985.

Jones, Ann Rosalind. "Writing the Body: Toward an Understanding of *l'écriture féminine*." *The New Feminist Criticism: Essays on Women, Literature, and Theory*. Ed. Elaine Showalter. New York: Pantheon, 1985. 361–77.

Kristeva, Julia. *Revolution in Poetic Language*. Trans. Margaret Waller. New York: Columbia UP, 1984.

Messerli, Douglas. Introduction. *"Language" Poetries: An Anthology.* New York: New Directions, 1987. 1–11.

Mulvey, Laura. "Visual Pleasure and Narrative Cinema." *Screen* 16.3 (1975): 6–18.

Owens, Craig. "The Discourse of Others: Feminists and Postmodernism." *The Anti-Aesthetic: Essays on Postmodern Culture.* Ed. Hal Foster. Seattle: Bay, 1983. 57–82.

Perloff, Marjorie. *The Poetics of Indeterminacy: Rimbaud to Cage.* Princeton, N.J.: Princeton UP, 1981.

Scalapino, Leslie. *Defoe.* Los Angeles: Sun, 1994.

———. *How Phenomena Appear to Unfold.* Elmwood, Conn.: Potes, 1991.

———. *Objects in the Terrifying Tense Longing from Taking Place.* New York: Roof, 1993.

———. *The Return of Painting, the Pearl, and Orion/A Trilogy.* San Francisco: North Point, 1991.

———. *that they were at the beach—aeolotropic series.* San Francisco: North Point, 1985.

Silliman, Ron. "'Postmodernism': Sign for a Struggle, the Struggle for the Sign." *Poetics Journal* 7 (1987): 18–39.

Stanton, Domna C. "Language and Revolution: The Franco-American Dis-Connection." *The Future of Difference.* Ed. Hester Eisenstein and Alice Jardine. New Brunswick, N.J.: Rutgers UP, 1980. 73–87.

Watten, Barrett. "Political Economy and the Avant-Garde: A Note on Haim Steinback and Leslie Scalapino." *Talisman* 8 (1992): 49–52.

9

Lyn Hejinian and the Possibilities of Postmodernism in Poetry

CHARLES ALTIERI

I have to indulge in condensed abstraction in order to explain the context in which I want to discuss Lyn Hejinian's poetry.[1] It seems to me that postmodernism is now dead, because the conceptual frameworks it generated are unlikely to generate any significant new ideas and because as we unfold the ideas that it has inspired we find them caught in what to me at least seem inescapable contradictions. But while this is a cause to lament the state of theory, it also manages to help right a situation made problematic when "theory" appropriated a postmodernism first developed within the arts for its own thematic purposes. It is the thematics that have died, and through that death we can see better how some of the art has the power to live because of how it grapples with concerns that produce disabling contradictions when squeezed into the machines provided by postmodern theories.

Let me briefly develop the five contradictions within this theorizing that I find most disturbing; then I will focus on the one I think most important for developing by contrast what we might call Hejinian's claims on postmodern society.

1. There is a contradiction between treating values as symptoms of postmodern society and creating values that can claim to empower changes within that society. Given global claims for the effects of postmodern simulacral structures, what can be said to

146

escape them or even transform them without simply turning back into what one is trying to escape? The more art reflects its culture, the less it can be said to offer possibilities of change. Yet why bother to be concerned with reflecting the culture unless one can show how such reflection helps facilitate some kind of alternative? Notice, for example, how Jameson's call for dialectical readings is on the verge of turning into an absolutely antidialectical social spectacle in which ideas are recycled as self-promotion by intellectuals thinking that only they can avoid a world in which marketing is the only reality.

2. It is probably impossible to correlate critiques of Enlightenment universals with rhetorics of participatory democracy. If postmodernism needs ideals of heterogeneity to save it from universals, from ideals of coherent selfhood, and from reliance on commonsense judgment, it then also needs an identity politics so that it can resist proliferating those differences and can develop grounds for working within its Englightenment heritage. However, that identity politics is very difficult to correlate with the constructivist and performative ideals that it requires to make that heritage sufficiently sensitive to the differences that in theory should proliferate.

3. Problems emerge in developing models of subjective agency that preserve singularity while rejecting bourgeois models of individuality. Take, for example, the contradictions that emerge within the now standard line of thinking that calls for breaking down the ego's armor (or loosening the hold of the male imaginary). Which of the many possibilities of dissolving fixed identity will one pursue, and how will one hold off the more extreme possibilities that now emerge as we hover between ideals of sublimity and of renewed sociality? Clearly, de-emphasizing the need for single coherent selves will help us accept fragmentation and come to better terms with vulnerabilities in ourselves and in others. But then why stop with a psychology that still cultivates traditional caring intimacy with others? Why not explore the more radical opportunities of self-dissolution that fully shatter any sense of individual ego and open onto radical sublime states of self-dispossesion (such as those Alphonse Lingis explores)? At

the other pole, the more collective the model of subjectivity, and the more strident the replacing of slogans about history (the buzzword of the eighties) by slogans about community (our new toy), the more there returns the pressure of the seductions, conventions, and collectivities which had initially to be undone by modern critiques of rhetoric and representation in order to get to the intricate interfaces between self and world where all the theoretical ladders start.

4. Ethical contradictions arise between ideals of opening ourselves to otherness and those calling for perfectionist versions of the self. At one pole postmodernism is perhaps the first large-scale cultural movement in the West since Augustinian Christianity to base ethical ideals on the overthrowing of the masculine performing and ordering ego. If we look at Mike Kelley's dolls or read popular theorists like Kaja Silverman who idealize castration or reflect on Levinasian ethics, we see that decentering seems inseparable from demasculinizing. From these ethical perspectives it is crucial not merely to respect the other, but to understand, in Levinasian fashion, that in some deep way the call from the other that positions the self is more primary, logically and temporally, than any impulse toward self-fulfillment. And then the deepest ethical adventure involves getting far enough away from the ego's demand for control to enter into proximity with what can be said to call to us in that other. Yet as we try to move in that direction we are haunted by the contrary pull, in the form of languages of empowerment or of coming to "own the self" (in Stanley Cavell's phrase) which shift the focus from how we listen to others to how we actively resist their seductions, especially those seductions that restore old power hierarchies under the guise of fostering community. We find ourselves confronted with both a good "other" whose call we must hear and a bad "Other" who reduces us to imposed categories and hence must be denied. But we cannot at once yield to castration and assert ourselves, nor can we quite fix any specifiable other to help us tell the difference between them.

5. Postmodernism's enabling versions of anti-foundational

constructivism end up sharply at odds with each other. At one pole there is pragmatism's sense that poststructural critiques of Enlightenment values seem unnecessarily caught up in the metaphysical tradition they are trying to deconstruct. What matters is simply adapting ways of talking that are justified in terms of the emotional and practical needs that beset specific communities. However, for deconstruction this minimalist confidence in antimetaphysical stances stems from problematic assumptions about our powers of judgment, our capacities to discern and follow the appropriate social emotions, and our willingness to accept the authority of specific communities. These assumptions may even depend on the very metaphysical beliefs they are employed to challenge. And anyone invested in deconstruction would argue against these pragmatists that deconstruction is not a statement of principle (to be treated as a metaphysics) but a process of endless self-questioning to keep us wary of just such restorations of easy faith in our "regular" practices.

I think one can find significant contemporary art grappling with all these contradictions. But there may be no richer grappling with any one of them than the work Hejinian does in dissolving fixed identity while preserving a range of values like individuality and intimacy which have derived from now outmoded depth-psychology versions of selfhood. Her poetry can be seen as having its origins in objectivist calls for a sincerity won by resistance to rhetoric and by rendering the elemental features of emotion within objective lyric events. But for her this sincerity comes to demand a self-consciousness so intricate and mobile that it forces poetry to a sense of discontinuities, gaps, and readerly participatory differences quite foreign to the original objectivist project. And correspondingly, form is no longer a dynamic objectivity but a relational process elaborating between writer and reader gaps and connections charged with the mind's awareness of a life not reducible to any other, less intense, combinatory mode.

The Cell realizes this sincerity by establishing a personal agency so vital in its silences, in its ways of repeating itself, and in its shifting attentions, that it convincingly inhabits the overt form of a lyric diary while refusing the dramatic confrontations between represented and representing selves fundamental to that form. Traditionally such a focus on the subject's experiences tempts authors to have each entry build to a climactic dramatic moment, as in Lowell's *Notebook*. But to Hejinian such climaxes lead away from what she is most interested in because the dramatic organization blinds the author to the most intimate features of repetition and change as life unfolds, and it greatly oversimplifies the play of voices that constitute self-consciousness within that unfolding. As Hejinian memorably puts it, "Personality is a worn egress to somewhere in particular," confining consciousness to pre-established ends and, ironically, telling introspection what it is bound to find. So she proposes instead those imaginative paths where poetry can take up the "chance of enhancement" (42), in part because what emerges in such chance puns provides good reason for seeking more mobile versions of subjective agency.

Once one grows suspicious of "personality," lyric self-reflection becomes a very different enterprise:

> A person decomposing the unity
> of the subjective mind by
> dint of its own introspection.

(157)

Introspection sets the mind against its own images—not simply to maintain ironic distance but also to dramatize the resonant forces that circulate around the desire for self-representation. As an example of what can emerge from this interplay between decomposition and redeployment of imaginative investments, consider the volume's penultimate poem. Its opening lines bypass all empirical situating of the ego in order to dwell on how many senses come into play within the act of seeing, or better, around the way sight is poised between what disappears and what appears:

> All sentences about the sense
> of seeing, the sense of
> embarrassment
> It could all disappear—instead
> it appeared
> My language
> My language is a genital—
> lets say that
>
> (214)

Seeing involves a sense of embarrassment because it leaves the subject open to and dependent on the supplementary processes that sentences bring into play. Even the syntax is ambiguous because seeing cannot not be given one stable position as it vacillates between serving as an element within an extended clause (whose concern for sense never achieves its verb) and serving as the focal unit that everything sentences about, as if the seeing were the wellspring of possible meanings. No wonder that the "it" could all disappear: one's sense of one's immediate world depends on the vagaries of these sentences and on the difficult interplay between the time of pure seeing and the work of sentencing. But "it" also can seem to come into focus, making language itself seem inseparable from the person's hold on the scene. And that satisfaction, framed by the fear of disappearance, invites the sexual analogies that her reference to genitals brings to bear.

"Let's say that" breaks the enchantment. If the poem can achieve the distance to treat these sayings as provisional, we have to wonder whether we have lost touch with the immediate impulses that have been shaping our investments in this "sense" of seeing. Language can sustain a thinking at one with "the composition/of things/distinctions steering sunlight," but such intensified self-consciousness can also get caught up in its own overdetermined sequences that now take over the poem. The poem turns to demonstrate those movements, but I will go directly to the moment when the poem turns back from its wanderings to develop its conclusion:

It could all disappear
Streets
With remorse for individualism, provoking
    scale
Dimension sinks
It's the event of seeing
    what I speak of with
    someone's eyes
The event of a carnality
    covered by eye
The light preceding along the
    yellow sides of night
A word is a panorama
    of a thing
It's the eye's duty to
    tell
It's relevant—though a person
    is implicated in the process
    it keeps in sight

(215)

These lines are not easy to interpret. They demand a good deal of guesswork. Yet in responding to that demand we find ourselves embodying a cardinal principle of Hejinian's poetic, its foregrounding of processes of "conjecture" that force us to recognize the apparently arbitrary or uncaused leap of proprioceptive activity fundamental to a person's making any part of the world her own. Conjecture, in other words, is inseparable from our sense of the ego taking up residence in a world that exceeds it, but that also provides a ground for its sense of its own free contingency, without demanding that the "I" build a melodramatic stage on which to interpret its independence (and hence make it dependent on the version of the self one postulates). Even sex for Hejinian is best figured as "the pleasure of inexactitude" (140) because the alternative is sex by the book, sex blind to the arbitrariness and playfulness by which we come to appreciate how our lives might remain open to, even hungry for, what we cannot control in other persons. Why should poetry be different, since it seeks the same correlation of intimacy and pleasure playing through the same absorbing interest in seeing exact attention create indefinable edges?

My conjectures project here a process of using this fear of disappearance to highlight what Heidegger might call "a worldliness of the world" constantly at risk of collapsing into public pieties and private psychodramas. The passage begins with a fear of landscape turning into mapped streets, which in their turn become instantly allegorizable as "remorse for individualism," since the demand for individuation produces endless repetition, as well as a feeling that agency is in fact lost. Since these are not the kind of fears that admit of heroic confrontations, all Hejinian can do is let the earlier querying within the poem generate a syntactic form around which some resisting energies can be gathered. So as dimension sinks, and hence as the specific image collapses, the poem replaces "it could all disappear" with another "it" construction leading beyond the eager scrutiny to a more general sense of how persons inhabit the eye. If the "I" must give up the hope of somehow establishing private access to the real, it can instead treat embodiment as simply accepting the carnality of its bodily functions. This enables one to identify with the eye without making demands that vision be tied closely to the demands of any specific ego. Instead this abstracting of the eye leads back to the panorama of words, as if words too opened into vision so long as we maintain enough distance from specific imaginary demands to explore the access language gives us to the ways that our unconscious beings are deployed in particular moments.

This intricate balancing of eye, I, and word finally takes on its full emotional and sexual implications in the last three lines:

> It's relevant—though a person
> is implicated in the process
> it keeps in sight[.]

We arrive at this sense of implication by recognizing that language is part of the eye's imperative, even when one brackets individual sensibility, because language allows vision its "sentences," in every sense of that term. Then once that process is grasped in its independence, one can return to the issue of how particular persons make investments in what they see. Rather than being the source of the seeing, the person is literally folded into what appears, so that one in effect learns about one's own desires in the very processes that allow vision to unfold a world.

Everything the poem implies about the force of language as bearer of investments comes into the foreground in the brilliant final pun on keeping materials in sight. For it seems as if the plenitude of the pun arises out of nowhere, a grace within language attuned to the situation it tries to articulate. The eye not only keeps objects in its sight, it also has stakes in those objects, so that it matters how over time the person treasures what is seen. Decomposing the ego into its carnal functioning then does not repress feeling but allows us to encounter its most elemental forms—forms that depend on a syntax that works with an "it" in the subject position, not an inferred "I." In fact it is that formulation that helps temper the fear of thought overdetermining sight with which the poem began. For it helps us see how simply holding objects before the eye can modulate into actively *keeping in* sight, as if the eye expressed a version of the containing force that can be associated with female genitals. And this active keeping then becomes a full willing of what the eye sees, even though there has been no introspection by which to organize that will. Here the power of commitment does not depend on some inner state but on a specific way of engaging in events that prevents our isolating that personal dimension as a unique and representable center. The only workable mirror for the self seems to consist in folding consciousness within its own embodied activities: anything more speculative may entail self-divisive idealism.

I have to be this abstract if I am to keep Hejinian in sight. But it is crucial that readers not confuse the speculation it takes to orient ourselves within the poem with the very different mode of expression by which the poetry itself engages the world. Hejinian can be as minimalist as she is about emotions because she relegates much of the work of feeling to a remarkably fluid, intricate, and resolutely undramatic play of tones. Such tone makes it possible to keep a mode of conjecture within experience which we easily lose if we push too hard to capture the entire process as someone's possession, and hence as an extension of personality. So I think it fair to say that Hejinian's poetry offers a dynamic alternative to the modes of self-reflection generated by both more analytic models of thinking and by the therapeutic alternatives postulated to save us from the self-division such thinking creates. In her work what makes us persons is not how we compose self-images but how the degrees and modalities of concern that tone embodies compose a world for our keeping.

As Hejinian's final poem in *The Cell* puts it, rather than worrying about a gulf between word and world, we might think of how we can orient ourselves toward a "consciousness of unconsciousness" attuned to the ways we are always already part of the sentences that our grammars afford us. Then, she adds in order to close with her characteristic twinkle, "It is good to know/so (217). That is, we may need only this playful cross of rhyme and pun in order to correlate the "so" of method with the "so" of alignment and adjustment, and hence to demonstrate what consciousness of unconsciousness can afford us. And then it even becomes possible to have poetry speak what we might call the legislative "let it be so" rarely achieved in postromantic poetry. Such blessing depends only on managing to keep lyrical intelligence responsive to the delights embedded in the panoramas language affords, as if in this alternative to specular self-reflection, in this gentle and mobile distance, may lie our peace.

NOTE

1. This paper is abstracted and somewhat changed from a longer essay, "What Is Living and What Is Dead in American Postmodernism: Establishing the Contemporaneity of Some American Poetry," *Critical Inquiry* 22 (Fall 1996): 764–89.

WORK CITED

Hejinian, Lyn. *The Cell*. Los Angeles: Sun, 1992.

PART III

Americas (Geography/Politics)

10

Reimagining "Empire's Westward Course": Amy Clampitt's A Silence Opens

CELESTE GOODRIDGE

Amy Clampitt has been variously described as a poet with a "nomadic imagination" (Costello 34), who is "neither place-bound nor placeless, but unsettled and open to astonishment" (34), as a naturalist who "lets her eye guide her while, simultaneously, a more penetrating vision scans the assembled terrain" (Jordan 30), as someone who has "restored ornament to poetry" (Spiegelman 18), and as a writer who "has studied and learned a great deal—from the landscape and lifeblood of literature, as well as from the encyclopedia of the eye's observations" (McClatchy 314). These assessments, which emphasize Clampitt's engagement with specific locales, her use of landscape as a site of knowledge, her cultivated baroque sensibility, her penchant for literary allusion or referentiality, her homage to other writers' lives, and her curious and attentive eye, attend to her late romantic poetic strategies in her first three volumes: *The Kingfisher* (1983), *What the Light Was Like* (1985), and *Archaic Figure* (1987). Beginning with *Westward* (1990), however, and gathering an added urgency in her last, posthumously published volume, *A Silence Opens* (1994), Clampitt's concerns change and widen, as she begins to confront and critique different representations of America and American history from the vantage point of witnessing this fallen "empire's westward course" (*Westward* 90) in the late twentieth century.

To date, little attention has been given to Clampitt's interest in and often subversive indictment of contemporary American culture and the American past. Bonnie Costello's "Amy Clampitt: Nomad Exquisite" provides a notable exception to most Clampitt criticism, maintaining that she ignores neither history nor contemporary reality, portraying "a culture of appropriation and exclusion which has failed to take account of its own restlessness, and the natural drift and variety of the world we inhabit" (34). Finally, however, Costello is most interested in Clampitt's "nomadic imagination," which roams through spaces, finding "a home in motion" (46), whose "odyssey is not a reclamation of the homeland or an indictment of the American past, but a testament to the human and natural ecology, 'the linked, perishable, humming webs' that define and redefine place" (38). In contrast, I seek to bring Clampitt's complex critique of "America" to the foreground in a consideration of her last book, arguing that in these poems Clampitt attempts to reconcile her lyric romanticism with her reading of contemporary "America" and its past in this historical moment. Increasingly for Clampitt, Emersonian transcendence and the ability to "see the miraculous in the common" (Emerson, "Nature" 55) can only occur if one first takes stock of all that interrupts or threatens to destroy the lyric moment. Thus, in the poems of *A Silence Opens,* Clampitt's desire for interiority, for a sense of "stillness at the center" (*Predecessors, Et Cetera,* "A Poet's Henry James" 70) now accommodates and even welcomes, in a way that her poems in *Westward* only began to, noise, imminent destruction, constant activity, clutter, and vulgarity in the spaces she inhabits. It is this dissonance between a desire for a still place, for connection and rootedness in the moment, and a recognition that this vulgar enterprise called America will impede and interrupt this desire, which I hope to make visible as a way of assessing Clampitt's refusal in her late poetry to remain simply wedded to an uncomplicated lyric romanticism. For Clampitt, this entails exploring her own sense of displacement, otherness, frailty, and exile as a prelude to transcending her sense of dislocation. This gesture may be viewed as something of a sleight of hand for those of us who might wish Clampitt to have more political agency, or at least sustained conviction about her agency. What I am suggesting, however, is that Clampitt, who is more than, but still inevitably, a romantic, finds a way of making historical and cultural displacement of herself and others a condition for her own survival in this moment and in so doing feels entitled to moments of transcendence.

In *A Silence Opens* Clampitt demonstrates that any assessment of American culture must come to terms with the rapacity of colonialism in the Western Hemisphere, with the institution and ideology of slavery, with economic exploitation, and with the silencing of Native American cultures and peoples in the United States. She is particularly concerned with an image of America and American history that involves making the gaps in what we know visible. Simply put, to appropriate or colonize the space called America is to displace people and things— to erase and obliterate that which was here before. Clampitt's urgency, particularly in a poem like "Matoaka," to make a scarred American past inseparable from a reading of the contemporary moment forces us to confront our own complicity in this past and may even startle us into a new relation to the present.

In these poems, Clampitt provides a critique of America and American culture in the late twentieth century which is both concerned with recovering a version of the past—what history has "taught" us and what historians have said happened—and with what our current historical/cultural moment can teach us about reading and rereading the past. She implies in several poems that the past does not stay past and fixed; records and narratives are always necessarily constantly being revised, literally and in our imaginations. A 1991 *Newsweek* article, Susan Miller's "Slavery: The High Price of Sugar," becomes the catalyst for "Hispaniola," a poem about the economic enterprise of turning sugar cane ("a reed/that brought forth honey/sans the help of bees" [7]) into sugar ("crystalline/appeasement of mammalian/cravings" [8]). This "topography/of monoculture" (7) led inevitably to ecological disaster ("huger and huger/deforestations" [8]) and brutal slavery:

appeasement of mammalian
cravings   slave ships
whip-wielding
overseers   world-class
indignity   the bubbling
hellhole of molasses pits

(8)

A rereading of Whitman's "As I Ebb'd with the Ocean of Life"
leads Clampitt to write "Paumanok," her meditation on how this
"fish-shaped island" has been used and misused. While at one
time "a bused-in,/moved-on proletariat once/stooped for" (9)
potatoes here, this island is now devoted to the cultivation of
wine grapes, an industry that has served to obliterate some of the
original plants (juniper, honeysuckle, bayberry, Virginia creeper,
goldenrod, and poison ivy) that once "would have rioted" in "a
patina of/perpetual motion" (9) on this island:

> where Paumanok's
> outwash plain, debris of glaciers,
>   frays to a fishtail,
>
> now give place to grapevines,
>   their tendency to ramble
> and run on, to run to foliage
>   curbed, pruned, trained
> into another monoculture—row
>   after profitable row
> on acre after acre, whole landscapes
>   strung like a zither

(9)

Walking through this landscape, dismayed by these profitable im-
ported rows of grapevines, Clampitt comes upon a "mowed/and
tended pocket,//last resting place of slaves . . . " (10)—a still
place that evokes those who have been silenced here. This al-
most missed, almost invisible trace of slaves, which has survived

in part because the graves are next to those of the masters—
"Seth Tuthill and his wife Maria,/who chose finally to lie here/
with their sometime chattels" (10)—serves to remind us of the
ur-labor in this landscape, implicitly linking the current capitalist
economy of wine making to the legacy of slavery.

Two other poems in the collection, "Discovery" and "Matoaka,"
provide more extended venues for Clampitt to reflect on various
cultural mythologies and to re-place herself as a consequence of
these musings. Events today—the latest launching of a NASA
space shuttle or the three-hundredth anniversary of the founding
of the College of William and Mary—force her to look back, to
revise and reimagine some version of the past. In "Matoaka," the
wrenching of Pocahuntus out of that place eventually called Vir-
ginia invites us to question our own complicity in that story three
hundred years later as we approach the end of the twentieth cen-
tury. At the same time, the poet's and our alienation and aimless-
ness at the end of this century necessitate and teach us how
to read and reread the fragments or ruins of Pocahuntus's life
story—a story that can never be known but will always necessarily
be endlessly retold. Clampitt's subversive vigilance toward the
world she finds herself in makes her at once nostalgic for a world
that has not "been trademarked/Cute by the likes of Walt Disney"
(5) and simultaneously attentive to "the cozy mythologies we've/
swindled ourselves with" (5). The willingness to undertake this
negotiation is emblematic of her sense of displacement—of be-
ing uprooted—and of her concomitant desire to be accountable
to the contours of this condition and the unexpected detours it
necessitates.

"Discovery" records such a journey. The occasion that prompted
the poem, Clampitt tells us in her note to it, was the launching
on January 22, 1992, of the space shuttle *Discovery*. Her note
reads: "Cape Canaveral, Fla., Jan. 22. Seven astronauts from
three countries sailed flawlessly into orbit today aboard the space
shuttle Discovery. . . . " (89). The poem deals with several real
and potential discoveries: the astronauts' potential discovery of
something in space, the manatees' discovery of warmer waters to

retreat to in the winter, as they "come upriver/to Blue Spring where it's/always warm" (5), the "discovery" of Florida in the sixteenth century, and the poet's recognition at the end of the poem of her affinity with the manatees.

The poem begins with a natural and seemingly habitual occurrence that happens at the same time the space shuttle is launched. Initially this event, the manatees' winter retreat to warm waters, stands in stark contrast to the astronauts' more daring and ambitious quest:

> The week the latest rocket went
> up, a pod (if that's the word)
> of manatees, come upriver
> to Blue Spring where it's
> always warm, could be seen
> lolling, jacketed, elephantine,
> breathing and drowning.
> As they came up for air,
>
> one by one, they seemed numb,
> torpid, quite incurious.
>
> (5)

These "numb,/torpid, quite incurious" (5) creatures initially appear thoroughly other, protected from human intervention, and self-contained by this landscape; their ultimate vulnerability and imminent destruction in the spring, when they leave these warm waters for the ocean, where humans in boats with propellers will scar, maim, and kill them with predictability, is kept at a distance. For a moment, in this pastoral cocoon, they might even escape being commodified by Walt Disney.

> No
> imagining these sirenians
> dangerously singing. Or
> gazing up yearningly. (So much
> for the Little Mermaid.) True,

> the long-lashed little ones
> might have been trademarked
> Cute by the likes of Walt Disney.
> His world's over that way, . . .
>
> (5)

Clampitt implies here that everything in Florida is tainted by "the likes of Walt Disney." Florida naturally accommodates both the industry of Disney World and that of aerospace. Like Wallace Stevens's Florida and Elizabeth Bishop's, Clampitt's is full of tricks, deceptions, and false promises. There are no escapes, just "the cozy mythologies we've/swindled ourselves with" (5) — mythologies that can be linked to the discovery of Florida in the sixteenth century.

> suitably for a peninsula where
> the cozy mythologies we've
> swindled ourselves with, on
> taking things easy, might even
> come true: sun-kissed nakedness
> on the beach, year-round, guilt-free
> hibiscus and oranges, fountains
> welling up through the limestone,
> the rumor of Ponce de Leon, having
> found the one he was looking for,
>
> living at ease in, some say
> Boca Raton, others Cadiz. A last
> bedtime placebo?
>
> (5–6)

Clampitt alludes here to the Spanish explorer Ponce de León, who, in 1513, seeking the fabled Fountain of Youth, became the first European to land in Florida. His unfulfilled quest, Clampitt implies, still marks this space/place, creating and enabling the fictions we delude ourselves with today. At the same time, reversing the usual assumption that the past haunts the present, Clampitt suggests here that the present also haunts the past: the existence of Disney World might enable us to reread the implications of Ponce de León's quest and the Spanish explorers who came in his wake. Disney World today might give us renewed access to Spanish colonialism, inviting us to question the benign story we continue to tell ourselves about Ponce de León's initial quest.

Clampitt then returns to the liftoff of the shuttle, which, like Ponce de León's search for the Fountain of Youth, holds some promise, captivating our imaginations, as it soars away from earth. An odd turn occurs, however, when through her language she implicitly draws an analogy between the astronauts and the pod of manatees observed in the first part of the poem:

> Still, we keep
> looking up. That clear morning,
> just warm enough for a liftoff,
> the fabulous itself could be seen
> unwieldily, jacket by jacket,
> in the act of shedding, as
> a snake does its husk, or
> a celebrant his vestments:
>
> the fiery, the arrowy tip of it,
> of the actual going invisible,
> . . . .
> while up in
> the belly of it, out of their
> element, jacketed, lolling
> and treading, the discoverers
> soar, clumsy in space suits.
>
> (6)

Like the manatees, who have left their element in search of warmer waters for the winter, the astronauts are out of theirs—"jacketed, lolling and treading"—and are perhaps as vulnerable as the manatees, who will very likely meet their demise when they venture back to the ocean. These astronauts were the first to be sent up after the *Challenger* explosion; the possibility that they will meet a similar fate hovers over the poem.

The important turn of the poem occurs, however, in the final stanza when the poet realizes an imaginative kinship or link between her existence and that of these mammals; this connection serves to remind her of own vulnerability and perhaps mortality, though it also seems to be restorative and healing.

> What are we anyhow, we warmth-
> hungry, breast-seeking animals?
> At Blue Spring, a day or so later,
> one of the manatees, edging
> toward discovery, nudged a canoe,
> and from across the wet, warm,
> dimly imaginable tightrope,
> let itself be touched.

The poet's discovery—which is not unlike Stevens's and Bishop's in some of their Florida poems—is that she can have a transcendent experience in this place that swindles and tricks us. This romantic experience of connection, which comes about seemingly unexpectedly as Clampitt confronts the implications of a commodfied Florida, becomes an anchor of sorts for her in this world. At the same time, it is not presented as merely an escape from the world of Disney World, with all its horrors, but rather as an experience that can coexist with the vulgarity. Nevertheless, it is tempting to see the ending as an escape from a sustained confrontation of Florida and its past—as a retreat into a moment of personal transcendence that threatens to ignore what has been evoked in the first part of the poem.

The other poem I will consider is "Matoaka," which was written specifically for the occasion of the three-hundredth anniversary of the founding of the College of William and Mary, and as such can be assumed to be addressed to a particular audience. Clampitt could not have been oblivious to the discomforting effect this poem might have had on an audience of people gathered together to celebrate the founding of an institution that contributed to the obliteration of native peoples in the state and that depended upon the revenues of tobacco farming: "tobacco money, sometime mainstay/of a college given royal grant/and charter" (19).

In the poem, Clampitt makes the history of this place called Virginia inseparable from the silencing of the Native American peoples and cultures who once inhabited it. Retelling the life of Pocahuntus, known secretly by her tribe as Matoaka or "Little Snow Feather," allows her to to call into question what history signifies, reveals, and silences. Clampitt takes a lifestory that has been overmarked by countless stories, plays, and poems, and most recently by a Disney film, *Pocahontas* (1995; though her poem predates this film), and makes this life almost unmarked, strange, confusing, and impenetrable, restoring in the process some of the dignity and mystery that have been erased in the multiple narratives, none of which is actually Pocahuntus's. (I say "almost" unmarked because Clampitt's own marking is inevitable, though she goes to some length to remind us of all that can never be known, of the silences that surround Pocahuntus and into which she retreats, even in the stories told by others about her.) At the same time Clampitt does not offer her narrative as the last one that will circulate or need to be told. Once again she is looking for a way for the present to haunt the past, a gesture that she would insist must be endlessly repeated.

The poem begins with an homage to the Indian place names that remain as traces in this landscape:

> Place names, the names of streams—
> the Rappahannock, the Roanoke, the Potomac,
> and that commemoration of sometime
>   majesty, the James,
>
> its tributary the Chickahominy,
> the Pamunkey and the Mattaponi, each
> what a people called itself once, subsumed in
>   a gazetteer, the names

half-overgrown by the long quasi-
anonymity that is history

(11)

Figures in this landscape have not survived in the same way; lives
in places keep changing. "Matoaka. A woman's name, though/
not the one we know her by,/or imagine we do" (12), has be-
come the legendary figure, Pocahuntus, whom we know through
Captain John Smith as a "well formed but/wanton" (12) child.
The legend that has circulated and been reproduced in various
narratives for various cultural agendas has been that she was a
mediator between her father's tribe and the English settlers, ac-
tually preventing the murder of Captain John Smith when he was
captured by Powhatan, Pocahuntus's father. This of course is part
of the story, but not the one we are telling now:

> A king's
> daughter as advocate: that was
> the story we told once, from which
> we've since recoiled
>
> (we being history) in favor of
> the hidden, discreditable motive,
> the flagrant fib. Who was she?
> Ask Paul De Man,
>
> for instance. Ask Nietzsche, Freud
> or Lévi-Strauss. . . .
> Ask any woman
>
> what she thinks, or thought she did.
> The stories we tell ourselves keep changing.

(12)

Clampitt suggests that we have recently revised the myth that
Pocahuntus was simply an advocate for the English settlers, some-
one who intervened, mediating conflicts gracefully and skillfully
between the settlers and the Powhatans. Instead we now see her

169

as someone who sold out as a go-between, who betrayed her origins, her culture, and her family. Clampitt, who implicitly and mockingly disassociates herself from Freud, Nietzsche, and Lévi-Strauss, who seek to explain origins, to recover ur-texts, will now tell another story. Her story, however, will privilege what we don't know, what can't be ascertained about motives and origins.

Moving away from the "Bronze-immobilized" (12) version of Pocahuntus—an allusion to the 1958 bronze statue that was presented by the United States to Saint George's Church in Gravesend, England, where Pocahuntus died—Clampitt suggests we must "begin again" and first tell the stories of Queen Elizabeth and her "hankering after/gold, fame, danger," Sir Walter Raleigh, who was "given leave/to name the shore he claimed," and the "Silence at Roanoke" after the settlement disappeared. "Such were the forms/and usages, now quaint, of royalty./Behind them, silences" (13). These events and others led to the enterprising John Rolfe who married Pocahuntus, thereby silencing her:

> Silence at Werewo-
>
> comoco, seat of Powhatan,
> who—as Captain Smith, his match
> in guile, did not forbear to say—
> had his own majesty.
>
> Silence at Henrico, the lands upriver,
> and at Varina, where John Rolfe
> planted the golden weed that one day
> would amount to money—
>
> Varina, where after many inner
> wrestlings, after consultations,
> mumblings and catechizings,
> he'd bring his bride,
>
> not as Matoaka or, any longer,
> Pocahuntus but, renamed in Christ,

>   Rebecca. What she called herself
>   by then is not recorded.
>
>   (14)

Clampitt alludes here to Pocahuntus's abduction by white colo-
nists in 1613; for some time before this she had been forbidden
by her father to see any of the colonizers. Captain Samuel Argall
decided, with the aid of some Indians, to abduct Pocahuntus and
to take her as a hostage, whose return would necessitate a last-
ing peace with the Powhatans. Pocahuntus was thus lured onto a
British ship and held prisoner. In response to the colonists' de-
mands, Powhatan was silent; ignoring their requests, he did not
seek his daughter's return. Shortly after this, Pocahuntus was
married to John Rolfe; she moved to Varina, began wearing En-
glish dress, and converted to Christianity. "What she called her-
self/by then is not recorded" (14). In 1615 her son, Thomas, was
born; King James was said to be outraged. What Pocahuntus felt
remains unknown.

What can't be known, determined, or seen becomes at this
point a haunting presence in the poem, as Clampitt makes visible
Pocahuntus's increasing lack of agency. Stripped of all volition,
she is "the mere sullied pawn/of statecraft and testosterone" (16):

>   What happened in the mind of John
>   Smith's nonpareil, a pagan
>   without a peer, grown nubile,
>   then the shining
>
>   jewel of imperial endeavor,
>   now the mere sullied pawn
>   of statecraft and testosterone,
>   who dares imagine?
>
>   After what dazzlements, what
>   threats, what stirred, fearful
>   increment of passion, as Mistress
>   Rolfe, she crossed

that threshold, who can guess?
Concerning what she thought, miasmas,
quagmires, white birds flying up,
      the Holy Ghost,

deter us. Who's the more lost?
She had, at any rate, her uses.
Newly installed as convert, nursing
      mother and great lady

up the river named for his
increasingly unseemly majesty,
see her embark, chief showpiece
      of colonial bravado.

                                        (16)

Stressing what we will never know—"What happened in the mind of John/Smith's nonpareil," "who dares imagine," and "who can guess"—Clampitt wonders who is more lost: Pocahuntus or those who used her as their "chief showpiece/of colonial bravado," Pocahuntus or we in this historical moment who still commodify our version of her existence as a cultural icon to be displayed and distributed?

In the remainder of the poem, Clampitt records a version of Pocahuntus's journey to England in 1616, a journey from which she failed to return. We still don't know what Pocahuntus thought, but we have "records of a sort"—European ones, of course—and portraits:

Now records of a sort begin:
of presentations, masques, levees,
of portrait sittings, wearing
      wig, ruff, mantle

of brocaded velvet; no less,
for a season, than the rage
of foul, fashionable London
      with its spiteful

> stares and whispers, its catarrhs,
> its bruited rifts and ruinings, . . .
>
> (17)

While there she meets Captain John Smith again, whom she had thought dead:

> She'd thought him dead. She'd never
> been so tired. There in London
> a silence opens: Captain Smith,
> repenting to have writ she
>
> could speak English, is witness
> of how she turned away—she who,
> out of a distance grown by now
> intolerable, had seen
>
> the world so called: brought face
> to face with majesty, with empire, by
> that silence she took their measure.
> Amicably, then,
>
> she acknowledged him, and Jamestown;
> as for his countrymen (in what tone
> and with what gesture?), they were a people
> that often lied.
>
> (18)

The nostalgic and elegiac musings about the world Pocahuntus has left and lost increasingly encode Clampitt's own sense of loss, her own sense of the impossibility of reading this place, without acknowledging her own displacement and sense of exile in this moment, and her complicity in the "colonial bravado" necessarily present in what we know to be a version of America:

> through
> a pomandered fog

of rooms and posturings arises,
stunningly vivid still yet
dim with distance, a figure
　　　long gone from Jamestown,

an ocean's retching, heaving
vertigo removed, and more: from
girlhood's remembered grapevines,
　　　strawberries, sun-

warm mulberries, leapfrog,
cartwheels, the sound of streams,
of names, of languages: Paumunkey,
　　　Chickahominy. . . .

　　　　　　　　　　　　　　　　　(17)

At the end of the poem Clampitt overtly acknowledges that to tell a version of who Pocahuntus might be in this moment, making the silences audible and the gaps visible in any version or history of her life, is to recover through this telling our own complicity in that silencing. At the same time, the very gesture of acknowledging and witnessing the past in this contemporary setting leads her to an imaginative kinship with Pocahuntus—one that transcends history. The poem ends with a disconcerting moment of lyric recuperation, as Clampitt invites her listeners to conjure up Pocahuntus in Lake Matoaka, which is found on the campus of William and Mary:

to move nearer,

in imagination, to the nub,
the pulse, the ember of what she was—
no stranger, finally, to the mystery
　　　of what we are.

　　　　　　　　　　　　　　　　　(20)

As in "Discovery," a moment of connection occurs in the wake of indictments of the American past and contemporary American life. Both poems end with a moment of stillness, with a turning inward—and as such turn away from or mute the dissonance of contemporary American life and the indictment of the American past that Clampitt has made visible. While these lyric turns are decidedly nostalgic and wholly romantic, they finally cannot be disconnected from the larger cultural and historical context in which they occur, constituting in the process an important revision of Clampitt's earlier poetic project.

WORKS CITED

Clampitt, Amy. *Predecessors, Et Cetera: Essays.* Ann Arbor: U of Michigan P, 1991.

——. *A Silence Opens.* New York: Knopf, 1994.

——. *Westward.* New York: Knopf, 1990.

Costello, Bonnie. "Amy Clampitt: Nomad Exquisite." *Verse* 10.3 (Winter 1993): 34–46.

Emerson, Ralph Waldo. *Selections from Ralph Waldo Emerson.* Ed. Stephen E. Whicher. Boston: Houghton, 1957.

Jordan, Barbara. "Vision as Appetite: Clampitt as Naturalist." *Verse* 10.3 (Winter 1993): 28–33.

McClatchy, J. D. *White Paper: On Contemporary American Poetry.* New York: Columbia UP, 1989.

Spiegelman, Willard. "Amy Clampitt's Drama of Syntax." *Verse* 10.3 (Winter 1993): 18–27.

II

Bishop in Brazil:
Writing the Un-renamable

SUSAN MCCABE

my poor old island's still
un-rediscovered, un-renamable
—"Crusoe in England"

In discussing Elizabeth Bishop in Brazil, I make the perhaps perverse claim that she writes about the country by not writing about it. Her Brazil poems resist landscape and instead focus upon the limits of the traveler's eye—vision of another culture always mediated by pre-vision and expectation. Troubled by her "accumulation of exotic or picturesque or charming detail," she writes to Robert Lowell in 1960: "I don't want to become a poet who can only write about South America. It is one of my greatest worries now—how to use everything and keep on living here, most of the time, probably—and yet be a New Englander herring-choker bluenoser at the same time" (*One Art* 383–84). In spite of the somewhat problematic desire to protect her "bluenoser" identity and still "use everything," Bishop will constantly acknowledge her outsider status and question the ethics of poetic "use." Her writing of Brazil resists the seductions of a descriptive mode, "the accumulation of detail," as guard against and criticism of the inevitable ethnocentrism of her North American perspective.

During her residence in Brazil, she will critique colonialist possession, a process that reflects upon her own impulses in representing the other. I will briefly examine several poems from the

Brazil period that reveal how Bishop's negotiation of her double state of exile and home underwrite this process, and how her almost complete denial of landscape in these poems emerges from such hybridity. "Crusoe in England," the focus of the latter part of this essay, starkly enacts a self-conscious indictment of the naturalist's gaze and Defoe's colonialist agenda. Although not her most obviously Brazilian poem, "Crusoe" becomes both cultural criticism and self-review in its recapitulation of her Brazil experience. Like her Crusoe, Bishop deflects Adam's legacy of naming with its dangerous potential for appropriative domination. While Bishop has been perceived as contributing to the tradition of poetry as naming, her celebrated gift of writing poems that "have written underneath, *I have seen it*" (Jarrell 235) obscures her subversion of naturalism (a subversion that implicates colonialist assumption); her sharp eye is precise in showing precisely where word slips from image, an arm out of an endless sleeve.

Bishop resided in Brazil almost continuously from late 1951 until 1966 with her Brazilian lover, the aristocratic and politically active Lota Macedo de Soares. During this time, she won the Pulitzer Prize for *North & South—A Cold Spring* (1955), wrote many of her first autobiographical pieces of her Nova Scotian childhood, translated *The Diary of Helena Morley* from the Portuguese (1957), and authored the Time-Life edition on Brazil in 1961[1]; and in 1965 *Questions of Travel* appeared, a volume divided into sections "Brazil" and "Elsewhere." Truly a poem of double exile, "Crusoe" was begun in Brazil in 1964 and finished in 1971 in the United States.

That Bishop struggled under the shadow of early traumatic events is by now a well-known fact: her father lost to death, her mother to madness, she was an orphan at eight months. She spent much of her life moving between locations, but paradoxically, while self-exiled in Brazil, felt she "must have died and gone to heaven" (September 16, 1952; *One Art* 246). Though she occupied a privileged position as a white, putatively middle-class American in Brazil, home, for Bishop, never escaped quotation marks; it remains provisional and ready for slippage. Edward

Said's notion of the exile's "plurality of vision" as "contrapuntal" is especially resonant here (*Representations* 105). If Brazil offered Bishop asylum from what Kalstone calls "the doom-laden predominantly masculine poetry world" of the United States (232), and permitted her to explore her traumatic childhood,[2] it also presented her with the significant challenge of negotiating her identification with otherness, of realizing what Adrienne Rich refers to as Bishop's "outsiderhood," a position "closely—though not exclusively—linked with the essential outsiderhood of a lesbian identity and with how the outsider's eye enables Bishop to perceive other kinds of outsiders and to identity or try to identify, with them" (Rich 125). These identifications, I would argue, become further complicated by her relationship to Lota, whose race and class would necessarily raise questions of unequal power for Bishop. She was perhaps less of an outsider in Brazil than in the United States in terms of her sexual choice and poetic priorities, but she was also more of one, both her class privileges and cultural disadvantages militating for an increased sense of "outsiderhood." Home, then, becomes "contrapuntal," always tinged with the knowledge of nonhome, of the dangers and exhilarations of travel and displacement. In discussing expatriates and marginals, Said writes (again quite resonantly here), "A true intellectual is like a shipwrecked person who learns how to live in a certain sense *with* the land, not *on* it, not like Robinson Crusoe" (*Representations* 59). Bishop's "homelessness," land always disappearing from under her, allows her the unstable perspective necessary for her later retroping of the Crusoe story.

Bishop repeatedly complains (especially in her early Brazil years) about difficulties in writing directly about the country, about her disorientation in cultural identity. To Lowell she writes, "I don't know whether it's a good idea to have to change all one's names for everything so late in life!" (n.d.; Millier 240) She warns Moore of deficiencies in the mail system (alluded to in "Arrival at Santos" when she speculates upon the possible "inferiority" of the glue),[3] and then describes "the really lofty vagueness of Brazil . . . where a cloud is coming in my bedroom window right this minute" (March 3, 1952; *One Art* 237): she is drawn to the "vagueness" and also somewhat irritated. In another letter, which refers to Lota's Petropolis house as "a large and elegant modern house on the side of a black granite cliff beside a waterfall," she says "the scenery is unbelievably impractical" (February 7, 1952; *One Art* 234). Impractical, primitive, excessive, too liquid—such ethnocentric terms recur in her reactions to Brazil's otherness. In fact, the poem "Questions of Travel" (*CP* 93–94) begins with irritation ("There are too many waterfalls here") and compares the mountains to "hulls of capsized ships," as if she were shipwrecked. She writes, in this same vein, to Pearl Kazin that she feels cut off from civilization, saying she felt "as if [she'd] undergone a sort of Robinson Crusoe experience" (November 30, 1956; *One Art* 332) The early Brazil poem "Arrival at Santos" (*CP* 89–90) refers to "a meager diet of horizon," to "frivolous greenery," and, once again, to "impractically shaped and—who knows—self-pitying mountains," yet the poem reproaches the tourist (implicating herself in the process) even surprised by "there *being* a flag"—by another continent having its own beingness. Although most of Bishop's more blatantly racist or classist remarks occur early in her years in Brazil, they never entirely disappear; in fact, when she returns to Ouro Prêto after Lota's death, she comments on how "they all speak so badly," referring to what she rates as her "slightly purer Portuguese" than that of one of her newly found servants (Saint Valentine's Day, 1970; *One Art* 512). Her relationship to the otherness of Brazil, then, does not follow a linear or predictable plot. "Crusoe," nevertheless, belongs to Bishop's unevenly evolving counterposition as cultural and self critic.

Bishop's Brazil writing, sparse in "exotic or picturesque or charming detail," seems written without faith in writing directly about landscape, or in transporting perceptions of this other place into poetry.[4] *Questions of Travel,* her book most partaking of her experience (at least chronologically) in Brazil, prepares us to expect that it might present the country in some naturalistic detail. The poems, however, are not rooted in the place of Brazil; rather, they represent the deflective and mediational vision hinted at in her previous work, "like what we imagine knowledge to be" (*CP* 64). As a traveler, as an exile, she cannot gain comprehensive knowledge or vision; the Brazil poems, in fact, connect the dangers of imagined knowledge with the dangers of appropriation, of delusive possession, of colonialism. In spite of her absorption in the natural details of the landscape in her letters about Brazil,[5] Bishop reminds us (especially in her poems) that landscape is never unmediated by cultural context, and so infuses her acts of naming with stringent self-consciousness.

"Arrival at Santos" (completed by 1952) initiates her meditations on displacement, the ongoing moment of deferral; the "Brazil" poems as a whole present the active awareness of homelessness as *the condition*. She interrupts her second stanza with ironic self-address:

> Oh, tourist,
> is this how this country is going to answer you
>
> and your immodest demands for a different world,
> and a better life, and complete comprehension
> of both at last, and immediately,
> after eighteen days of suspension?

Suspension, syntactic as well as phenomenological, rather than comprehension becomes foregrounded. The desire for a new world, for "a better life," must meet disappointment. Even as it remains in neat rhyming quatrains, the poem questions any epistemological stability; the home of her fellow traveler appears to slip on the page: "Her home, when she is at home, is in Glen Fall." The next stanza begins with the withheld and falling *s*, and we slide into the discomfort of the traveler who fears linguistic incomprehension and alien customs, needs not being met, a "port" mentality of transit and ephemerality.

The title poem of the volume, "Questions of Travel," further explores the motives of travel—"Should we have stayed at home and thought of here?" Images of the Brazil landscape continue to be spare; only the waterfalls remain an overwhelming presence, liquid the element in which these poems float—the watercolorist's blurred and spilling shapes, with "those streaks, those mile-long, shiny, tearstains" mirroring the exile's loss. An ethical imperative restrains her: "Is it right to be watching strangers in a play/in this strangest of theatres?" Incorporating what she knows of travelers and explorers before her, Bishop questions her own suspect desire to cross the equator:

> What childishness is it that while there's a breath of life
> in our bodies, we are determined to rush
> to see the sun the other way around?
> The tiniest green hummingbird in the world?

When does sighting the "tiniest green hummingbird" become exploitive desire to exoticize, to fix in formaldehyde as object of strangeness and difference? Darwin, in *The Voyage of the Beagle*, a book quite familiar to Bishop, was ecstatic over hummingbirds he sighted in Rio (41). And before Darwin, Emerson had exulted in the ornithological sublime, in identificatory naming, as in his drawing "an occult relation between the very scorpion and man" and in his declaring, "I am moved by strange sympathies, I say continually 'I will be a naturalist'" (111). The transparent eyeball becomes what it sees through a naturalism based on inclusion and empathy; nevertheless "the hummingbirds little & gay . . . Trochilus delalandi from Brazil" are enclosed in "wise cabinets" and rival Raphael *only* as they become artifact and dead nature (110).

Bishop must refuse this kind of naturalism, its passion for fixing and naming. Her traveler in "Questions" records in her exile's notebook, *"Is it lack of imagination that makes us come/to imagined places, not just stay at home?"* Such an inquiry makes naturalism poignant and absurd. We come to places we have read about and can't shake loose the preinscriptions. But the alternative leads to the same: staying at home is another effort of imagination. Home is culturally circumscribed (*"the choice is never wide and never free"*) and dislocated, in the process of being reconstructed at every turn: the perpetual traveler and exile know this.

That our perceptions are always mediated and limited is the recognition of "Brazil, January 1, 1502" (*CP* 91–92), a necessary poem in the prehistory of "Crusoe" as it reveals "complete comprehension" as illusory and the naming of another culture as misnaming violation. The conquerors (with whom Bishop admits complicity) fabricate the landscape: they (we) can never get to the thing itself. A poem written later in her stay in Brazil (1959), the poem explains, in part, what I see as a resistance to landscape and a rejection of the pastoral eye. Her criticism of colonialism inevitably implicates her own outsider's eye. The language of her first two stanzas is painterly, nature is made into a canvas, its immediacy a matter always of mediation. She begins, "Januaries, Nature greets our eyes/exactly as she must have greeted theirs:/ every square inch filling in with foliage —." "[O]ur eyes" do double with "theirs," those conquerors who "fill in" and construct nature.

A central image of the poem (or so she writes Aunt Grace) are the lizards (Millier 302); this natural image configures in microcosm the power relations of conqueror and conquered, master/slave, "*L'Homme armé*" and the female Indian, relations the poem wants to question: "The lizards scarcely breathe; all eyes/are on the smaller, female one, back-to,/her wicked tail straight up and over." We are breathlessly prepared for the poem's elaborate conceit: the making of nature into art resembles the conquerors' making over the land, their refiguration of it with their own fabrics; they never touch the thing itself. Bishop deftly subverts the moment of conquest, inscripted also as rape:[6]

> [the soldiers] ripped away into the hanging fabric,
> each out to catch an Indian for himself—
> those maddening little women who kept calling,
> calling to each other (or had the birds waked up?)
> and retreating, always retreating, behind it.

A telling counterpoint to this poem and prelude to "Crusoe" is Bishop's record in her Time-Life book of the "discovery" of Brazil by Portuguese navigator Cabral in 1500; she quotes his scribe Caminha, " 'On this day at the vesper hour we caught sight of land, that is, first of a large mountain, very high and round, and of other lower lands. . . . To this high mountain the captain gave the name of Monte Pasoal [Easter Mountain], and to the land, Terra de Ver Cruz [Land of the True Cross]'" (*Brazil* 26). Such naming looks forward to Crusoe's "time enough to play with names," the homophonic mistaking allowed as one volcano he "christened Mont d'Espoir or Mount Despair." With her narration of Cabral's landing, Bishop includes a map published a year after his return, annotating, "The coastline of Brazil is not much more than a guess, but Caminha's groves of trees are there, lined up as formally as in a Portuguese garden and under them sits a group of macaws, presumably to give explorers some idea of what to expect." Appealing vagueness turns to artifice; discovery quickly becomes imposition, the birds calling to one another, the designating otherness of an otherwise ever-receding shoreline. Bishop's blocks in writing about landscape, at least in part, become an awareness, almost strategic, that the naming gaze loses the thing looked at.

While Bishop resists naturalist description, she is nevertheless attracted to the work of other naturalists, especially in her reconfiguring of the Crusoe story. She read (among other books) Sir Richard Burton's *Explorations of the Highlands in Brazil,* Darwin's *Origin of the Species* and *The Voyage of the Beagle,* and Charles William Beebe's *Galápagos: World's End.* Yet even as she admires Darwin's "solid case" of "heroic observations," "his eyes sinking or sliding giddily off into the unknown" are what truly compel her ("Letter to Anne Stevenson," *Elizabeth Bishop and Her Art* 288). She even recommends to Moore a rather obscure book, Konrad Guenther's *A Naturalist in Brazil,* quaintly subtitled *The Record of a Year's Observation of Her Flora, Her Fauna, and Her People.* Bishop will quote from Guenther's subtitle in "Crusoe," significantly leaving out "her people," an omission gesturing toward both her experience of isolation and her sense of naming as dehumanizing possession. While taxonomy can exhilarate, her Crusoe is haunted by "ages" of such work, trapped upon "infinities/of islands":

> knowing that I had to live
> on each and every one, eventually,
> for ages, registering their flora,
> their fauna, their geography.

As much as islands themselves obsess her ("my brain bred islands," her Crusoe ambivalently declares), along with the trope of survival and self-sufficiency they represent, their geographies can enact xenophobia, a separating off from and projection upon an unrenamable other (Defoe's Crusoe lives in almost continuous fear of being devoured by savages). Not only did Bishop visit and live on many islands—Nova Scotia, Florida's Ten Thousand Islands, Aruba, San Juan Islands, England—her great-grandfather's ship foundered at Sable Island. Bishop even describes Brazil as if it were an island, remote and having an inaccessible interior (*Brazil* 55), a shaping conception, as we have seen, of "Brazil, January 1, 1502"; her knowledge of Brazilian history makes her suspicious of fetishistic naming of another culture, of enisling it within clear boundaries so that the outsider herself (with her colonialist fathers) becomes islanded or shipwrecked rather than the always remappable land itself.

The poem begun in Brazil in 1964 as "Crusoe at Home" and finished in the United States in 1971 as "Crusoe in England" (*CP* 162–66) is a highly palimpsestic moment in her thinking about exile and colonial encounter as well as about the risks of naturalist endeavor. In its recapitulating her experience of Brazil as it is lived in absence, the poem (like her other Brazil pieces) denies direct relationships between the topography of Brazil and her poetic images. The sources for the poem are dizzyingly multiple: Millier tracks the waterspouts and snails of the poem to a canoe trip to Florida in 1939, the goats and volcanoes to a trip to Aruba in 1957 (446–48); Lorrie Goldensohn references Bishop's trip to Galápagos in 1971 as the poet follows in the footsteps of Darwin (249); Bonnie Costello describes "Crusoe" as a "spatial distillation of her many travels—to Key West, Brazil, Haiti, the Galápagos, as well as Cuttybank" (208); we should also consider Bishop's trip up the Amazon in 1960 as well as her journey to Darwin's home in Kent in 1964 (Millier 355). In an early letter in which she complains about not being able to write about Brazil, she "plunged into Darwin and Burton and *A Naturalist in Brazil*—before she wrote" (Millier 259). The travels of reading and of imagination blur with her literal excursions, and the personal transpositions between these different arenas make delimiting sources problematic. She often wrote of a place before she actually traveled to it: she knows Darwin's journal before she treks to the Galápagos; she knows the Amazon of her "The Riverman" through Charles Begley's *Amazon Town* (Lota objects to the poem on grounds of its inauthenticity, or detachment from lived experience). In a letter to Frani Blough Muser, she says she wrote Crusoe two years before she went to the Galápagos and was glad that the tortoises hissed the way she said they did (December 14, 1974; *One Art* 591); yet even with such fortuitous correspondences, landscape remains heterogeneously mediated.

To examine "Crusoe" as it is composed over time and with its plural origins foregrounds the motif of displacement and exile the poem allegorizes; in the process, Defoe's novel becomes decentered, his narrative, however significant, only one among many of the poem's strands. With the eye of the expert exile, Bishop remakes the long history of Crusoe's iconic persistence and Defoe's text, one of the most colonialist of all time: "None of the books has ever got it right," the first stanza ends in condensed rejection of the eighteenth-century writer's authority, and her Crusoe's island is "still un-renamable," beyond discovery. When asked by George Starbuck if the poem converged with her rereading of the novel, she replies, "No. I've forgotten all the facts. . . . I reread it all one night. . . . All that Christianity. So I think I wanted to re-see it with all that left out" (Starbuck 18). Even her filtering of experience through Defoe is mediated by forgetfulness, and "all that" amounts to quite a bit: her Crusoe has no storm-soaked Bible or gun, by far the most valuable items in Defoe's inventories. Perhaps more inspiring to Bishop than the novel is her discovery that a restoration of an eighteenth-century slave church in Ouro Prêto had uncovered a mural of Crusoe, "umbrella, goats, and all—gilt on red lacquer panels" (Millier 446–47). The doubleness of such a restoration—Crusoe emblazoned as both exile and colonialist—would have to be apparent to Bishop (who would see her own double position) in her thinking about master/slave relations. Bishop will also translate Carlos Drummond de Andrade's "Infancy" (1963) with the lines "A small boy alone under the mango trees,/I read the story of Robinson Crusoe,/the long one that never comes to an end" (*CP* 258). What would it mean for a Brazilian to read Crusoe and be trained in its plot? The values of self-reliance within captivity compel, but the novel abides in its endless expanse of solitude, moralizing, and subjection. As "Infancy" reminds us of "lullabies long ago in the slave-quarters—and never forgot—," the child in the poem rereads the novel—as Bishop will do—discovering within it a suppressed narrative of enslavement. "Infancy" ends with the lines "And I didn't know that my story/was prettier than that of Robinson Crusoe." Prettier? "He had a pretty body," Bishop's Crusoe understatingly says of his Friday.

Bishop most significantly revises Defoe in her rendering of the Crusoe-Friday relationship; Friday becomes for Bishop unrenamable ("Accounts of that have everything all wrong"): he once had a name, but Defoe's imposition of one places the original under limitless erasure. I emphasize this particular revision as it vividly underscores Bishop's insistent denial of the naming of landscape as a concomitant refusal of naming as possession. Before turning my attention to Friday, however, I need to elaborate on Bishop's biographical status while writing the poem, and her ambivalent identifications and rejections of Defoe's Crusoe.

When Bishop drafts the poem in 1964, she feels perhaps her most liminal in her home with Lota: it is the year before she accepts a teaching job at the University of Washington, the year Lota's emotional and physical health is deteriorating after extensive involvement in Brazilian politics. In 1967 Lota reunites with Bishop in New York and dies of an overdose of Valium, after, in Bishop's words, "at least 13 happy years with her, the happiest of [her] life" (*One Art* 470). When she returns to Brazil to reclaim her recently purchased Ouro Prêto home, she is treated poorly by her Brazilian neighbors, who blame her and make her into a "scapegoat," as she puts it in a letter (January 4, 1968; *One Art* 489). Exile—Return—Exile: the emotional map of "Crusoe" that speaks for an otherness only the redispossessed can know (Crusoe and Friday now become interchangeable possible identifications for her). Bishop's Crusoe, who will "whoop and dance among the goats" (unlike Defoe's, who prides himself on killing them), dreams of "slitting a baby's throat/mistaking it/for a baby goat" (the most violent image in the poem); to slit the goat's throat metonymically slides into the human one: Bishop succinctly condenses an identification between those who sacrifice and those who become sacrificed, of both the exiled Crusoe and the "unrenamable" Friday. I will return to the goats as they are transposed from her visit to Aruba onto Brazil, as they become emblematic of her exile.

An islanded lesbian artist outside of mainstream tradition, Bishop problematically identifies with aspects of Crusoe's exile, aspects Defoe doesn't know his character possesses. By recuperating not the text, which bored her, but Crusoe as reusable figure, she celebrates the individual who can "make do," who is committed to transforming the limited materials of a restrictive environment. In an early notebook entry (1934) with yet another mention of Crusoe, Bishop refers to the island as trope for necessary acts of invention: "On an island you live all the time in this Robinson Crusoe atmosphere; making this do for that, and contriving and inventing . . . A poem should be made about making things in a pinch" (quoted in Costello 207–8). An island is estranged from the mainland and lives rooted, oxymoronically, in water. It is the emotional landscape for separation, solitude, and drifting, yet also for "making things do," for independence, autonomy, stability (qualities often attributed to the masculine). Her later poem, however, will modify this "island feeling" and upset boundaries between self and other, ending as it does with its emphasis on the necessary relationship of Crusoe and Friday.

In spite of the potentially favorable aspects of Crusoe as myth of self-making, Defoe's text must be read, to use Martin Green's language, as "a pharisaical" one that "lets [Defoe's] civilization speak through him quite freely," that belongs squarely to the adventure genre, which has "inspired nationalism and imperialism and cultural chauvinism," and, to quote him further, functions as "the liturgy . . . of masculinism" (2). Bishop overturns such "liturgy" in making connection and homoerotic allure pivotal for her Crusoe. As she invades the territory of the adventure genre, which traditionally excludes women (it is "reading for men, not for readers"; Green 5), Bishop rejects as well a mythos of white supremacy and the imperialist imperative. Adventure turns into elegy and self-criticism. Solitude, in Bishop's version, truly occurs not in exile but upon recuperation by "civilization."

Defoe's materialist hero is always intent upon fortifying his shelters, while Bishop's denies any conventional need for shelter—the "home-made" knows no roof or doors but rather the community of exiles, without set borders: "Home-made, home-made, but aren't we all?" her Crusoe exclaims. Hélène Cixous offers a helpful gloss on reading Bishop's rejection of ownership and physical possession; in her terms, borders are artificial and generate a nationalistic "*home-neid* (home-envy)":

> This home-neid is not only the need for a land and roof. It is primarily a need for the proper, for a proper country, for a proper name, a need for separation and, at the same time, a rejection of the other; it is less a need of difference than a distaste for difference, a desire to leave coupled with a desire to expel. A harsh, trenchant desire not to be you. (130)

Bishop must give up (again and again) the "neid" for the "made," the home in the making, in its provisional tenuous existence. Richard Poirier pertinently assesses Defoe's novel as "a sort of idyllic parable of man's gaining merely economic control over an environment out of which he could try to make anything he chose," and as such "has no interest whatever in the merely visionary possession of the landscape" (8–9). While Bishop revokes possession altogether in the poem, her more "visionary" and "home-made" relationship to the island threatens to make it a prison colony without reciprocal interchange, without the "difference" of an other.

Here I must turn to Defoe's treatment of otherness as embodied in Friday. Crusoe in Defoe's novel leaves his profitable plantations in the Brazils to pursue greater wealth through slave trading (having been shipwrecked once already and taken as a slave). Human life is quantified and catalogued among other objects, as he boasts of "how easy it was to purchase upon the coast, for trifles, such as beads, toys, knives, scissors, hatchets, bits of glass, and the like, not only gold dust, . . . elephants' teeth, etc., but Negroes for the service in Brazils, in great numbers" (37). His marooned condition does not teach him to recognize the significance of relationship; after fifteen years of solitude, his sight of "a man's naked foot" leads him only to bolster his fortifications and arsenal. Not until his twenty-fourth year islanded does he decide (that if he is to escape) he must "get a savage into [his] possession" (192). The first encounter between Crusoe and Friday (who "lays his head flat upon the ground, close to my foot, and sets my other foot upon his head") is an emblem of abjection, a renaming that erases identity:

> In a little time I began to speak to him and teach him to speak to me; and first, I made him know his name should be Friday, which was the day I saved his life. I called him so for the memory of the time; I likewise taught him to say Master, and then let him know that was to be my name; I likewise taught him to say *Yes* and *No* and to know the meaning of them. (199–200)

Defoe has already described Friday as possessing "all the sweetness and softness of an European in his countenance," and he is therefore diagnosed (in the above passage) as recuperable through learning "appropriate" names.

In her well-known essay "Can the Subaltern Speak?" Gayatri Chakravorty Spivak reminds us that in terms of the "question of the consciousness of the subaltern, the notion of what the work *cannot say* becomes important" (*Marxism and the Interpretation of Culture* 287). Like Defoe, Bishop will never be able fully to conceive of Friday's language, which lives within the spaces and mesh of colonialist and patriarchal discourse. As I have earlier noted, in spite of her vigilant recognition of the dangers of colonialism in herself, Bishop nevertheless continues to voice ethnocentric judgments. Relevant to her later revision of Defoe's Friday, she complains, for instance, to the Barkers, that Friday is the day everything goes wrong with the hired help in Brazil and unfavorably compares "the primitive people" with "the good servants of England" (February 25, 1954; *One Art* 290).

The subversion of Defoe in "Crusoe," however, becomes a way of self-consciously redefining such a perspective. Friday "saves" Crusoe, and does so through what never gains full articulation. Bishop offers a minimal eleven lines (all appear in the poem's last stanzas) specifically to revisit Friday's importance.[7] As excised and withheld, he becomes primary as Bishop narrates:

> Just when I thought I couldn't stand it
> another minute longer, Friday came.
> (Accounts of that have everything all wrong.)
> Friday was nice.
> Friday was nice, and we were friends.
> If only he had been a woman!
> I wanted to propagate my kind,
> and so did he, I think, poor boy.

Bishop manages to insert homoerotic desire, yet with "poor boy" risks returning to Defoe's language of dominance; the phrase, however, is undercut by the following stanza of a solitary line, the blanks surrounding it made potent: "And then one day they came and took us off." The poem ends by returning us to an other; Friday's repeated name transforms into an unrenaming with the disjunctive dash: "—And Friday, my dear Friday, died of measles/ seventeen years ago come March." These words call for the poem to be reread with this accentuated loss in mind, all the recounted experiences inflected by both the unspeakable significance of Friday's presence and the loss of him. Bishop's "island industries" preclude thinking of relationship in terms of mastery, the poem framed as it is by her relationship to Lota and her loss of it: things only fleetingly hold meaning through acts of connection, not through naming or ownership.

Both Bishop's home in Brazil and her loss of it make her live with a necessary distance from objects and landscape so that she never hopes to claim them fully. Things, of so much value to Defoe's Crusoe, become quite explicitly nothing. The last stanza refuses cultural consumption, the making of lived experience into museum artifact, inevitably epitaphic and disembodied:

The local museum's asked me to
leave everything to them:
the flute, the knife, the shrivelled shoes,
my shedding goatskin trousers
(moths have got in the fur),
the parasol that took me such a time
remembering the way the ribs should go.
It still will work but, folded up,
looks like a plucked and skinny fowl.
How can anyone want such things?
—And Friday, my dear Friday, died of measles
seventeen years ago come March.

"The memory of the time" is kept into the future ("come March")
by Friday, whose death inscribed after a catalogue of things, for-
bids the making of him into artifact. The parasol "will work" (us-
able even if it can't protect), but out of its context of exiled home-
making, without the communion with an other, it turns into dead
nature. The dis-invested poet challenges, "How can anyone want
such things?" Bishop is always somewhat suspicious of objects,
and especially in "Crusoe" they become porous emblems of per-
ishability.

The objects in "Crusoe" have been only vital as they have lived
in their active, present tense, in their "remembering" as an act
of creation, and perhaps, only becoming animate with the gaze
and "living soul" offered by the other. I am not suggesting that
Bishop denies art any potency; it is just that she is radically re-
defining it in terms of her losses, necessarily converting an ad-
venture into an elegy. Significantly, Bishop is both reaching her
height as a poet (*Geography III* is arguably her best volume) and
giving up her "art," at least in the senses of art as mastery or
as possession. Pragmatic utility founders without imaginative en-
actment or emotional fulfillment. After being asked to leave the
house of Petropolis in 1966 under the advice of Lota's psychia-
trist, Bishop makes a catalogue of what is left over from her ship-
wrecked relationship into a draft called "Inventory": " 'out in half

an hour,' 'after fifteen years with a few dirty clothes in a busted suitcase, no home any more, no claim (legally) to anything here'" (Millier 384). Things lose their borders for the disenfranchised lover.

In subverting Defoe's colonial enterprise, Bishop foregrounds the eye as always mediating what it sees, unbelieving a landscape can be named, known, framed, so to speak, and then possessed. She cannot be a naturalist like Darwin or Emerson; neither can she be a landscape poet in the Wordsworth tradition. Her amnesiac, tradition-wrecked Crusoe midpoem bemoans:

> Because I didn't know enough.
> Why didn't I know enough of something?
> Greek drama or astronomy? The books
> I'd read were full of blanks;
> the poems—well, I tried
> reciting to my iris-beds,
> "They flash upon that inward eye,
> which is the bliss . . . " The bliss of what?
> One of the first things that I did
> when I got back was look it up.

Looking it up doesn't help; the thing itself emaciates. We think we find William Wordsworth's words, but they are really Mary Wordsworth's, acknowledged in a footnote (McCabe 199). Language darkens, and the denied and missing word, *solitude,* floats to the surface. To forget is to remember to the islanded poet who discovers exile. "I tried reciting to my iris-beds," Crusoe says after confessing in the previous stanza what lies beneath the blanks of his landscape, under "the one variety of tree": "Snail shells lay under these in drifts/and, at a distance,/you'd swear that they were beds of irises." The iris-beds are, in fact, imaginary, of "the inward eye," not consolatory but deflected experience. I make much of the irises—risk fetishizing them even—because they are the only "real," albeit, slender link (in the poem) to the nature of Brazil as Bishop knew it: she grew them in her garden in Petropolis (*One Art* 328). The irises are mediators, truly the snail that "creeps" and spreads its "bright violet-blue," the color of exile.

The most notable features of her Crusoe's landscape—indigenous to Aruba—are the goats and the volcanoes (Millier 446–48). As I have indicated, the goats further contribute to the deflective rendering of landscape of "Crusoe" as well as to the motif of exile. Bishop's Crusoe, who regrets not knowing enough of "Greek drama or astronomy," nevertheless becomes a Dionysian, enacting an alchemical rite of fusion with the natural world and the origin of a new poetic scale.

> There was one kind of berry, a dark red.
> I tried it, one by one, and hours apart.
> Sub-acid, and not bad, no ill effects;
> and so I made home-brew. I'd drink
> the awful, fizzy, stinging stuff
> that went straight to my head
> and play my home-made flute
> (I think it had the weirdest scale on earth)
> and, dizzy, whoop and dance among the goats.
> Home-made, home-made! But aren't we all?

In dancing among the goats, this Crusoe becomes a goat, a stanza later declaring, "I was a goat, too, or a gull." As I have already stated, there is no direct mention of killing a goat in the poem; but one of his souvenirs (would-be museum articles) of the island is the "shedding goatskin trousers." As Bishop modifies them with the parentheses, "(moths have got in the fur)," she reminds us that as objects they are not exempt from mortality. Crusoe's scene of play in the above quote calls up an image of Dionysian revelry, often associated with the goat figure; also significantly, the goat—connected to ancient fertility rites—becomes inseparable from the birth of tragedy. Pan with his pipes is the antecedent source of poetry usurped by Apollo (Graves 76).

In his tracing of the origin of tragedy, Roberto Calasso turns us back to Dionysus, who reveals to an old Attican gardener, Icarius, the secret of the vine, and as the story proceeds, "it becomes, apparently, Icarius' responsibility to introduce the juice of the vines. One evening, drinking among shepherds, he falls into a slumber; the other shepherds, suspicious of him, slay him." The myth waxes even stranger and perhaps more reverberatingly as Calasso provides Icarius' memory as he lies dying: "One day he caught a goat eating some vine leaves. He was overcome by anger and killed the animal on the spot. Now he realized the goat had been himself" (39). Calasso adds, "Aristotle says that early tragedy was the singing and dancing of goats"; to simplify drastically, a rupture in nature or liminal moment occurs, when those dancing and wearing skins become goats. To be a satyr, one must first slay the goat.

Nietzsche offers further potential illumination to Crusoe and his goats in *The Birth of Tragedy*, as he describes the satyr as "the ecstatic reveler enraptured by the proximity of his god, the sympathetic companion in whom is repeated the suffering of the god, wisdom's harbinger speaking from the very heart of nature, emblem of the sexual omnipotence of nature, which the Greek was wont to contemplate with reverence" (985–86). In contrast, Bishop's amnesiac, culturally bereft Crusoe (whose knife becomes as meaningful as a "crucifix") does not possess the ability to enter fully into the natural; his goats are too tame and refuse to embody transcendent meaning: the goat that stands on the doubly named volcano—hope and despair—looks back at Crusoe without reflecting him: "His pupils, horizontal, narrowed up/and expressed nothing, or a little malice." This landscape has been drained of the "sexual omnipotence of nature"; we are even deprived of what Nietzsche refers to as the "counterfeit tricked-up shepherd" that has come to replace the true Dionysian in modern times. The significance of these excursions for Bishop's Crusoe lies in their adumbration of sacrifice and exile. Bishop's guilt over Lota's death reinforces her sense of exclusion: she ruminates in letters, just after the loss, upon her guilt, writing, for instance, to Dr. Amy Baumann, "oh—oh—if only I'd done something better, said the *right* thing, stayed up & watched her all night. I can't stop blaming myself for all the things I know I did wrong—in the past, and probably, without realizing it, on that Sunday" (October 11, 1967; *One Art* 475).

Genesis is often cited as a reworked source for "Crusoe"—in its interest in naming. But Leviticus, in its underscoring of the dynamics of guilt and sacrifice, seems equally present through its narrative of the "two he-goats": "Aaron shall bring forward the goat designated by lot for the LORD, which he is to offer as a sin offering; while the goat designated by lot for Azazel shall be left standing alive before the LORD, to make expiation with it and to send it off to the wilderness for Azazel" (Lev. 16:9–10). Bishop (through her Crusoe) becomes the scapegoat, sacrificed up in the name of her transgressions, sent into the wilderness "marked for Azazel," the name for removal and banishment. What is being expunged and rejected is, in part, paradoxically what Bishop celebrates; her exile is always already exiled, exiled previous to the island and exiled upon return to the so-called mainland. To recall the earlier Cixous quotation, Bishop counteracts that "rejection of the other" and "distaste for difference" involved in the "home-neid." Bishop's "home" with Lota looks back at her, "the living soul" gone—as fragile, temporary tent. In crossing the border that apparently separates the wilderness from civilization, the native from the foreign, the master from the slave, she discovers an interchangeability that subverts rigid structures erected by a patriarchal discourse. Another meaning of goat is the "emissary," with the double definition of the biblical "scapegoat" and the Greek figure of a being "sacred to Hermes as messenger of the Gods" (deVries 218). Is this an accidental overlapping with Iris, that other messenger? If so, it is a profoundly felicitous "mistaking"; both figures represent the liminal zone Bishop is so engaged by. If Bishop's position in Brazil as an outsider invigorates her disinvestment in objects and naming, her expulsion from this semiparadise accentuates her liminality.

Brazil, in this light, has reoriented Bishop, just as the island has her Crusoe; she cannot think about relationships in terms of mastery. The exile is never at home. Bishop tells of Cabral leaving two men as prisoners, left to convert the savages: "This was the usual Portuguese practice; no one knows how many hundreds of these wretched men were dropped along the coast by later expeditions" (*Brazil* 28). Defoe's Crusoe also leaves two men as prisoners—after teaching them survival tactics—upon his "rescue"; he later compulsively returns in order to supply wives and check on his colony. Bishop read Chekhov's *Journey to Sakhalin*, a journal of the writer's visit to a prison island; he apparently had copies of *Robinson Crusoe* sent to the exiles. "The exile knows that in a secular and contingent world, homes are always provisional. Borders and barriers, which enclose us within the safety of familiar territory, can also become prisons. . . . Exiles cross borders, break barriers of thought and experience," Said writes (*Representations of the Intellectual* 104). Bishop's "Crusoe"—in its self-review and its revision of Defoe—celebrates the traversing and deflective rather than the appropriative eye. Otherwise our islands become prisons, otherness only what we forcibly rename it.

NOTES

1. She disavowed the book because she felt the editors wanted only to inscribe their preconceptions of Brazil. In an interview with George Starbuck, she says of it, "It was edited by Time-Life Books and they changed a lot of it" (11).

2. Bishop refers to a "total recall" in the fall of 1952 which culminates with "In the Village" in 1953 (Millier 252).

3. Elizabeth Bishop, *Complete Poems* 89. All poetry citations to be taken from this volume abbreviated as *CP.*

4. Marilyn M. Lombardi refers to Bishop's response to a question about whether cataloguing and endless taxonomy were not "the poet's duty or his burden": Bishop was to declare "that many poets don't like the fact that they have to translate everything into words" (140). The process of conversion and metamorphosis implicit in translation becomes a potentially cannibalistic one, from Lombardi's point of view.

5. Her letters can be quite vivid and assertively descriptive as when she writes to Ilse and Kit Barker (February 25, 1954; *One Art*): "The water is a pale green, straight down off the top of the mountain, with a few yellow leaves floating on it, and many blue dragonflies and gorgeous, or tea-tray, butterflies" (293); at the same time, such letters often cast doubt upon the powers of representation, especially in relation to Brazil. In another letter to James Merrill (and in anticipation of the

kinds of disproportions in scale depicted in her Crusoe's landscape) she explains, "The 'Samambaia' mentioned at the top of the page is a giant fern, big as a tree, and there are toads as big as your hat and snails as big as bread & butter plates, and during this month butterflies the color of this page and sometimes almost as big flopping about" (February 1, 1955; *One Art* 303). Even in this description, however, Bishop makes nature textual, "the color of this page."

6. Robert Dale Parker, in discussing the connections between the poem and Bishop's translation of Clarice Lispector's "The Smallest Woman in the World," foregrounds "the conflict between genders" as "even more constant than the conflict between explorers and explored" (96).

7. In his afterward to *Becoming a Poet,* Merrill paraphrases Bishop saying there was once "lots more" Friday material (257).

WORKS CITED

Bishop, Elizabeth. *Brazil.* New York: Time-Life, 1962.

———. *The Complete Poems: 1927–1979.* New York: Farrar, 1979.

———. "Letter to Anne Stevenson." *Elizabeth Bishop and Her Art.* Ed. Lloyd Schwartz. Ann Arbor: U of Michigan P, 1983.

———. *One Art: Elizabeth Bishop Letters.* Ed. Robert Giroux. New York: Farrar, 1994.

Calasso, Roberto. *The Marriage of Cadmus.* Trans. Tim Parks. New York: Knopf, 1993.

Cixous, Hélène. *Three Steps on the Ladder of Writing.* Trans. Sarah Cornell and Susan Sellers. New York: Columbia UP, 1993.

Costello, Bonnie. *Elizabeth Bishop: Questions of Mastery.* Cambridge: Harvard UP, 1991.

Darwin, Charles. *The Voyage of the Beagle.* New York: Harper, 1959.

Defoe, Daniel. *Robinson Crusoe.* New York: Black, 1941.

deVries, Ad. *Dictionary of Symbols and Imagery.* Amsterdam: North Holland, 1984.

Emerson, Ralph Waldo. *Emerson and His Journals.* Ed. Joel Porte. Cambridge: Harvard UP, 1982.

Goldensohn, Lorrie. *Elizabeth Bishop: The Biography of a Poetry.* New York: Columbia UP, 1991.

Graves, Robert. *The White Goddess.* New York: Farrar, 1948.

Green, Martin. *The Robinson Crusoe Story.* Pennsylvania: Penn State UP, 1990.

Jarrell, Randall. *Poetry and the Age.* New York: Knopf, 1953.

Kalstone, David. *Becoming a Poet: Elizabeth Bishop with Marianne Moore and Robert Lowell.* New York: Farrar, 1989.

Lombardi, Marilyn M. *The Body and the Song: Elizabeth Bishop's Poetics.* Carbondale: Southern Illinois UP, 1995.

McCabe, Susan. *Elizabeth Bishop: Her Poetics of Loss.* Pennsylvania: Penn State UP, 1994.

Millier, Brett. *Elizabeth Bishop: Life and the Memory of It.* Berkeley: U of California P, 1993.

Nietzsche, Friedrich. *The Philosophy of Nietzsche.* Trans. Clifton P. Fadiman and Helen Zimmern. New York: Random, 1954.

Parker, Robert Dale. *The Unbeliever: The Poetry of Elizabeth Bishop.* Urbana: U of Illinois P, 1988.

Poirier, Richard. *A World Elsewhere: The Place of Style in American Literature.* New York: Oxford UP, 1966.

Rich, Adrienne. "The Eye of the Outsider: Elizabeth Bishop's *Complete Poems.*" *Blood, Bread & Poetry.* New York: Norton, 1986.

Said, Edward W. *Representations of the Intellectual.* New York: Pantheon, 1994.

Spivak, Gayatri Chakravorty. "Can the Subaltern Speak?" *Marxism and the Interpretation of Culture.* Ed. Cary Nelson and Lawrence Grossberg. Urbana: U of Illinois P, 1988.

Starbuck, George. "'The Work!' A Conversation with Elizabeth Bishop." *Ploughshares* 3.3–4 (1977): 11–29.

12

Family Values and the Jewishness
of Linda Pastan's Poetic Vision

SANFORD PINSKER

Linda Pastan's unpretentious, rigorously crafted poetry is like the
Jews themselves—easy to recognize but difficult to define. As a
survey of contemporary American poetry in the *New York Times
Sunday Magazine* (Dinitia Smith, "The Poetic Pantheon," Feb. 19,
1995) puts it, she is an "earth mother" (whatever that is supposed
to mean) and thus properly belongs in the company of other
"earth mother" poets such as Sharon Olds and Molly Peacock.
But that simply won't do, not only because each of these voices
is quite unlike the others, but also because Pastan's sanctification
of the ordinary is much wider and her vision much deeper than
most of what travels under the wide umbrella of earth mother-
hood.

Earth mothers, as I understand the term, do not usually worry
about the niceties of sustained metaphor, much less about the
intricate shaping that free verse, at its most achieved, demands.
Rather, earth mothers simply *are*: natural, spontaneous, alto-
gether tied to the rhythms of the world and their bodies. All this
is, no doubt, lovely, but Pastan is hardly an avatar of Molly Bloom.
Granted, she celebrates the domestic condition—just as she
sometimes broods about it—but what matters to her finally is
the shape of individual word choices, line breaks, and the poem
itself.

I have chosen to focus on Pastan's Jewishness because it is a

199

rich, complicated source of one recurrent vein of her material—
sometimes explicitly so, sometimes in less obvious ways. As Gerald
Stern argues:

> The critical issue for twentieth-century Jewish-American poetry
> is whether, and to what degree, it can be perceived as separate
> from twentieth-century American poetry itself and whether, what-
> ever peculiarities the Jewish-American poets can be construed as
> having, taking them as a group, these "peculiarities" are the re-
> sult of their Jewishness rather than other factors, such as age,
> geographic location, aesthetic or philosophical commitment, and
> such—or another way of putting it is to ask whether those very
> commitments (age, philosophy, etc.) are more overriding for
> those poets than their Jewishness.[1]

Born in 1932, Pastan belongs to that generation of Jewish
American poets that includes Jerome Rothenberg, Allen Gross-
man, Jack Hirshman, Grace Schulman, and Marge Piercy—quite
different poets in posture and poetics, but all of them retaining
vestiges of a Jewish identity. Indeed, how could they not, coming
as they did at a point in Jewish American history when accultura-
tion had not yet slipped into assimilation? Still, the *expression*
of that Jewishness took a wide variety of forms, as Gerald Stern
points out in his thumbnail sketch of poets who came of age in
the early l97os:

> The poetry ranges from Rothenberg's revived Yiddish vision and
> his underground and tribal chants, to Grossman's mystic and
> mythological visions, to Hirschman's lucid and powerful per-
> sonal and political recollections, to Pastan's family memories, to
> Marshall's dramatic and biblical poems.[2]

"Family memories" do indeed form a spine of Jewishness that
runs through many of Pastan's poems. She is acutely conscious
that families are generational and, moreover, that the ghosts of
the heart abide. Hence, even when the objects of a poem are not
explicitly her Russian Jewish grandparents or her parents, Pastan
sees history as a template that binds present to past, and past to
present. Granted, her vision does not take the preferred form

among the Orthodox—insisting that all Jews received the Commandments at Sinai in a moment transcending time—but given the setting of the Jewish Museum and its famous exhibition on the Lower East Side, 1887–1924, one quickly realizes how many ways a poet might have gotten the material wrong, either by sentimentalizing the sepia photographs of that time and place, or by falsifying what they signify. In this regard what T. S. Eliot said about inferior poems from the Christian tradition applies with equal force to those from a Jewish American ethos: namely, that they are marked by emotions people would like to have rather than by the more complicated ones they actually do. When Eliot wrote about religion and literature, he was not concerned with literary works written by well-meaning people sincerely desirous of "forwarding the cause of religion." Such writing came, Eliot felt, under the heading of propaganda. Rather, what he meant to champion was "a literature which should be *un*consciously, rather than deliberately and defiantly, Christian."

I realize full well that Mr. Eliot has rather fallen out of favor, and that his pronouncements no longer have the ring of authority they once had. But there may yet be value in remembering—or hearing for the first time—what he had to say about the assets and liabilities that come with the territory of a defined religious tradition. And indeed, his suggestion about literature that is *un*consciously Christian not only hearkens back to his more famous dictum that "the bad poet is usually unconscious where he ought to be conscious, and conscious where he ought to be unconscious," but also points us to what makes Pastan such an accomplished Jewish American poet.

Perhaps I am suggesting little more than that good poets must, above all else, be honest about the emotions they present. With this in mind, look at the ways in which Pastan radically compresses the distance between nameless immigrant children and "the faces of our fathers," between the *endure* in line one and the *lightly* of line two. "Light," of course, is what was noticeably missing in the crowded squalor of tenement life, but it is hauntingly present in "the faces of our fathers/who have grown old before us"—a turn of phrase that weds the "before" of a preserved past with intimations of a future in which we too will surely become old ourselves. Hence, the laundry that hangs "like a portent" over everything, and the memories of faces we take home "like piece-work." In short, the fabric of their world is woven, once again, into our own, for this is the lesson of history—namely, that

> . . . our children's sins
> still fall on the old Jew
> in a coal cellar, on Ludlow Street
> in nineteen hundred.[3]

"The Law of Primogeniture" puts the same matter a slightly different way. Here, she describes a grandson as having her father's mouth "with its salty sayings" and her grandfather's "crooked ear/that heard the soldiers coming." That the boy is blissfully unaware of these connections is true enough; he pushes his bright red fire truck toward "a future he thinks he is inventing/all by himself," but Pastan knows better. History is an abiding force, one that shapes who we are and figures greatly in what we will become.

Russian grandparents not only figure importantly in her mythic construction of the slow inexorable movement toward as-similation, but they also pop up in what can only be called unex-pected places. For example, "The English Novel," Pastan's deli-cious send-up of literary conventions and their comic distance from her own experience ("I used to think chilblains were a kind of biscuit"), starkly reverses direction in its last haunting lines. There, the point is less that in the English novel "everything was brocade and velvet," rather than our own unfortunate polyester, but that certain disturbing cultural facts must also be allowed a place in our reckoning of the "familiar":

> And all the familiar faces we notice at the movies
> or across a restaurant, couldn't they be our half brothers
> or cousins, lost once in the deep and mysterious gene
>> pool—
> descendants, some of them, of Emma and Mr. Knightley,
> or the ones with Russian faces descended from Ladislaw

maybe,
who could have come from a place just a few hours
    by carriage
from the shtetl where my great-great-grandmother
somehow acquired her blond hair and blue blue eyes?[4]

Here is cultural chronicling far removed from the niceties of literary history, for what Pastan alludes to is nothing less than the violence—the rape—that generations of officially sanctioned anti-semitism comes to. No doubt another poet might have made the same point in a more direct, in-your-face manner, but one wonders, first, if the result would have been more effective and, second, what costs—to the poem itself—would have been extracted in the process. No doubt those who hanker for redder meat can make a case for the incendiary poem I have imagined, but I think the subtle blending of two traditions (the culture of English literature on one hand, and that of tsarist Russia on the other) packs the more significant punch. Why so? Because understatement allows for wider, deeper recognitions; and also because the sheer artistry required for successful understatement makes for more satisfying poems. As "The English Novel" ably demonstrates, one need not be forced into a choice between aesthetics and social consciousness. Pastan's poem has aspects of both, without abandoning its sense of playful satiric humor or its commitment to social justice. In short, in an age when too many poets err on one side or the other of what shapes up to be an important ongoing debate, Pastan reminds us that a poem can be as playfully serious as it is seriously playful.

Roughly the same thing is true of subjects filled with sand traps, but that Pastan finds especially congenial nonetheless. I am, after all, hardly the first critic to point out that poems about one's Jewish grandparents often degenerate into sentimental exercises, an easy mounting up of predictable detail and tugs on the heartstrings. Small wonder, then, that the editors of *Response* magazine threw up their hands and issued the following advisory: they would no longer publish poetry "on the following subject matter: the Holocaust, grandparents, Friday night candle lighting, . . . Jerusalem at dusk." Pastan's poem—significantly enough, entitled "Response"—makes it clear that these outlawed elements can, in the right hands, be combined into a poem of enormous skill, considerable wit, and, not least of all, great power. It is so lucid, so impeccably crafted, as it fuses its disparate, at first glance, unlikely elements into an image of singular power. Pastan begins in the negative, as if to mock conventional expectations. Thus, it is *not* dusk but rather morning; and the grandparents (who figure so prominently in the poetry of sentimentalists) are also not there. They have "disappeared/in the Holocaust"—taking their Sabbath candles with them. At this point, the speaker conflates the image of candles into that of poetry as she implores her fellow bards to "light" their poems. The tone is decidedly ambivalent here—at once reverential and mocking. After all, bards of the busy-busy, cliché-slinging school hate to miss a Jerusalem sunset. For them, it ends up every bit as much a souvenir of a week in Jerusalem as, say, an ashtray from the King David Hotel or an Arab headdress that must satisfy the less talented traveler.

At the same time, however, Pastan's line about lighting poems (instead of candles) is deeply serious, for the ritual of candle lighting is a means by which she juxtaposes the world of East European Jewry and the Holocaust that obliterated it. Meanwhile, it is dusk—not only in Jerusalem but in the larger sweep of Western history—and Pastan's lines remind of us of how much has been packed into our nightmarish century, and also into her poem:

> Already the sun is leaning
> towards the west
> though the grandparents and candles
> have long since burned down
> to stubs.[5]

Compression—the element Ezra Pound found central to the modernist spirit—is much in evidence here, as are the usual suspects one rounds up in the making of an achieved poem: imagery, verbal tension, and, perhaps most of all, voice. But in the

quiet yoking of Sabbath candles, the Holocaust, and one's grand-
parents, Pastan adds a peculiarly Jewish twist (one I would define
as an abiding consciousness of history's cunning) to the meta-
physics.

Something of the same spirit—call it playfully serious or seri-
ously playful—is at the very heart of "A Short History of Judaic
Thought in the Twentieth Century." No doubt Pastan has the
story of Hillel in mind (he was once asked to explain the essence
of Judaism while standing on one foot), but her Talmudic wiz-
ardry points us toward the dark wisdom that, I would argue, is
the proper province of poetry. Put another way: I have no par-
ticular quarrel with Hillel's insistence that one should "do unto
others as you would have them do unto you" or even with his
conclusion that "all the rest is commentary," but Pastan's riddling
poem gets us to richer places in the heart. She sets up the poser
by pointing out that the rabbis permitted us to remove a dying
person from a burning house, even though one is normally for-
bidden to touch a dying person. Context apparently makes the
difference; but Pastan's outraged speaker will have none of it:

> Barbaric!
> I say,
> and whom may I touch then,
> aren't we all
> dying?
>
> You smile
> your old negotiator's smile
> and ask:
> but aren't all our houses
> burning?[6]

To answer a question with a question (what, I ask, could be more
Jewish than that?)—but, I hasten to add, there are questions and
questions. My grandfather used to tell me that a fool can throw
a stone into a lake where not even a dozen scholars could find
it. The same thing is true for most riddles/questions: they are
not worth considering, much less trying to answer. To her credit,

Pastan knows the difference, and, even more impressive, she gives her antagonist the poem's most intriguing line/question.

In a related vein, my grandfather explained the mysteries of Genesis this way: God created the heavens and earth because he could. He created man because he liked a good story. And women were created, he would insist with a wink, to thicken the plot. Perhaps he had my grandmother in mind, perhaps not; what is certain is that his remarks packed more wisdom, then and now, than most of what currently passes for gender studies.

For Pastan, grandparents also complicate in wonderfully rich and haunting ways. Pastan might not share my grandfather's earthly midrash about Eve, but she at least joins him in the long tradition of giving biblical characters a decidedly human face. Indeed, Eve, in Pastan's term, has "aspects"—properties that ripple outward from her biblical and/or mythic incarnations to contemporary avatars. In this sense her Eve poems join those about Rachel as representative tokens of Pastan's Jewish American imagination. Consider, for example, the opening lines from "Aspects of Eve": "To have been one/of many ribs/and to be chosen." *Chosen* is, of course, a charged word—perhaps *the* charged word—of Jewish history, at once an indicator of the specialness that results from accepting the yoke of Law and an occasion for the irony that sees this destiny against the persecution it provoked. My hunch is that Pastan is using the word *chosen* in both senses—as compliment as well as complaint. True enough, Eve's various "aspects" do not include the victimization, patriarchal exploitation, and plain unfairness that often figure in more militantly feminist renderings; rather, Pastan's Eve's bones knock at the closed gates of Eden's garden "which unexpectedly/open." Whatever "radical" might mean (here, I suspect it refers to a vision at the very root of human history), this is surely a vision that rearranges, if not completely overturns, the Eve associated with the temptation and Fall.

By contrast, Pastan's ruminations about Rachel spring from the existential fact that this is her daughter's name. In "Rachel," it is, significantly enough, sound pattern—the "sake/of the syllables"—that initially attracted them to the name. But names are finally more than a collection of pleasing utterances; they are also markers that place one into a certain history: the ship that searches for the survivors of the *Pequod* in *Moby-Dick;* the biblical matriarch who "waited at the well"; and finally, the "small daughters of the Holocaust" who followed their "six-pointed stars/to death," and who were, all of them, known as Rachel.

This strand of mythmaking might have been yet another way for Pastan to talk about her inveterate Jewishness; but I have chosen to focus on the family, partly because it is an abiding subject and partly because in naming those who came before, Pastan has come to find a voice that is distinctively, powerfully her own:

> My grandfather gave me a name
> in Hebrew I never heard,
> but it died with him.
> If I had taken that name
> who would I be,
> and if he calls me now
> how will I know to answer?[7]

Klezmer music, or, if you will, the Yiddish blues, is largely played in minor keys. It has, for our purposes here, an elegiac lilt. And so too do many of Pastan's best poems. They are "Jewish" without aggressively announcing their Jewishness, just as they are crafted without unduly calling attention to their craft. "The Hat Lady" strikes me as the best instance of what I have just tried to describe, and makes a fitting conclusion to this essay. For if my central argument about the Jewishness of Linda Pastan's vision makes any sense at all, one should feel it reflected in the haunting lines that speak memory through the objective correlative of "a childhood of hats." There, uncles in homburgs and derbies mingle freely with "the yarmulke my grandfather wore/like the palm of a hand." Only her father went "hatless/even in winter."

By contrast, spring ushered in the Hat Lady, who came "to measure my mother's head." Each season was marked, made memorable, by its distinctive hat: the dove gray felt one that "settled like a bird/on the nest of my mother's hair," the pillbox, the navy straws. Taken together, these are the hats of a certain mother, at a certain time and place.

And when that mother first ages, and then slowly succumbs to the ravages of cancer, the imagery formerly associated with the Hat Lady takes an abrupt, heart-cracking turn:

> Last years when the chemicals
> took my mother's hair, she wrapped
> a towel around her head. And the Hat Lady came,
> a bracelet of needles on each arm,
> and led her to a place
> where my father and grandfather waited,
> head to bare head, and Death
> winked at her and tipped his cap.[8]

Once again, the mixture of fact and mythmaking, Judaism and Christianity, cultures highbrow and low-, blend into an elegy of great beauty and enormous power. Pastan accomplishes this by compressing the sweep of history from the Orthodoxy of her imagined grandfather (his yarmulke, significantly enough, cradling his head) to the bareheadedness of her culturally assimilated father; the various hats her mother wore when she was "in fashion" and the turbans that replaced them when chemotherapy took its toll. Members of an entire family—and the cultural worlds they occupied—are thus presented, along with intimations of that place where "my father and grandfather waited,/ head to bare head."

Pastan is best known as a poet who gives particular attention to the "ordinary" and, as such, she is often numbered in the school of Emerson and Dickinson. True enough, but I would hasten to add that this sense of the ordinary is grounded in a resistance to the abstract which has deeply Jewish roots. For, in this tradition, there was little sense in talking about the Good, the True, or the Beautiful as if they were metaphysical constructions alone. Rather, they showed themselves in stories that tell "what happened next" when a carriage driver made his way into a strange town or when a widow found herself unable to buy Shabbos candles.

In this sense my grandfather was surely right when he insisted that God created man because He liked a good story. Families thicken the plot—something that writers from Homer and Shakespeare to Dickens and Faulkner have always known. Much the same thing is true for poetry—and especially if the lines are as clear and as well crafted as those in Pastan's work decidedly are. Does this, then, make her an authentically Jewish American poet? The answer is simultaneously Yes and No—for while it is certainly true that Pastan's oeuvre embraces a wide range of subjects (this essay focuses rather self-consciously on those with definably Jewish themes), it is also true that one recognizes both a specificity and a *tam* (taste) that strikes me as altogether "Jewish."

A final word about "family values": this term, unfortunately, has been appropriated by politicians who care a good deal more about voter approval than they do about the specific people— grandparents, fathers, mothers, children—who populate the loves, conflicts, and commonsensical humanity that makes Pastan's poetry so distinctive and so humanely valuable.

NOTES

1. Gerald Stern, "Poetry," *Jewish-American History and Culture,* ed. Jack Fischel and Sanford Pinsker (New York: Garland, 1992) 485.

2. Stern 493.

3. "At the Jewish Museum," *PM/AM: New and Selected Poems* (New York: Norton, 1982) 28.

4. "The English Novel," *An Early Afterlife* (New York: Norton, 1995) 33.

5. "Response," *PM/AM: New and Selected Poems* (New York: Norton, 1982) 108.

6. "A Short History of Judaic Thought in the Twentieth Century," *PM/AM* 70.

7. "A Name," *PM/AM* 6.

8. "The Hat Lady," *Heroes in Disguise* (New York: Norton, 1991) 32.

13

Castings for a (New) New World: The Poetry of Joy Harjo

JANET MCADAMS

*If I am a poet who is charged with speaking the truth (and
I believe the word poet is synonymous with truth-teller),
what do I have to say about all of this?*

I should be writing poems to change the
world. They would appear as a sacrifice of deer for the starving.
Or poems of difficulty to place my name in the Book of Poets. I
should get on with it.

I take my epigraphs from Joy Harjo's two most recent volumes of
poetry, *The Woman Who Fell from the Sky* and *In Mad Love and War.*
In each of these books—and throughout her work—Harjo fore-
grounds the question of the poet's role in the world. She is a
consciously *public* poet, deliberately writing against the highly pri-
vatized poetry that constitutes the "dominant mode"[1] of contem-
porary U.S. poetry. Institutionalized mainstream U.S. poetry has
remained falsely "unmarked," and its ahistorical, private dimen-
sion has had a curiously normative effect that has attempted
to erase "other" poetries within its borders. Those of us in the
United States, particularly those of us who study and teach at
academic institutions, must confront the pervasive support, fi-
nancial and otherwise, given to this poetry—and these poets.[2]
Ironically, though, despite the enormous institutional powers'
supporting the wave of highly personal verse that has been domi-
nant in the United States, it is the dominant mode of private,

self-expressive poetry that should compose the marked category, since it is both minor and "other." Running counter to it is nearly every other poetic tradition outside the borders of the United States, as well as the many "marginalized" writing communities that persist within its borders. Among those communities is that of Native American writing.

Brian Swann has written, "More than most poetry being written today, Native American poetry is the poetry of historic witness" (xvii). Swann's comment appears in his introduction to the *Harper's Anthology of Twentieth Century Native American Poetry*, a collection published in 1988 when the great wave of self-absorption that had plagued "mainline" American poetry—to use Swann's terminology—was only beginning to ebb. Swann's comment notwithstanding, a dilemma has arisen for many of these marginalized "U.S." poets. Because of the dominance for nearly thirty years of the private mode, "voice" as a rhetorical gesture has become so pervasive that even poets attempting to write beyond the personal find themselves trapped within it, because of their own unconscious beliefs as to how voice must be constructed, because of the kinds of expectations of voice that readers bring to the page, *and* because of what strategies of voice are "successful." Present-day interest in "witness poetry" is strong both in "mainline" institutions and in marginalized poetic communities, which increasingly disrupt and displace these institutionally based centers. A curious reversal further complicates these issues of centered and marginalized, dominant and "other" poetries. As this wave of witness poetry has arisen from the center, the parameters of it have become increasingly inclusive and "multicultural." Yet this inclusiveness has not necessarily disrupted the center. Rather, many poets writing from the margins have been included, even as their more radical writings and writing strategies have been either excluded or contained within dominant mode writing practices.

In this essay, I argue that Harjo is attempting to write a poetry of "witness," even as I am conscious that the need for this peculiarly ahistorical and local "marking" of the category of so-called witness poetry exists only within the boundaries of the United

States. I use Harjo's most recent collection of poetry to investigate the ways contemporary poets bring private experience to bear on public issues, and I consider Harjo's work in relation to public and private modes. I am especially interested in examining the dramatic stylistic changes between Harjo's earlier work and her 1994 *The Woman Who Fell from the Sky*, a collection distinctive for its earnest and flat declarations and for its foregrounding of public concerns. I do not mean that Harjo is not a powerful and fine poet or that her poems lack a strong and effective political message, for both these things are true. Yet, as I will discuss in greater detail later in this essay, her earlier two books, *She Had Some Horses* (1983) and *In Mad Love and War* (1990), are equally political. They too "bear witness," unless we define "witness" within narrow rhetorical boundaries. If bearing witness is a straightforward declamation from an insistent poet/speaker, a "telling," then it is clearly not the only possibility for the political poem. The political poem may also be a performance, a "showing," of what has happened, what might happen, what should happen.

In the heyday of extremely private poetry, how do poets effectively erase the boundary erected between private and social experience in particular texts? Further, through the work of such poets as Harjo, is the poem being restored to its status as social text in "mainline" circles, so that poetry and poets once again "bear witness"? Or has the postconfessional dominant mode appropriated and contained strategies of poetic "witness" so that public experience can be rendered only when it is first filtered through private experience? As the center broadens to include more of its others, do dominant mode writing strategies influence and contain marginalized writing communities?

In this essay, I examine this issue of "witness" in relation both to *The Woman Who Fell from the Sky* and to Harjo's two earlier collections, *She Had Some Horses* and *In Mad Love and War.* These earlier books may be read as two strongly connected parts of the same project. Focusing on them, I first ask how, for Harjo, poetry might "change [this] world" into something else. For despite her insistence in "Deer Dancer" (*Mad Love* 5–6) that "in [English] there

are no words for how the real world collapses," her poems con-
stitute a project of reclamation through that very language. The
world is recast and unified in English, so that the "real" is indeed
collapsed into the sacred. Further, I will assess how Harjo posi-
tions herself as a poet—that is, how she perceives the poet acting
and reacting to the world. Here I note in particular her words
from the first epigraph to this essay, that the poet is a "truth
teller."

I. HOW THE REAL WORLD COLLAPSES

In Harjo's poetry being able "to speak, to have voice" is necessar-
ily dependent on the recognition not only of all the voices with
which she speaks but of the places from which they emerge. Only
through the construction of a new space in which past and pres-
ent, white, Indian, and urban existences converge is survival
made possible. Harjo has said that she writes poetry because

> I feel strongly that I have a responsibility to all the sources that I
> am: to all past and future ancestors, to my home country, to all
> places that I touch down on and that are myself, to all voices, all
> women, all of my tribe, all people, all earth. . . . In a strange
> kind of sense it frees me to believe in myself, to be able to speak,
> to have voice, because I have to, it is *my* survival. (quoted in
> Coltelli 55)

The pronoun *my*, thus does not mark an identity that is individual
and apart from others but one that arises from and encompasses
a collective. Her words emphasize the importance of poetry's
function as a social text while insisting that the voice that speaks
for the collective—or, rather, collectives—is finally a highly indi-
vidualized one. Because it is female, Indian, and poetic, Harjo's
voice lies at the intersection of a number of marginalities. These
poems, however, do not reproduce her marginality as a confining
subjective alienation. Instead, they reimagine and remake the
world by laying out the poet's bifurcated *literal* existence in a so-
ciety that is both white and Indian and then delineating a third
space, located in "genetic memory," which overlaps her Indian
present and begins to seep into her life in the white world.

Harjo's 1990 volume, *In Mad Love and War,* documents the poet's exploration of her different pasts and presents. Her quest is inspired and guided by Deer Woman, who first appears in the book's second poem, "Deer Dancer" (5–6):

Nearly everyone had left that bar in the middle of winter except the
hardcore. It was the coldest night of the year, every place shut down,
   but
not us. Of course we noticed when she came in. We were Indian
   ruins. She
was the end of beauty. No one knew her, the stranger whose tribe we
recognized, her family related to deer, if that's who she was, a people
accustomed to hearing songs in pine trees, and making them hearts.

                                                  (5)

The poem is set in a "bar of broken survivors," and the woman is, ostensibly, just someone in a red dress who wandered in late one night. The people in the bar recognize her tribe, even though she is a stranger to them. As Harjo has explained, "Those people of that tribe who knew families . . . know what family she belonged to, but they didn't know who she was which was odd because if you knew *that,* you usually knew who the person was" ("Interview," videocassette). What she becomes, however, is a locus onto which the "Indian ruins" can project their nostalgic longing for a past in which survival was not the most critical issue. At the same time, however, there is a "woman inside the woman who was to dance naked in the bar of misfits." She is Deer Woman,[3] a mythic figure who has arrived to remind these survivors of their past and to bring "deer magic."

The poem delineates one world, that of the bar and the "hardcore" customers who find themselves there, in the "club of shotgun, knife wound, of poison by culture." The culture poisoning these customers is present both in the maudlin country and western songs that play on the jukebox and in the experience of the speaker's brother-in-law, who "hung out with white people, went to law school with a perfect record, quit." It is a profoundly troubling scene when one considers the devastating effect alcohol and alcoholism have had on Indian people, for, most of all, the

people in this poem are poisoned by what is being served at
the bar.

Thus, the image of names carved into the table functions to
link epidemics of the past with this contemporary epidemic and
to conflate the fallen of the past with the fallen of the present.
The poem, as well, introduces a third space, the past *as it is present*
in this room, for these particular Indian people. The appear-
ance of the Deer Dancer both signals the presence of this past
and embodies it: "The way back," the speaker tells us, "is deer
breath on icy windows." Her unexpected tabletop dance sum-
mons the past:

> The next dance none of us predicted. She borrowed a chair for the
> stairway
> to heaven and stood on a table of names. And danced in the room
> of children
> without shoes.
> . . . .
> She was the myth slipped down through dreamtime. The promise of
> feast we
> all knew was coming. The deer who crossed through knots of a curse
> to find
> us

(6)

The images here are double-edged, denoting the present, con-
noting other worlds: the "stairway to heaven" echoes an ear-
lier line in the poem, "Some people see vision in a burned tor-
tilla, some in the face of a woman." Salvation, that is, Christian
salvation, is invoked even as the image is undercut with heavy
irony.[4]

The Deer Dancer's very presence forces the speaker to begin
to question the world she inhabits. "That's what I'd like to know,"
she asks. "What are we all doing in a place like this?" The ques-
tion is a moment of revelation for the speaker, but the speaker's
epiphany is obstructed by language, for in English, there "are no
words for how the real world collapses." The effect of impos-
ing the colonizers' language has been well documented;[5] in these

poems, the speaker remains ambivalent, conscious of her own investment in that language even as she recognizes what it has obliterated.

This struggle to remember, understand, and document the past, even when one must do so in a foreign language, is pervasive in *In Mad Love and War.* "Grace," which opens the collection, is a prayer spoken by a dispossessed poet writing from a secularized and divided world, reckoning with "stubborn memory" in a "cheap apartment":

> We still talk
> about that winter, how the cold froze imaginary buffalo on the stuffed
> horizon of snowbanks. The haunting voices of the starved and
>   mutilated
> broke fences, crashed our thermostat dreams, and we couldn't stand it
> one more time. So once again we lost winter in stubborn memory,
>   walked
> through cheap apartment walls, skated through fields of ghosts into
> a town that never wanted us, in the epic search for grace.
>
>   (1)

All of this volume—and Harjo's work in general—could constitute the "epic search for grace" she mentions, which entails recognizing "something larger than the memory of a dispossessed people." She insists, in the same way she insists in several poems in *Mad Love,* that the "something larger" was/is there, that she *knows.* In "Grace," she claims, "We have seen it." In "Deer Ghost," she writes:

> I don't care what you say. The deer is no imaginary tale
> I have created to fill this house because you left me.
> There is more to this world than I have ever let on
> to you, or anyone.
>
>   (*Mad Love* 29)

Pronouns are used very differently in these three poems. In "Deer Ghost," the speaker is writing as a recently abandoned lover, thus the singular pronoun is particularly emphatic, and the insistence on this "something larger" is a way of turning away from the ex-lover, back to "home," to "the ways of my people." Thus, there are two abandonments in this poem, that of the speaker who leaves her own world for the lover's, and that of the speaker who is then herself abandoned. The closing stanza suggests a particular aspect of betrayal. When she says, "There is more to this world than I ever let on/to you," the necessity of assimilating to her non-Native lover and thus hiding her Indianness is apparent. Her "passing" as non-Native is a betrayal of her own heritage and ancestry.[6]

This "something larger" is associated with the elusive, shadowy female figure who appears in "Crossing Water" (*Mad Love* 46). The poem takes place on a dance floor in New York after an encounter with a woman as ephemeral as the one who appeared in "Deer Dancer": "A woman chased by spirits kept asking you to dance,/made a gift of her hands . . . She was/a witness but I don't have her name." These figures—and the poems in which they appear—are linked further when the speaker insists later in the poem that she "should be writing poems to change the/world. They would appear as a sacrifice of deer for the starving." The notion of sacrifice links the poet's offerings to traditional hunting practices, in which deer (and other animals) allowed themselves to be killed by hunters so that human beings would not perish. The poems thus allow themselves to be consumed by the starving, those hungry for sustenance charged with something other than material. The line following undercuts the speaker/poet's self-importance: "Or poems/of difficulty to place my name in the Book of Poets. I should get on with it."

The poem yokes the seemingly incongruent acts of the "mixed" contemporary Indian poet whose life and work are informed by traditional value systems and ways of telling about the world yet who also participates in white Western institutionalized writing practices. Indeed the speaker/poet does not "get on with it," but instead walks back across the floor to find her lover. It is significant that the speaker is wearing "shoes the color of hearts," the ruby slippers necessary to traverse the distance between this Oz of her making and the "real world." The image of the shoes also forges a connection between the women of this poem and the woman in "Deer Dancer," who wore "a stained red dress with tape on her heels." Both poems are informed by hunger and sacrifice. The speaker of "Crossing Water" offers her poems as "a sacrifice of deer for the starving." As in "Deer Dancer," there is recognition that the place where the speaker and her lover have been is too magical and thus out of place in the mundane world in which she lives. The troubling note of empiricism bears mention: "I add her to the evidence. We were there." At the beginning of the poem, the speaker returns to the dance floor to try to "detect" whether what she remembers happening really happened.

This dilemma, trying to sort out "what really happened," is confounded by the difficulty, even the impossibility, of trying to articulate certain experiences in an "other" language. In "For Anna Mae Pictou Aquash" (*Mad Love* 8), a poem about the Micmac AIM activist murdered on the Pine Ridge Reservation, Aquash cannot be "free," her spirit cannot escape to the "dappled stars" until she is buried a "second time in Lakota, a language that could/free [her]." In "We Must Call a Meeting" (*Mad Love* 9), the speaker says, "Give me back my language and build a house/Inside it." In "Heartshed" (*Mad Love* 63), the oppressor's language is resisted through silence: "Lean up against me full with the words that have/kept you silent. Lean with the silence// that imagines you."

The notion that the past cannot be recovered and reconstructed inside the language of the oppressor persists throughout the book, and while a return to her own indigenous language (and by this I mean the indigenous language of the Muscogees— Harjo's first language is English) is finally not the solution Harjo proposes, she clearly recognizes just how empowering an *other* language can be:

> We all watch for fire
> for all the fallen dead to return
> and teach us a language so terrible
> it could resurrect us all.
>
> (*Mad Love* 18)

In "Song for the Deer and Myself to Return On" (*Mad Love* 30), the speaker finds herself in "downtown Denver" wishing to return to the "hammock of [her] mother's belly." However, she can return only through the agency of the deer, whom she must summon in their/her language, Creek: "I sang the song Louis taught me:/a song to call the deer in Creek." After the deer arrive, "wonder[ing] at finding themselves/in a house near downtown Denver," the speaker realizes she and they must discover the words that will enable their return: "Now the deer and I are trying to figure out a song/to get them back, to get all of us back,/because if it works I'm going with them."

This foregrounding of language is a departure from Harjo's earlier poems where voice is essentialized as if it exists outside language. In "Motion" (*Horses* 54) she writes, "we exist/not in words, but in the motion/set off by them." Lines in "Skeleton of Winter" (*Horses* 30–31) suggest that voice can precede language: "I am memory alive//not just a name/but an intricate part/of this web of motion." In "Remember" (*Horses* 40) language seems to arise from the self and not vice versa: "Remember that you are this universe and that this universe is you./Remember that all is motion, is growing, is you./Remember that language comes from this."

This conflict between language and voice is evaded in "New Orleans" (*Horses* 42–43) as the speaker returns to the South to find "evidence/of other Creeks, for remnants of voices" and to uncover the voices of "ancestors and future children buried . . . in the Mississippi mud" and the "stories made of memory."

In "New Orleans" the speaker is on a journey toward the original home of her tribe, but she makes it only as far as New Orleans, a city notable for the many different cultures that coexist there. While the physical journey ends in New Orleans, the temporal one persists as far back as de Soto, and de Soto becomes a natural locus for every aberration imposed by the Conquest, including slavery:

> But he must have got away, somehow,
> because I have seen New Orleans,

the lace and silk buildings,
trolley cars on beaten silver paths,
graves that rise up out of soft earth in the rain,
shops that sell black mammy dolls
holding white babies.

(44)

Ironically, the image in which Harjo locates the idealized, pre-Conquest past is "a blue horse/caught frozen in stone in the middle of/a square," ironic because the square in which she stands is Jackson Square, so named to honor Andrew Jackson, the agent of Muscogee dislocation, and it is his horse depicted there. "I know it wasn't just a horse/that went crazy," she says, and the line reverberates throughout the poem, particularly in the stanza above, with its hodgepodge of cultural artificialities like the trolley car rails or New Orleans's elaborately constructed graveyards, which attempt to contain the dead and the past.[7]

The speaker blames and resists the past in this poem. That the past is rendered in terms of someone else's narrative—the story of European conquest—is hardly irrelevant to the speaker's resistance, but she remains trapped in and by that narrative, in a world and a past constructed by the colonizer. In *Mad Love,* however, when the deer show her an alternate past and lead her back to it, she discovers an*other* narrative that makes other endings possible. What Harjo must reconstruct is a narrative that does not exclude her own history; furthermore, she must construct a space that accommodates the different settings—to further extend the metaphor—from which that narrative arises.

In "Original Memory," Harjo uses Rabbit, a trickster from Muscogee mythology and the agent of the creation of human beings. The poem begins with the Muscogee creation myth, which signals the reader that *other* stories are important here. Like "Deer Dancer" the poem mediates among various pasts and presents, among Rabbit, popular songs on the radio, third world politics, the blues, and so forth; and the speaker moves among these spatial and temporal locations. She is "early on some morning that will pass as fast as the earth spins at 18.5 miles per second," but she is moved by her understanding that the day is "a repetition." The poem relies on humor—"the morning . . . will pass quicker if one is making love with someone desired and forbidden"—but undercuts the humor and any simple understanding of love—"slower if one is being tortured by someone who claims to do it out of love, love for the state, the state of political affairs."

The speaker inhabits different worlds in this poem, which may exert the same pressures on her as they have throughout these poems. However, she now appears able to move in and out of them easily:

> When I am inside the Muscogee world, which is not a flip side of
> the Western time chain but a form of music staggered in the on-
> going event of earth calisthenics, the past and the future are the
> same tug-of-war. Love is always love but we're convinced there
> isn't enough there either, so we pull ourselves out of our ceremo-
> nial spiral of prayer, understood relationship, into this other
> world because whatever world we are entering or leaving we are
> still looking for love. (47)

"Love" is ostensibly what is common to all these worlds and therefore what could possibly unify them. But at first Harjo's use of the word *love* in this poem is ironic, limited to its Western manifestations, including contemporary versions of courtly love in the popular songs that play on the radio, patriarchal love, which "demands . . . utmost respect and servitude and calls it love," and, of course, "love for the state," with its terrible uses and consequences. Despite the word's corruption and debasement, though, the speaker persists in believing in "love," even though "there isn't enough there."

Unifying the different worlds operating in this poem is the trickster Rabbit. Rabbit appears in order to bring humor into grim situations and to offer laughter as a way of reckoning with tragedy and disempowerment, just as Deer Woman offers the past as a means of mitigating the present. In "Original Memory" Rabbit's contemporary manifestation is the saxophone:

> Last night, I played saxophone duets with a friend. This was not
> in Muscogee world (though as elements interplay throughout
> the evening, I am never far away). . . . In the world of the
> jammed city I am flying on a saxophone with someone who is
> not my lover, trying to leap past 4/4 time to understand it. Was
> it love? Or are all events imaginary? In this world the turn of
> events is praised by love songs: either Bobby Caldwell sweetly
> with "What You Won't Do for Love," or a pale madonna skip-
> ping on the vanishing stage of your love. And that is the cere-
> mony. We sip wine, do a hit of courage, each of us imagining an-
> other spin of the wheel, and take up our horns again. Rabbit,
> who invented the saxophone and who must have invented our
> imaginary lovers, laughs through millennia. And who are we to
> make sense of this slit of impossible time? (47–48)

Through the music the speaker hears and makes as she plays the
saxophone she experiences an epiphany and discovers "this slit
of impossible time" in which the past and present converge. Once
this "impossible time" has been discovered, the speaker is able to
construct this third space, which collapses linear time and physi-
cal space. The poet's quest to uncover her past and construct a
new space in which to locate identity hardly follows a straight line.
There are a number of missteps, attempts to locate identity else-
where, as in "The Real Revolution is Love" (*Mad Love* 24–25),
where she awakes "in a story told by [her] ancestors" ready to
begin her quest but aware that Managua is not the place to do
it; or in "Deer Ghost" (*Mad Love* 29), when she "failed and let the
fire go out," not understanding the appearance of the deer after
she has abandoned her home for a lover, even as she finally real-
izes that the "deer is no imaginary tale" and that "there is more
to this world than I have ever let on."

Clearly there are wrong paths in attempting to redeem the
"split world," as Harjo characterizes it in "Legacy" (19). "Legacy"
relates the story of a prison riot in West Virginia and the murder
of an inmate:

> In Wheeling, West Virginia, inmates riot.
> Two cut out the heart of a child rapist

and hold it steaming in a guard

because he will live

to tell the story . . .

In this poem, there are two "camps." In one camp the
ers/have cooked up/a stench of past and maggots," while
other/love begins a dance." In this poem, love is recast to incl
the perverted love of the "child rapist," refigured as the "be-
trayed lover" once his heart has been cut out. The poem's ending,
"And I understand how lovers can destroy everything/together,"
suggests the interconnectedness of love and hate, of creation and
destruction. These heretofore polarities are reimagined as parts
of a continuum. This poem picks up the threads of betrayed
love in the rest of the book especially, in the way the speaker
has had to betray her own world to be with the white lover who
leaves her.

The first section of the book details not only "real wars," as in
the Nicaragua poems and the references to the conquest of Na-
tive peoples, but the speaker's "war" with the lover who has now
left her, the "mad love" affair that has brought her so much grief.
The book has four parts, the opening and closing "prayers," re-
spectively "Grace" and "Eagle Poem," and the two main sections,
"The Wars" and "Mad Love." But these threads of love and war
run throughout the poems and are not contained by the sec-
tions. As she writes in "The Real Revolution Is Love," "We are
Anishnabe and Creek. We have wars/of our own." But in what
sense can the "real revolution" be "love"? How might this alter
Harjo's manifesto for the role of the poet? And is the love broadly
conceived here contingent upon the sort of romantic/sexual love
detailed in many of the poems? In this poem, global politics are
enacted on a small scale, at the microscopic level, as the players
sit around a table that is a continent, at this gathering of indige-
nous people from many different parts of the Americas. But,
as she explains, the speaker and the other people in this poem
remain separate: "I do what I want, and take my revolution to
bed with/me, alone." The magical elusive third space of "Cross-
ing Water" and "Original Memory" does not emerge in this

to being a different world.
"not a foreign country, but
em has an edge of despair
Harjo's work, in which the
as the present-day "tortuous
recognition and mapping of
way of calling for and laying
gue in the next section, the
ifferent strategies for telling

VITNESS:
ANGE THE WORLD

in *In Mad* ___ cknowledges Leslie Silko for
"teaching her the importance of story"; yet it is in *The Woman
Who Fell from the Sky* that Harjo fully embraces traditional story-
telling, both in the form of the poems themselves and in the con-
textualizing strategies she employs. *Woman* is a curiously ar-
ranged book. The poems are long and prosaic, and each is
followed by an explanatory note, which attempts to place the
poem within a matrix of referents. The book's packaging is un-
usual. It comes in a sort of gift box and is accompanied by an
audio-cassette on which Harjo reads the book nearly verbatim.

The intratextuality in *The Woman Who Fell from the Sky* gener-
ates a kind of "play"—between genres, voices, and so forth—that
shifts the text slightly so that it is never exactly the same each
time the reader returns to it. With this strategy, Harjo is follow-
ing the lead of many contemporary American Indian writers who
have published volumes that mix genres and write within genres
that are themselves mixed. Luci Tapahonso's *Saani Dahataal: The
Women Are Singing* contains lyric poems, short prose narratives,
and anecdotal stories that have the ring of oral narratives, as does
Carter Revard's *An Eagle Nation*. Ray Young Bear's *Black Eagle Child:
The Facepaint Narratives* is a book that has been classified as a novel,
as poetry, as autobiography. This mixing and disrupting of genres
occurs, in part, because traditional oral storytelling does not
fit easily into any traditional Western literary genre, but instead

encompasses many aspects of song and lyric, and of narrative. Among these Native-authored texts that mix genres and thus draw upon oral traditions in an overt way, Leslie Marmon Silko's 1989 *Storyteller* is perhaps the most striking and influential. A collection of short stories, family photographs, transcribed oral narratives, and poems, *Storyteller* attempts to replicate an orality in written form. The text unravels the expected individualized authorial voice and instead presents a multiplicity of voices.[8]

The production and performance of oral storytelling is highly contextual. These narratives are not static or fixed. Rather, they are generated according to the occasion, in relation to the audience present. They change and evolve over time to suit the needs and desires of the community to which they are addressed. Furthermore, as Navajo poet Luci Tapahonso has noted, the authorship of oral narratives is collaborative. Describing one of her collections of poetry and stories, Tapahonso explains, "This writing, then, is not 'mine,' but a collection of many voices that range from centuries ago and continue into the future. . . . I view this book as a gift from my mother and father, both of whom embody the essence of Navajo elders—patience, wisdom, humor, and courage. It is a collaboration of sorts . . . " (xii).

Harjo's "endnotes" in *The Woman Who Fell from the Sky* and the pairing of written and audio texts attempt to generate context, since an important aspect of traditional stories is their inclusion of a number of different storytellers who pass the story down from generation to generation and contribute to it within the same generation. In *The Woman Who Fell from the Sky*, the sequence of poems and the italicized afternotes constitute two different, interlocking threads. The matrix formed by these two threads, their relation to each other, to Harjo the writer, and to the persona speaking, is weblike. The accompanying cassette presents a parallel oral version creating a rich intratextuality. The text is open ended and accessible because of its multitextuality; each story is told several times, in different ways.

Like *Storyteller, The Woman Who Fell from the Sky* thematizes questions about the function of poetry, of art. Each poem is followed by an explanatory note, in which the origin and purpose of each poem is detailed. Interestingly, these notes serve to further un-ravel the boundaries between genres. The division between the poems themselves and their "afternotes" are marked by the use of italics; however, on the cassette that accompanies the printed volume, Harjo's reading style makes no distinction between these different "genres." She reads with a decidedly uninflected style, suspending words at the end of each line. Her reading style is "artificial," by which I mean to say she contrives a poetic voice distinct from a conversational, everyday tone.

The narrative sequencing of poems in this volume compli-cates its structure even further. The book divides neatly into two separate but intertwined parts. The first suggests the long de-scent into destruction, while the second provides for affirmation and the possibility of healing and resurrection. The first half of *The Woman Who Fell from the Sky*, entitled "Tribal Memory," begins with several creation story poems—"The Creation Story," "The Woman Who Fell from the Sky," "The Naming"—then shifts to poems about the colonization or conquest of the New World, and moves on to poems that mourn that colonization—"Mourn-ing Song" and "A Postcolonial Tale." The section ends with the apocalyptically titled "Letter from the End of the Twentieth Cen-tury," which segues easily into the second half of the book, "The World Ends Here."

This doom-laden title is undercut by the last poem in the vol-ume, *"Perhaps* the World Ends Here" (my italics), a gesture that typifies Harjo's pervasive irony. Furthermore, this poem is pre-ceded by two pieces whose titles signify their striking hopeful-ness, "Promise" and "The Dawn Appears with Butterflies." The celebratory "Promise" (62–63) anticipates the birth of Harjo's granddaughter; "The Dawn Appears with Butterflies" (64–67) is equally celebratory, even as it describes preparing to bury a friend who has died. The juxtaposition of these two poems, com-ing as they do nearly at the end of the book and at the end of the section entitled "The World Ends Here" (68), suggests other interconnections, such as birth and death or family broadly con-ceived to include both actual blood relatives and close friends. *The Woman Who Fell from the Sky* is an ambitious project—and one clearly requiring, to borrow a term from Czeslaw Milosz, "a more spacious form."[9] These formal innovations and the recurrence of certain words such as *witness* and *truth* instantiate the public dimension of Harjo's text. In her use of these long prosaic lines, Harjo forges new, and lays claim to old, territory. The most obvious American precursor here is Whitman, the inclusive poet, whose use of long lines seems crucial in order to "contain multitudes." Further, Harjo is following many important American women poets who forge a sort of Whitmanesque pluralism in their work, such as Adrienne Rich, who chooses to "cast my lot with those/who age after age, perversely//with no extraordinary power/reconstitute the world" (*Dream* 67).

In the poem "Perhaps the World Ends Here" (68), Harjo locates herself in the domestic and seemingly mundane world: "The world begins at a kitchen table. No matter what, we must eat to live./ . . . We chase chickens or dogs away from it. Babies teethe at the corners. They scrape their knees under it." The poem's central conceit of the kitchen table symbolically pushes "Woman" to the center, while babies, chickens, men circle the periphery. Men and women are *made* here. "Wars have begun and ended at this table," the poet writes. Clearly, the political and the private are indivisible. There is no public dimension separate from the personal, no abstract apart from the concrete. The table is the meeting place of birth and death: "We have given birth on this table, and have prepared our parents for burial here." The poem constitutes a prayer or blessing, spoken at mealtimes, in the room that is the heart of the family, which, in turn, is the heart of the community. It is an inclusive prayer: " . . . we sing with joy, with sorrow. We pray of suffering and remorse. We give thanks."

As with many of the poems in *In Mad Love,* the pervasiveness of the sacred and its complex interweaving with the secular are important concerns in "The Woman Who Fell from the Sky" (5–10). At the same time, the poet's desire to tell a story distinguishes this poem from earlier work in which narrative emerges indirectly or is only referred to. The poem is remarkable in its ability to call into question the idea of "the poem" itself and to compel its reader to revise his or her reading practices. Characterized by the same magical disbelief of "Deer Dancer" and "Crossing Water," the poem constitutes a new articulation of the poetic projects begun in *She Had Some Horses* and *In Mad Love and War*. A prose narrative, the poem is divided into short, separate paragraphs, and peopled with such characters as Saint Coincidence, the woman herself who is "neither a murderer nor a saint" but "rather ordinary" and a "strange beauty in heels."

The "strange beauty" appears to be the same woman of "Deer Dancer" and "Crossing Water." As with these two poems, "recognition" is an important consideration in "Woman":

> Saint Coincidence thought he recognized her as she began falling toward him from the sky in a slow spin, like the spiral of events marking an ascension of grace. There was something in the curve of her shoulder, a familiar slope that led him into the lightest moment of his life. (5)

Yet the focus of this poem is not the women in it, not the woman who falls mythically from the sky, not the "strange beauty" disappearing across a parking lot, not the girl from the Indian boarding school. Rather, the poem finally belongs to Saint Coincidence, a Vietnam veteran:

> Saint Coincidence, who was not a saint, perhaps a murderer if you count the people he shot without knowing during the stint that took his mind in Vietnam or Cambodia—remembered the girl he yearned to love when they were kids at Indian boarding school. (5)

But this is no sloppily romantic tale. The boarding school girl "whose spirit knew how to climb to the stars" is also the girl who suffers a "severe beating" at the school and survives only because "myth was as real as a scalp being scraped for lice." With this line the poem turns, lurching suddenly from the mythic to the real. The heretofore "Saint Coincidence" and the unnamed falling woman become Johnny and Lila, real people with mundane names. Yet the story does not move clearly into the particular— that is, into an individual and isolated tale. Rather, it becomes a parable. Johnny's story is that of many Indians—boarding school, alcohol, the military, the imposition of a foreign name and language on his existence.

III. THE MYTH SLIPPED DOWN THROUGH DREAMTIME

Deer Woman is the "myth slipped down through dreamtime," hence the agent that deconstructs the boundary between the secular and the sacred, the conscious and the unconscious, a boundary imposed on the poet by the white world. Rabbit, though, is the persistence of myth in the secularized white world. "I did not tell you," the speaker says to her daughter in "The Book of Myths" (*Mad Love* 55), "when I saw Rabbit sobbing and laughing/as he shook his dangerous bag of tricks/into the mutiny world outside Hunter." Deer Woman returns the speaker's past to her, but Rabbit gives her a place to stand that comprises her two worlds and leads her here:

> Across the frozen Bering Sea is the invisible border
> of two warring countries. I am loyal to neither,
>
> only to the birds who fly over, laugh at the ridiculous
> ways of humans, know wars destroy dreams, divide the
>
> country inside us. . . .
>   The war was over; it had never
>
> begun. And you were alive and laughing, standing beneath
> a fat sun, calling me home.
>
>   (55)

For, after all, this is what the poet has sought, a way to live without divided loyalties, to discover a way of constructing "home" outside of nationalism and boundaries, and to reinvent the past. Harjo has written that Oklahoma, the home of many Native writers, "is a dream, an alive and real dream that takes place inside and outside of the writer" ("Oklahoma" 44). The desire to map this dream propels Harjo's poems.

Harjo is mapping a "third space"; her poems suggest that this new world is all around us, if only we look hard enough. This seemingly magical collapsing of time and space is evident in *She Had Some Horses* and pervasive in *In Mad Love and War.* In *The Woman Who Fell from the Sky,* this process is less apparent. In that volume, the poet's role as "truth teller" ironically reinscribes her voice as individual, at times containing the public dimension of her work. In the opening "prayer" to *The Woman Who Fell from the Sky,* Harjo writes, "We sing our song which we've been promised has no beginning or end." Her task as a poet, I would argue, is to recognize and articulate the space in which this song can be sung, a space in which the borders between past and present and between the secular and the sacred are erased.

NOTES

1. *Dominant mode* is Charles Altieri's phrase. He writes: "A mode becomes dominant when the ethos it idealizes develops institutional power—both as a model for the ways in which agents represent themselves and, more important, as the basic example of what matters in reading and in attributing significance to what one reads" (8).

2. Walter Kalaidjian has noted that this "lyric solipsism has led to verse writing's professional domestication within the university" (4), and that "the nexus between academe and poetry writing is vital to the formation of the postwar verse canon" (20).

3. Paula Gunn Allen, in *Grandmothers of the Light,* described Deer Woman as a "supernatural who appears as a human woman and as a doe by turns" (236).

4. Janice Gould writes that the "reference to the 'vision in a burned tortilla' is an inside joke that people in the Southwest might recall: a woman in the small town of Cuba, New Mexico, saw a vision of Christ in a tortilla one Easter. This is the sort of thing that makes news in our parts" (812).

5. See Jorge Noriega, "American Indian Education in the United States: Indoctrination for Subordination to Colonialism." Tzvetan Todorov also provides a valuable discussion of the imposition of written cultures onto oral ones in *The Discovery of America: The Question of the Other.*

6. I do not mean to suggest that the speaker in this poem has literally "passed" as white, but rather that she has downplayed her Indianness to suit her lover.

7. Nancy Lang has noted the "careless Anglo supremacist behavior" documented in this poem, as in "the contemporary rock shop salesman and the historic Spanish explorer deSoto, both of whom exert a strong but superficial power over deeper, more private native Creek and natural world powers" (46).

8. Arnold Krupat has written: "There is no single, distinctive, or authoritative voice in Silko's book nor any striving for such a voice (or style); to the contrary, Silko will take pains to indicate how even her own individual speech is the product of many voices" (163).

9. Milosz uses this term for his 1986 *Unattainable Earth*, the published version of his writer's notebooks from 1981 to 1984. *Unattainable Earth* contains Milosz's own poems, fragments of letters, miscellaneous quotations, and poems by Whitman and Lawrence (xiii).

WORKS CITED

Allen, Paula Gunn. *Grandmothers of the Light: A Medicine Woman's Sourcebook.* Boston: Beacon, 1991.

Altieri, Charles. *Self and Sensibility in Contemporary American Poetry.* Cambridge: Cambridge UP, 1984.

Coltelli, Laura. *Winged Words: American Indian Writers Speak.* Lincoln: U of Nebraska P, 1990.

Gould, Janice. "American Indian Women's Poetry: Strategies of Rage and Hope." *Signs: Journal of Women in Culture and Society* 102 (1995): 797–817.

Harjo, Joy. *In Mad Love and War.* Middletown, Conn.: Wesleyan UP, 1990.

———. *Interview.* By Lewis MacAdams. Dir. Lewis MacAdams and John Dorr. Videocassette. Lannan Foundation Literary Series, 1989.

———. "Oklahoma: The Prairie of Words." *The Remembered Earth: An Anthology of Contemporary Native American Literature.* Ed. Geary Hobson. Albuquerque: U of New Mexico P, 1979. 43–45.

———. *She Had Some Horses.* New York: Thunder's Mouth P, 1983.

———. *The Woman Who Fell from the Sky.* New York: Norton, 1994.

Kalaidjian, Walter. *Languages of Liberation: The Social Text in Contemporary American Poetry.* New York: Columbia UP, 1989.

Krupat, Arnold. *The Voice in the Margin: Native American Literature and the Canon.* Berkeley: U of California P, 1989.

Lang, Nancy. "'Twin Gods Bending Over': Joy Harjo and Poetic Memory." *Melus: The Journal for the Study of the Multi-Ethnic Literature of the United States.* 18.3. (1993): 41–50.

Milosz, Czeslaw. *Unattainable Earth.* Hopewell, N.J.: Ecco P, 1986.

Noriega, Jorge. "American Indian Education in the United States: In-doctrination for Subordination to Colonialism." *The State of Native America: Genocide, Colonization, and Resistance.* Ed. M. Annette Jaimes. Boston: South End P, 1992. 371–402.

Revard, Carter. *An Eagle Nation.* Tucson: U of Arizona P, 1993.

Rich, Adrienne. *The Dream of a Comman Language: Poems, 1974–1977.* New York: Norton, 1978.

Silko, Leslie. *Storyteller.* New York: Arcade, 1989.

Swann, Brian. "Introduction: Only the Beginning." *Harper's Anthology of Twentieth Century Native American Poetry.* Ed. Duane Niatum. San Francisco: Harper, 1988. xiii–xxxii.

Tapahonso, Luci. *Saani Dahataal: The Women Are Singing.* Tucson: U of Arizona P, 1993.

Todorov, Tzvetan. *The Discovery of America: The Question of the Other.* Trans. Richard Howard. New York: Harper, 1984.

Young Bear, Ray A. *Black Eagle Child: The Facepaint Narratives.* Iowa City: U of Iowa P, 1992.

14

Mixing It Up in M. Nourbese Philip's Poetic Recipes

CRISTANNE MILLER

Cooking, or culinary preparation, transforms food into a dish—salade Niçoise, Wienerschnitzel, lemon meringue pie. Almost always, this involves a process of combination, mixing one ingredient with another, and often a process of transformation as well: liquids may become solid when baked, airy when beaten, gelatinous when boiled; the "raw" becomes "cooked."[1] A recipe provides the formula for such changes. Because eating is more than a matter of gustatory pleasure—indeed its nutritional necessity makes it, as Gian-Paolo Biasin puts it, a "metonymy of the real" (4)—a recipe is also more than a bourgeois set of instructions for tastier, less fattening, or more gourmet dishes. At its most basic, a recipe is a formula for transforming the raw or inedible into the edible, and it is produced through a conjunction of historical, economic, communal, and individual factors. Recipes meet necessities and desires: what is available, or cheap; what must be used before it spoils; what can or can't be grown in, or imported into, a region; what are the eating patterns, taboos, and tastes of the cook, the family, the community; and who else will be present for the eating—that is, the occasion marked by serving this food. A recipe, in this sense, is both a part of, and a response to, a complex story or process of life. As the English idiom "a recipe for success" or "disaster" suggests, recipes are analogous to other forms of life-instruction; they tell us how—or how not to—live.

M. Nourbese Philip's use of culinary metaphor in her writing functions on many of these levels, but most directly as a form of embodied record, or history, for African Caribbean people, especially women. In her work, food functions as crucially material, and as representative in its materiality. Philip writes about making food, passing on recipes, and how food may stimulate memory, feeling, and thought as well as taste buds. For her, however, cooking also functions as a primary scene and metaphor for exploring the broad cultural dynamics of capitalism, colonialism, and indeed all power relationships as they are inflected by the "ingredients" of race, gender, location, and a historical community. Moreover, and especially through the flexible orality of the tongue, Philip emphasizes the interconnections of aesthetic judgment, language structures, and sexual desire and oppression with the more obvious orality of taste.

M. Nourbese Philip is herself an African Caribbean poet from the island of Tobago, now living in Toronto. Not widely known in the United States but increasingly noted in Canada for her stylistic innovations and activism, Philip combines elements of postmodern formal experimentation with an engaged political stance—indeed, makes those aspects of her work inseparable.[2] Through her interrogation of linear narrative, lyric poetic voice, consistent tone and diction, and "standard" English, Philip challenges the apparent naturalness underlying and disguising oppressive relations of power. Philip's experiments with form hence affirm African Caribbean, African American, and women's communities, rather than reproducing the touted ahistorical and apolitical experimentalism of a poststructuralist collage of styles.[3] To vary slightly Françoise Lionnet's use of Sidonie Smith: writers like Michelle Cliff, Christa Wolf, Maxine Hong Kingston, and M. Nourbese Philip "use postmodern fictional [and poetic] techniques that . . . 'challenge the ideology of individualism and with it the ideolog[ies] of [race and] gender'" (324).

A short story about cooking, "Burn Sugar," lays out in narrative form many of the elements of this cluster of relationships. Here, Philip's narrator reconstructs from memory her mother's recipe for black, burnt sugar cake. As she remembers both the transformation of ingredients under her mother's supervision and her mother's strength in the prolonged beating of those ingredients, the speaker questions processes of transformation and relations of interdependence generally. She and her mother, she speculates, are both "ingredients" in some unspecified recipe— as different from each other "as the burn sugar was from the granulated" (14, 17). The daughter lives in North America, the mother in the Caribbean; the daughter uses a plastic bowl, the mother mixes in a pail; the daughter doesn't have to wash her butter to get the salt out, and the eggs she buys "never smell fresh like they suppose to—like those back home" (19). Yet both have "the same source" and both are involved in the same "ritual of transformation and metamorphosis" through what amounts to violence—the burning and beating of ingredients for the cake (17). Does change "ever come gently . . . so much force or heat driving change before it," the daughter wonders (15).[4] The story seems to give contradictory responses to this central question. Despite their "differences," and the "burning" transformation one of them has apparently undergone, change from mother to daughter seems to be gentle, just as the daughter's own "change to womanhood" was: "There wasn't no force there, or was there? too old and ancient and gradual for she or her to notice as she watch the Mother and wait" (15). The surprising gentleness of these changes, however, stands in marked contrast to the associations called up by making this typically Caribbean cake—beginning with the necessarily ambivalent relation of African Caribbeans to sugar itself, that product and breaker of slave lives, as it burns from white to "bitter" black, the cake's key ingredient.

This cake is not easy to make, and the memories it calls forth ("each black mouthful bringing up all kind of memory," 12) suggest that neither cooking nor nourishment has been easy in this culture. The daughter insists, "(gently of course)," to her mother:

> just listen—the burn sugar is something like we past, we history, and you know that smell I always tell you about? . . . is the smell of loneliness and separation—exile from family and home and tribe . . . is the same smell of . . . the first ones who come here

rancid and rank with the smell of fear and death. (18; ellipses
mine)

Like the cake, the bakers themselves have been produced through
a history of violent transformation—enslavement, rape, reloca-
tion to a different continent—and eating the one brings analogi-
cal association, represented as physiological memory, to the
other.

The daughter's "exile" in North America, although chosen (to
the extent that one can regard movement determined by trans-
national capitalism's extensive postcolonial system as chosen),
reflects in relatively mild form the horrific exile of her enslaved
ancestors from Africa.[5] To her, the cake mailed by her mother
from the Caribbean every year has a peculiar odor that she iden-
tifies with the exile itself, as quoted above. Making the cake her-
self is, then, an act of crucial significance, marking her continuity
with a historically distant past and a geographically distant com-
munity. Philip suggests that the burning of the sugar for this cake
ritualistically repeats the violence performed on enslaved Afri-
cans in the Americas and hence marks a community's determi-
nation not to forget that past. Through culinary burning and
beating, that past of violence is transformed into a product
not only digestible but of distinctive and prized flavor. The cake,
then, ritualizes history and politicizes taste.

Although Philip's story follows the preparation of this cake in
great detail, it provides no recipe. We know there is sugar (burnt
and granulated), eggs, butter, a curl of limeskin, and rum, but
we don't know either the measurements or how to proceed—for
example, with burning the sugar, a complex and delicate opera-
tion. Philip offers a taste of this distinctively African Caribbean
cake to all readers while withholding the formula for its produc-
tion. This withholding underlines the different relationships of
the author (and narrator) of this story to various members of her
mixed audience: those familiar with the cake and any version of
its recipe will see enough in the story to recognize the narrator's
description as authentic.[6] Those unfamiliar with but intrigued
by the "taste" must obtain the recipe, or learn more about the

creative production of African Caribbean culture, for them-
selves; those unfamiliar and uncomfortable may find that the
story—a metonymy for the burnt sugar cake itself—indeed has
a bitter taste, or sticks in their throats.[7]

For Philip the "taste" of the "tongue"—generally, and for this
particular cake—develops from and reveals intersections of ex-
perience, history, politics, and culture. To the mother, embedded
in her Caribbean world, it is "only black cake[,] child, is what you
carrying on so for?" (18). To the reader, perhaps especially a non-
Caribbean reader, the cake may also represent the unknown, the
untasted—even while every ingredient is commonly available. To
the cuisines of Europe, a burnt ingredient is indigestible, to be
discarded; to a people with a background of scarcity and enslave-
ment—as the daughter sees it—even (or especially) burnt sugar
is prized—a "magic liquid; is like it have a life of it own—its own
life—and the cake need it to make it taste different . . . strong,
black and bitter it going make the cake taste like no other cake"
(14; ellipses mine).

Just as taste is connected to history, for Philip the orality of
eating is closely linked to the orality of producing language and
of sexuality, and the point at which these discourses converge—
literally and metaphorically—is the tongue. As Philip writes in
a multiple-choice quiz concluding the poem "Discourse on the
Logic of Language":

> In man the tongue is
> (a) the principal organ of taste.
> (b) the principal organ of articulate speech.
> (c) the principal organ of oppression and exploitation.
> (d) all of the above. (*She Tries Her Tongue* 59)[8]

The next question of her quiz underlines the phallic—hence sex-
ual and authoritative—nature of language implied in "(d)" (the
correct answer to the first question) by identifying the tongue
with the penis—"a tapering, blunt-tipped, muscular, soft and
fleshy organ." Despite the physiological blurring (unlike the
tongue, the penis has no muscles), Philip makes her point clear:
the tongue expresses relationships of power, and both language

and "taste" are composed from those relationships. The tongue also expresses love and gives pleasure, but these functions are never divorced, for Philip, from the tongue's historical and political embodiment and maneuverings, or from her own texts' rapid discordant and connective strategies.

In "Discourse on the Logic of Language," Philip questions the historical and psychological dimensions of the tongue's production of language: what is the long-term impact of forcing a people (Africans) to adopt as native a language (English) that is "etymologically hostile" to them (*ST* 15). Manifesting visually the multiple ways in which language may confront its speakers and readers, Philip uses five distinct print types and configurations of words on a page in this poem. Here there is no clear textual norm or hierarchy of sequence—no recipe for reading: each reader must decide what to read first, and how to order the poem's remaining material or ingredients. On the far left margin of the first (left-hand) page, the poem contains a storylike narrative about a mother licking her newborn child and then blowing words into her mouth. This section is printed all in capital letters vertically down the margin so that one must physically turn the book to the side in order to read it; it is continued on the margin of the second left-hand page. Center page comes a fragmented lyric claiming English as both "mother tongue" and

a foreign lan lan lang
language
l/anguish
 anguish
—a foreign anguish. (*ST* 56)

This section alternately claims English as either or both mother and father, or foreign, tongue. Moving right on the same (first) page, one next encounters the first of two slave edicts, both proclaiming that slaves may not speak their African languages, and the second (on the next left-hand page) recommending "removal of the tongue" for such prohibited speech. In intellectual counterpoint, the first right-hand page describes the work of two nineteenth-century doctors who identify the parts of the brain responsible for various aspects of speech, one of whom "proved" that white men had larger brains and were therefore superior to women, and to all peoples of color (*ST* 57).

These sections are juxtaposed with no links except those the reader intuits between the separate pieces. For example, the reader must choose whether to read the story of the mother and child first, as a kind of urtext, or later, as a response to the mutilation of African tongues threatened in other sections of the poem. The mother's licking both marks the child as her own and gives the child the taste of her whole ancestral line: "SHE TOUCHES HER TONGUE TO THE CHILD'S TONGUE" and then blows "HER WORDS, HER MOTHER'S WORDS, THOSE OF HER MOTHER'S MOTHER, AND ALL THEIR MOTHERS BEFORE—INTO HER DAUGHTER'S MOUTH" (58). The intimacy of such touching shocks with its sensuality: it suggests the power of taboo, or deeply spiritual, rituals. And indeed, this maternal nourishment and (literal) inspiration—the inverse of cannibalism, the prototypical European descriptor of "native" island barbarism—does counter the script of colonialism.[9] Through this interposed, disrupted narrative, Philip's poem may suggest that even within a language of colonization etymologically hostile to its colonized speakers, there will be words of powerful affirmation and ancestry, making English indeed a mother tongue as well as a "foreign anguish." Like the bitterness of the burnt sugar, the anguish of English may even give it a distinctively intense or "prized" flavor, but only for those speakers who can taste their own history in its structures.

Philip's poem "Universal Grammar" centers on the kind of memory community suggested by the mother-child section of "Discourse on the Logic of Language." Here again, Philip uses distinct language patterns, or voices, on the right and left pages of her text to signal the ambivalent relation of her speaker to English and the multiple discourses that structure that language. The poem begins with isolated words—on the left with apparently unconnected definitions ("Parsing," "The," "smallest," "cell," "remembers")—and on the right with "Man"—all words that become key to sentences in the poem. In reflective tones, Philip asks: "when the smallest cell remembers . . . how can you . . . lose a language"; on the other side of the page, she builds a cumulative sentence, apparently spoken by a different type of voice, in several European languages: "*The tall, blond, blue-eyed, white-skinned man is shooting/an elephant/a native/a wild animal/a Black/a woman/a child/somewhere*" (*ST* 67). In both sentences, language is directly linked to physical life—either as the cells of the body itself "re-member" a language lost to active memory, or as the shooting man kills. Philip underlines the link between linguistic presence and shooting by repeating the first part of the sentence in several languages of colonization.

"Universal Grammar" ends with facing pages: on the left-hand stands a redefinition of "Parsing" at the top and a definition of "raped" at the bottom of an otherwise blank page; on the right-hand side stands the completed sentence about the shooting "Man" and then, following a solid black line across the page, a quotation from the imaginary text "*Mother's Recipes on How to Make a Language Yours or How Not to Get Raped*":

> Slip mouth over the syllable; moisten with tongue the word. Suck
> Slide Play Caress
> Blow—Love it, but if the word
> gags, does not nourish, bite it off—at its source—
> Spit it out
> Start again (67)

Through these subversive "recipes," as well as through its interstitial form, this poem offers a revolutionary response to the process of forced learning, or to any other process analogous to the violence of shooting and rape. You do not have to swallow what enters your mouth, or passively accept shooting; choose your own nourishment, Philip advises. The revolutionary aspect of this recipe stems from the fact that it demands action—even threatening action—not what one associates stereotypically with cooking or women. Moreover, it links those activities often taken for granted as trivial (choosing what to eat, or passing on recipes) with radical resistance to victimization. Philip here suggests that even the apparently least powerful may exercise some degree of choice; even the process of deciding what words or ingredients to take as your own may be revolutionary. Where "Discourse" presents the radical nourishment of the daughter with her mother's and maternal ancestors' words, "Universal Grammar" presents the mother giving more obviously defensive advice to her daughter. At the same time, however, through its own model of handing down "recipes," this conclusion also suggests that the mature speaker will know not only what words and actions to reject as detrimental to her being and development but also what words, or strategies, she might pass down to others. Parallel to the laws of grammar and definition suggested in the poem's title and earlier passsages stands this law of strategic resistance and affirmation—perhaps not "universal" but certainly communal in its operation.

That Philip focuses intimate sharing in these two poems and in "Burn Sugar" on the relations of mothers and daughters has some basis in the traditional (and still commonly justified) assumption that women are responsible for the work of ordinary, daily culinary preparation and feeding, but also in the material realities of a slave past. As Françoise Lionnet observes, the "matrilineal filiation" governing slave societies provided "the only possible means of retracing memory and charting the contours of a historical past that, in the Caribbean, is both submarine and subterranean" (339).[10] The radical separation of slave families made the bond between mother and infant often the only link between an individual and her or his ancestral line. Philip's various scenes of instruction between mothers and daughters reflects the crucial role of this link in slave history, and restores some measure of honor to the mother or older female.

For Philip, the mother's body, or the history of a people, manifests itself in the daughter's memory, which is in turn manifested in her language and the repeated labor of her daily life. As Brenda Carr puts it, "Philip puts pressure on memory as a juncture between the lived body and its placement in community and global histories. She conceptualizes memory as a resistance strategy" (84). Or as Philip herself writes in "Echoes," "Memory . . . has a potentially kinetic quality and must impel us to action" (*Frontiers* 20). The sharing of recipes, like the sharing of "taste" and breath, signifies the possibility of maintaining or recovering memory and of further physical and imaginative production for the Caribbean "daughter." For Philip, as for other African American women who use food in their writing "as a marker of cultural identity" (Lionnet 338), one's relationship to food production may emblematize affiliation, authority, fertility, and the strength of connections drawn from a (traditionally and still predominantly) female lineation of knowledge and identity. Goldman writes, in this regard, of the importance of food in manifesting the repetitive "conscious labor" of women in cultural production, as opposed to the either unconscious or publicly acknowledged labor of men usually emphasized (190–192). Through her use of recipes and cooking, Philip both recuperates a sense of agency for women, who are often represented as subjects in name only, and represents the relation between individual "subjectivity and ethnicity as a conscious, practiced one" (Goldman 191).

A recipe then, as "Universal Grammar" makes clear, may imply or embody one's relation to multiple aspects of cultural production. In this context, it is important to remember that a recipe is a flexible set of instructions. It is a suggestive grid of ingredients, the use of which entails strategic maneuvering (how do I make up for the ingredients I don't have?) and imagination. As Debra Castillo writes,

> A recipe is not a blueprint, and any experienced cook will concur that it is almost impossible to stick to the script, even the first time through. It is less a formula than a general model; less an axiom of unchanging law and more a theory of possibilities; more a springboard than a restricting cage. (xiii)

For Philip, one's language most importantly manifests one's relation to such a cultural "theory" or "springboard." Like the receiver of a recipe, the tongue moves according to certain phonological and grammatical guidelines but with its own idiosyncratic inflection in producing intelligible sound. As the development of multiple demotic versions of English attests, the tongue may also affect more radical transformations of those guidelines.[11] To the extent that all speakers reproduce language, all—in Philip's poetic—become "mothers" as well as "daughters" in the system of language culture, and hence may themselves affect and foster such transformations once instructed in their possibility. Among other things, this metaphor replaces the phallic master/father with the cooking mother as instructor in manipulations of the tongue—not a simple inversion of the gendered binary, but a reminder that in the history of enslaved Africans a child followed the condition of its mother, regardless of its paternity, and that mothers were primary contributors to the construction of every aspect of what remained richly nourishing in that culture.

While many feminists writing on the politics of food production and use focus on "men's control of women's labor" (Hartmann 114) or on the myth that "males need more and better food because they do more work" (Steinem 194), Philip calls attention to women's agency in the cultural dynamics of food production and, analogously, in the production and distribution of goods and power. Such a focus results in both the obvious empowerment of women and the more general affirmation of the quotidian and of materiality—the two spheres most consistently degraded in relation to cultural production and most consistently linked with women and people of color.[12] Somer Brodribb, for example, writes of the long history of devaluing products and work involving the direct labor of bodies—especially hard manual labor, reproduction, and cooking/feeding—as a strategy to promote the value of the products of an elite class of men: "How to elaborate masculine creativity and power in the face of matter's forming potential is the practical and theoretical enterprise of patriarchy" (120). Postmodernism, in Brodribb's analysis, is simply another stage in this ongoing "enterprise," a stage that takes the form of celebrating "dematerialized knowledge" (126) to the detriment of materialized, embodied, raced, and gendered bodies and knowledge.[13] Writing about Philip's work, Brenda Carr identifies "the social practices, discourses, and power relations of empire-building and colonialism—that historical matrix which Philip calls down in her writing—[as] one of the most pernicious manifestations of such disembodiment" (88). Philip, she declares, "activates the possibility of intervention in the disembodied and anti-body formations that dominate Western culture," including those of postmodernism that transfer engagement with the body to engagement with a text abstracted into the realm of European philosophical discourse (88).

Cooking, an archetypal activity of materiality, in its mundane repetitions and its production of material nourishment, stands in extreme contrast to traditional notions of power and genius, and yet, as Friedrich Engels notes in *The Origin of the Family, Private Property and the State*, "according to the materialist conception, the determining factor in history is, in the final instance, the production and reproduction of immediate life" and "the production of the means of existence" (in Hartmann 113). One sees some vestige of this power in the levels of individual responsibility and choice entailed by cooking as the daily feeder of a household— not as a paid restaurant professional or special occasion cook; one plans menus, chooses ingredients, serves the food. The revolutionary potential of such power is clearer, however, in its radical uses: for example, one can only imagine how many poisonings or mysterious sicknesses may have been brought on by slave cooks, or unhappy housewives. According to historian Deborah Gray White, poisoning constituted a covert form of resistance among slave women (White 79), and Eugene Genovese describes the relation between slaves and slaveholders in the kitchen as one of "the culinary despotism of the quarters over the Big House" (543).[14] Cooking is a service and the cook is by definition a server if not a servant; she may, however, as the dynamics of slavery suggest, also transform this service into one of her own empowerment. Perhaps in order to avoid the inequality of power relations traditionally associated with food preparation and service, and with women, Philip focuses her cooking scenes around the moment of transmitting knowledge (sharing recipes), transforming ingredients, and marking relationships between women. In her work—as for Engels—food production and the exchange of information about food are potentially revolutionary activities.

"Mother's Recipes" in "Universal Grammar" teach both "how not to get raped"—an issue of concern primarily for women—

and "how to make a language yours"—an issue affecting every speaker, but particularly those whose relationship to their native tongue is complicated by a history of oppressions. Through her poem's title, its repeated definitions—indicating the extent to which even simple "rules" and idioms may carry oppressive messages for some speakers—and its direct reference to "THE THEORY OF UNIVERSAL GRAMMAR," Philip ironizes the assumptions of objectivity and naturalness in language structures that hierarchize the positionality of its many speakers. In one section, she mimics the tones of a linguistic textbook describing language acquisition: "OUR CHOICES OF GRAMMATICAL POSSIBILITIES AND EXPRESSIONS ARE, IN FACT, SEVERELY LIMITED; IT IS THESE VERY LIMITATIONS THAT ENSURE WE LEARN LANGUAGE EASILY AND NATURALLY" (*ST* 65). At the pragmatic level, this is true: African Americans learn to speak English as quickly and well as any other speakers, by the same physiological and mental processes. Yet through the context of the poem, Philip implies that the enforced necessity of such learning made this process far from "easy and natural" for Africans transported to the New World. Sander Gilman observes broadly that "adapting to a new language, as did African blacks in slavery, the Irish following Cromwell, or the Jews in the Diaspora, means at least a period in which the novelty of the language makes a sensitive speaker aware of the hidden agenda of Otherness present in the language to be adopted" (14). Philip suggests, more radically, that the use of English (or other colonial languages) continues to be psychologically difficult for "a sensitive speaker" even generations after that original period of acquisition. The limitations of English grammar indeed enable linguistic acquisition, but other limitations of the language hinder celebratory expression of the lives of people of color. At the same time, however, as Philip describes in "Dis Place," the African presence and experience have become inscribed within all European and Euro-American texts. Body becomes text; "the Body African dis place—'place' of exploitation inscribes itself permanently on the European text. Not on the margins. But within the very body of the text where the silence exists" (23).[15]

Such inscription takes place in the more fluid patterns of spoken English as well as in formal texts, and its forms may be loud as well as silent. As Philip describes it, the African forced to learn English "developed strategies to impress her experience on the language. The formal standard language was subverted, turned upside down, inside out, and even sometimes erased," thereby making of English a "metaphorical equivalent of the havoc that coming to the New World represented for the African" (*ST* 17). As I suggested earlier, Caribbean English is an obvious form of such mixing. As with other transformations discussed above, the demotic results in part from violence, what Philip calls "the linguistic rape and subsequent forced marriage between African and English tongues" (*ST* 23). For Philip, however, the most important combinations of linguistic ingredients occur not in the past but in the present negotiation of various registers of English, all of which are marked by the historical intermingling of Anglo-Europeans and Africans, in different degrees. Philip seeks to force the acknowledgment of the silenced, gendered, raced body of history, of African and female presence, within the apparently neutral contemporary text and thereby to transform English into a language capable of expressing a fully embodied, cognizant subject position in the context of historical and contemporary circumstances that continue etymologically and physically to colonize the African American—and especially the African American woman's—body.

The "recipe" concluding "Universal Grammar" provides for such transformation. By presenting this recipe in the context of rape, however, Philip implies that making full use of such instruction requires more than knowing its grammar, or a list of ingredients: the speaker/cook must be courageous in asserting her right to her own safe physical space, a space marked by physical boundaries but also emblematic of space, or freedom, to speak, think, and create. For Philip, a person's whole relationship to language and to taste is mediated by the experiences and the social construction of her body.[16] The boundary between speech and silence is, for her, not the Western rational boundary of intellect and body (or male and female) but of embodiment and invisibility, in which unempowered or forced silence violates the crucial place or space of the physically positioned self. For this reason, Philip implies, rape should be a matter of particular concern to the poet. Rape is an act of violence typically performed by men against women, and so prevalent that by a conservative estimate one in four women in the United States or Canada will be raped during her lifetime.[17] Rape both constitutes and signifies an invasion of all that is most personal, hidden, private, all that represents a vestige of personal control. The prevalence of rape in most cultures signifies that a woman cannot mark her own boundaries, cannot declare her self or any space in which she stands "safe," and, even more radically, cannot declare any cavity of her body hers alone—that is, she is at best always potentially violable, permeable. At the same time, rape can be seen as functioning oppositionally to the kind of violent change signified by cooking—where the ingredients are indeed foodstuffs to begin with, even if cast-offs from the master kitchen, which considers them inedible, and, transformed through the violence of cooking, become forms of nourishment and delectation. Rape forces presence or knowledge of hierarchical power, in constrast to the communal passing on of knowledge that sustains through shared cooking, eating, and the textual/memorial form of recipes.

Philip defines rape as follows:

> raped—*regular, active, used transitively the again and again against women participled into the passive voice as in, "to get raped"; past present future—tense(d) against the singular or plural number of the unnamed subject, man* (*ST* 66)

Cooking involves the participation (not the "participled . . . passive voice") of women in determining what may be eaten, in what forms. Understanding how to respond to the *in*edible, however, is another aspect of culture, and here Philip's orders to the linguistic daughter are explicit: "bite off" and "spit out" what "does not nourish" and then "start again." By presenting this castrating and retaliatory, as well as loving, response to language learning as though it were cited from a recipe book, Philip gives a comic twist to her point that one's relationship to language is always at least in part a relationship of power, and power is manifested in and on bodies: whether or not one allows oneself to be *"participled into the passive voice"* by legal codes and common speech, whether or not one "bites" off what does not nourish, whether or not one passes on one's own recipes for creative survival, one assumes a stance of verbal and physical power (or powerlessness).

In "Managing the Unmanageable," Philip comments on the conclusion to "Universal Grammar": "I was suggesting in this excerpt from the imaginary *Mother's Recipes* the link between linguistic rape and physical rape, but more than that the potential for unmanageability even when faced, as a woman, with that ultimate weapon of control—rape. *Mother's Recipes* was an attempt to place woman's body center stage again as actor and not as the acted upon" (299). Later in this essay, Philip restates this crucial shift from passive to active as related to a conceptual shift in the difference between standing on a margin and on a frontier. Less interested in occupying already established, hierarchical positions of power than in discovering new, more egalitarian and liberating forms of power relationship, Philip repeatedly attempts to move women and all people of color from the margins of textualized, unembodied silences to various active frontiers: "From margin to frontier—is a deceptively simple act requiring no movement or change, but only the substitution of one word for another. It is an important and liberating first step, this substitution of words and meanings, but to make that authentic leap from margin to frontier demands nothing less than a profound revolution in thinking and metamorphosis in consciousness" (300). Like learning to reject what does not nourish, and pass on what does, reimagining one's own relationship to systems of power and language is key to Philip's "recipes."

NOTES

1. Claude Lévi-Strauss, "The Culinary Triangle."

2. Lynette Hunter sees the engagement of a community anchored by actual social problems and willing to act on them as key to Philip's writing; her address to readers is "based on an understanding that the

conventional strategies that tend to habituate and make comfortable need to be disrupted in order to address the social immediacy of reality" (258).

3. Kumkum Sangari's provocative "The Politics of the Possible" explores such difference in depth. As he writes, textual hybridity that is grounded in the historical-material politics of race, gender, and postcolonialism does not signify postmodernism's "recurring renovation of style" as aesthetic principle but rather "the restless product of a language history of miscegenation, assimilation, and syncretization, as well as of conflict, contradiction, and cultural violence" (158). Brenda Carr elaborates: "Like miscegenation, the mixing of cultural forms, traditions, and languages violates the taboo against mixed genres and categories of all kinds . . . In *She Tries Her Tongue*, miscegenation of form runs a kind of textual interference, incites a collision of discourses" (82, 83).

4. Ellipses are Philip's unless indicated. Perhaps as part of her discussion of change, Philip slows down the rhythms of prose by using ellipses and repetition to create a structure of rhythmic elaborating phrases more common to poetry than to prose, and characteristic of demotic speech in the Caribbean.

5. Philip links these two exiles autobiographically in her essay "A Piece of Land Surrounded," which describes her 1991 return to Tobago for a year.

6. On the other hand, Philip's story also implies that the daughter in her exile *cannot* make the "authentic" cake—as her circumstances of production and life differ so greatly from those of the Caribbean. As Anne Goldman puts it, the food itself is invested "with a cultural register ultimately inaccessible to the non-native" or exiled native, even one who does possess the complete recipe (180). Unlike a recipe, which exhorts the holder to reproduce it, Philip's story calls attention to the boundaries both within a community, historically defined, and among various communities of readers, while using the materiality of taste and repetition to authorize the subject's process of identification. The daughter reproduces her Caribbeanness and affiliation with the mother as well as her difference from the mother and distance from the Caribbean in making the burnt sugar cake. See Goldman 184, 190–91.

7. In a telephone conversation, Philip speaks of wanting her work to "stick in the craw" of some readers while more easily nourishing others (June 7, 1996). Lynette Hunter writes of this aspect of Philip's work, and states that Philip's various readers will inevitably position themselves differently: "some of those positions will be enabled and others alienated" (257).

This partial withholding in Philip's text also corresponds to other writing experiments in the Caribbean. Focusing on Gabriel García Márquez, Kumkum Sangari writes that the use of enigma to structure a text counters the "familiar Orientalizing trope" marking the "native" her- or himself as enigmatic (mysterious, inscrutable, feminine) and hence structures the text itself, formally, as female: "The form becomes a critique of the content (the subjection of women to the violating codes of a chauvinist society), and functions to protect the already violated woman from further violation or further surveillance . . . [T]o maintain the text as enigma is also to maintain a resistance to being construed as an object of scrutiny . . . it exercises power by sustaining insecurity [in its reader] and by openly refusing to surrender its 'meaning'" (171). Sangari here considers only the relation of the text to a foreign or potentially violating audience.

8. Hereafter, I abbreviate *She Tries Her Tongue* as *ST.*

9. In his 1492 diary Christopher Columbus transposes the words *Caritaba* and *Caniba,* and then claims that the people of nearby "Caniba" "ate human beings" (217). Columbus's "caniba"—no doubt stimulated by his belief that he was in China, in the realm of the "Khan"—becomes the root for cannibal, emblematic representation of all barbarism for European "discoverers." In his classic essay on the Caribbean, "Caliban," Roberto Fernández Retamar discusses this etymology (6).

10. In "Managing the Unmanageable," Philip writes that "when the African came to the New World she brought with her nothing but her body and all the memory and history which body could contain. The text of her history and memory was inscribed upon and within the body which would become the repository of all the tools necessary for spiritual and cultural survival" (298). As the site of reproduction, the mother's body marked the child legally for slaveholders and culturally through its own coding ("the smallest cell remembers").

11. Unlike the more commonly used terms—"nonstandard" or "creole" English—"demotic" English implies the appropriateness of its own forms through its Greek root, *demos,* "the people." Philip consistently uses "demotic" to designate Caribbean English.

12. Christine Battersby, for example, summarizes the myth that "women's 'chief destination' is the 'perpetuation of the human species,' and that is why they have evolved as down-to-earth creatures with minds that tend 'to the concrete, the easily visualizable.' '[T]he genius's pursuit is essentially "idle" hence the true woman, the true mother has a mentality incompatible with such kind of creative activity'" (21; quoting Andrew Gemant).

13. As part of her evidence, Brodribb quotes both Jean-François Lyotard and Julia Kristeva. The former claims that the maternal is "the source of the message, that which gives the message its existence and gives the author authority. The sender imprints its destination on the message and on the recipient his destiny.... Whether the message is a sentence, a visible image, a building, a child, a richness, a meal, an article of clothing—we, postmoderns, renounce attributing to it an origin, a first cause" (126). Kristeva writes that "for man and for woman the loss of the mother is a biological and psychic necessity, the first step on the way to becoming autonomous ... Matricide is necessary to the survival of the self" (132–33).

14. Genovese refers here not just to the fact that slaves not only cooked the food, but that their preferences for spices brought from Africa (sesame seeds and oil, and red pepper) and for foods they had developed for themselves out of their own small supplies (for example, chitterlings and collard greens) influenced the taste of slave owners as well: "They were able to bend the taste of the Big House toward that of the quarters because the slaves as a class, including the rudest field hands, had quietly been making a life for themselves that included a healthy concern with cooking" (543).

15. See D. Emily Hicks for a discussion of Philip's language in relation to embodiment and colonialism.

16. As I suggested earlier, it is possible to read "Universal Grammar" as indicating that Philip, like many French feminists, sees the unempowered speaker position as always feminine in its relation to hegemonic power, the one who can be raped in relation to the one who can force words (or other forms of the phallus) down. For Philip, however, the phenomenon of rape is not just a metaphor of lack of empowerment; as she discusses at length in "Dis Place," rape is and long has been a serious and real problem for women (especially women of color) that distinguishes their life experiences from those of men—regardless of other aspects of men's relative (un-)empowerment. Philip is always as interested in the actual, historical experience of the flesh as in the manifestations of one's contextual embodiment—to the extent that these are differentiable.

17. A 1980 study conservatively estimates that "under current conditions, 20–30% of girls now twelve years old will suffer violent sexual attack during the remainder of their lives," and this figure does not include girls under twelve who have already suffered sexual assault (Lee 5). A 1991 U.S. Department of Justice report estimates that every six minutes a man rapes a woman (*Washington Post,* Dec. 8). According to a

1979 study, black women are more likely to be raped during their lifetimes than are white women (Doyle and Paludi 191).

WORKS CITED

Battersby, Christine. *Gender and Genius: Towards a Feminist Aesthetics.* Bloomington: Indiana UP, 1989.

Biasin, Gian-Paolo. *The Flavors of Modernity: Food and the Novel.* Princeton: Princeton UP, 1993.

Brodribb, Somer. *Nothing Mat(t)ers: A Feminist Critique of Postmodernism.* North Melbourne, Australia: Spinifex, 1992.

Carr, Brenda. "To 'Heal the Word Wounded': Agency and the Materiality of Language and Form in M. Nourbese Philip's *She Tries Her Tongue, Her Silence Softly Breaks.*" *Studies in Canadian Literature* 19.1 (1994): 72–93.

Castillo, Debra A. *Talking Back: Toward a Latin American Feminist Literary Criticism.* Ithaca, N.Y.: Cornell UP, 1992.

Columbus, Christopher. *The Diario of Christopher Columbus's First Voyage to America 1492–1493.* Abstracted by Fray Bartolomé de Las Casas. Trans. and ed. Oliver Dunn and James E. Kelley, Jr. Norman: U of Oklahoma P, 1989.

Doyle, James A., and Michele A. Paludi. *Sex and Gender: The Human Experience.* Dubuque, Iowa: Brown, 1985.

Genovese, Eugene D. *Roll, Jordan, Roll: The World the Slaves Made.* New York: Random, 1976.

Gilman, Sander. *Jewish Self-Hatred: Anti-Semitism and the Hidden Language of the Jews.* Baltimore: Johns Hopkins UP, 1986.

Goldman, Anne. "'I Yam What I Yam': Cooking, Culture, and Colonialism." *De/Colonizing the Subject: The Politics of Gender in Women's Autobiography.* Ed. Sidonie Smith and Julia Watson. Minneapolis: U of Minnesota Press, 1992. 169–95.

Hartmann, Heidi. "The Family as the Locus of Gender, Class, and Political Struggle." *Feminism & Methodology.* Ed. Sandra Harding. Bloomington: Indiana UP, 1987. 109–34.

Henley, Nancy, and Cheris Kramarae. "Gender, Power, and Miscommunication." *Problem Talk and Problem Contexts.* Eds. N. Coupland, H. Giles, and J. Wiemann. Newbury Park, Calif.: Sage, 1991. 18–43.

Hicks, D. Emily. *Border Writing: The Multidimensional Text.* Minneapolis: U of Minnesota P, 1991.

Hunter, Lynette. "After Modernism: Alternative Voices in the Writings of Dionne Brand, Claire Harris, and Marlene Philip." *University of Toronto Quarterly* 62.2 (1992–93): 256–81.

Lee, Ellis. *Theories of Rape: Inquiries Into the Cause of Sexual Aggression.* New York: Hemisphere, 1989.

Leonardi, Susan J. "Recipes for Reading: Pasta Salad, Lobster à la Riseholme, Key Lime Pie." *Cooking by the Book: Food in Literature and Culture.* Bowling Green, Ohio: Bowling Green State U Popular P, 1989. 126–37.

Lévi-Strauss, Claude. "The Culinary Triangle." *Partisan Review* 33 (1966): 586–95.

Lionnet, Françoise. "Of Mangoes and Maroons: Language, History, and the Multicultural Subject of Michelle Cliff's *Abeng.*" *De/Colonizing the Subject: The Politics of Gender in Women's Autobiography.* Ed. Sidonie Smith and Julia Watson. Minneapolis: U of Minnesota P, 1992. 321–44.

Philip, M. Nourbese. "Burn Sugar." *Imagining Women.* Ed. The Second Story Collective. Toronto: Women's, 1993.

———. "Dis Place The Space Between." *Feminist Measures: Soundings in Poetry and Theory.* Ed. Lynn Keller and Cristanne Miller. Ann Arbor: U of Michigan P, 1994.

———. *Frontiers: Essays and Writings on Racism and Culture.* Stratford, Ontario: Mercury, 1992.

———. "Managing the Unmanageable." *Caribbean Women Writers: Essays from the First International Conference.* Ed. Selwyn R. Cudjoe. Wellesley, Mass.: Calaloux, 1990.

———. "A Piece of Land Surrounded." *Orion* (Spring 1995): 41–47.

———. *She Tries Her Tongue, Her Silence Softly Breaks.* Charlottetown, P. E. I.: Ragweed, 1989.

Retamar, Roberto Fernández. *Caliban and Other Essays.* Trans. Edward Baker. Minneapolis: U of Minnesota P, 1989.

Roman, Camille, Suzanne Juhasz, and Cristanne Miller, eds. *The Women and Language Debate: A Sourcebook.* New Brunswick, N.J.: Rutgers UP, 1994.

Sangari, Kumkum. "The Politics of the Possible." *Cultural Critique* 14 (Fall 1987): 157–86.

Steinem, Gloria. *Outrageous Acts and Everyday Rebellions.* New York: New American Library, 1983.

White, Deborah Gray. *Ar'n't I a Woman: Female Slaves in the Plantation South.* New York: Norton, 1985.

15

Kozmic Reappraisals: Revising California Insularity

MARIA DAMON

I. ISLANDS

... the culture of the Peoples of the Sea is a flux interrupted by rhythms which attempt to silence the noises with which their own social formation interrupts the discourse of Nature.... the cultural discourse of the Peoples of the Sea attempts ... to neutralize violence and to refer society to the transhistorical codes of Nature. Of course as the codes of Nature are neither fixed nor even intelligible, the culture of the Peoples of the Sea expresses the desire to sublimate social violence through referring itself to a space that can only be intuited through the poetic, since it always puts forth an area of chaos. In this paradoxical space, in which one has the illusion of experiencing a totality, there appear to be no repressions or contradictions; there is no desire other than that of maintaining oneself within the limits of this zone for the longest possible time, in free orbit, beyond imprisonment or liberty.

—Antonio Benítez-Rojo 16–17

> Who can stay crazy
> under all this pressure
> it makes you wanna wear a short dress
> n hang it up . . .

—Jessica Tarahata Hagedorn,
Danger and Beauty 56

Early colonial maps of California showed it as an island, because the conquistadors, coming upon Baja west of Mexico, saw only a body of land beyond a bay so long they didn't know it ended. And subsequent conceptions of California have continued to portray it as somehow sequestered from the rest of the continent, as if its specialness depended on lack of contact. However, conventional concepts of insularity—islandness and island consciousness—contrast with what I know of California poetry, which is that it is highly interactive, generative, and exportable to the rest of the world. There is an emergent understanding that island, peninsular, and coastal cultural expression is particularly dynamic and complex, constantly stimulated and changed by cross-traffics and pollinations from afar; books by Antonio Benítez-Rojo, Robert Wilson and Wimal Dissenyake, and Sylvia Watanabe, among others, are theorizing this already intuitively well-established observation. One might say, to hazard a conflation of two recent buzzwords, that coastal communities are both what Mary Louise Pratt has termed a "contact zone" (a phrase she in turn borrowed from sociolinguist Ron Carter; Pratt 6–7) and what Hakim Bey has called a "temporary autonomous zone," or TAZ. A coastal or insular community is a temporary autonomous contact zone.

In this essay I want, however sketchily, to hypothesize a perspective that might be useful to considerations of regional poetries and of the relationship between poetries and specific social and/or antisocial orders, conditions, and practices. Thus, if we consider poetry as the region in this look at regionalism—specify it as an insular or peninsular region, revise our understanding of that topos, and grant the antidiscursive potential (Karlheinz Stierle writes: "*La poésie lyrique est essentiellement anti-discours*" [Stierle 431]), if not actuality, of poetry—we can begin to understand the Bay Area of California in the 1970s as, paradoxically, a poetic realm beyond time-space that permits its poets voyage thereto for briefer or longer stays, on condition that those poets stay in contact with the nonpoetic non–Bay Area. Furthermore, I would suggest that such a coastal environment, in its "becoming" and devolving, fluidly unstable nature, may permit a wider scope of cultural experimentation on the part of folks who have been traditionally "dispossessed"—in the context of this essay, women, and more specifically the women of color in Northern California who came to artistic maturity in the relatively open years preceding the Reagan era. An implicit archipelagic permission to "mix it up" is healthy for arts communities, and can make for unpredictable challenges to hurtful hierarchies (witness the relatively early success of the Haitian revolution under Toussaint L'Ouverture, compared with similar uprisings on the U.S. mainland). I will be drawing most of my citations from the work of Jessica Hagedorn and Ntozake Shange, though I will also include a partial catalogue of the "Third World" (as they then called themselves) women and men who made up the rich fabric of creative activity that nurtured these two now better-known writers and performance artists.

Poetry is a coast, a liminal discourse between the culture of cosmopolitan harbor cities and the wildness of the ocean, between the seeming stability of land and the seeming fluidity of the sea, between the semantic, semiotic, and sonic worlds, spirit and matter, body and breath. People pass through poetry as through a port of call, they're called into poetry and out of conventional discourse—that is, they are extra-pellated rather than interpellated. The Kozmic Doowop Commune multicultural art scene of the Bay Area 1970s—the ostensible topic of my essay— was a poetic time-space that took from and gave back to its participants, and sent them further into the world to continue their cultural guerrilla work.

California, and Northern California in particular, has since the nineteenth century been a haven for nonconformists of all kinds self-exiled from straight society, and for people oppressed in most other national contexts: antisemitism, for example, was relatively unheard of there until the Klan's revival in the 1930s, and many Jewish families, such as Gertrude Stein's and Alice Toklas's, moved there for that reason (see Rosenbaum). It was outside of the North-South division of the Mason-Dixon line and thus did not have a tradition of anti-Black institutions. It has also been the landing place for people forced to leave their homelands due to poverty (one could consider the desperation of the gold rush in this context, as well as the overseas immigration from other Pacific areas), political crises, or other social catastrophes; and it is the original homeland of people who did experience slavery and ethnicide at the hands of missionaries and who, if they did survive, were made to feel like strangers in their own place. In the early to mid-twentieth century, the Bay Area developed a strong anarcho-pacifist community and spirit that continued into the present through various incarnations, and the longshoremen's strike in the 1930s crystallized a strong sense of workers' importance. This sense of heterogeneity and motion continues. The constant confluences and meetings of these individuals and these groups are precisely what prevent California from ossifying into the stasis implied by conventional metaphors of insularity. It is this characteristic that makes it a place for fruitful and unusual collaborations, intellectual and cultural cross-pollination, and lively heterogeneity. And while I want to distance myself from the dramatically romanticized bifurcation of nature from culture on which Benítez-Rojo's passage relies, I nonetheless find fertile the suggestions that "Peoples of the Sea"—immigrant cultures, island cultures, coastal and ocean rim culture—may participate in a heightened sense of the poetic, and this in a cosmopolitan, liminal way.

This liveliness has become particularly meaningful to me since my move from California seven and a half years ago, to the Upper Midwest, a region whose traditional progressive populism is negatively counterbalanced by and in fact is dependent on a faith in sameness, ascetic stoicism, and aesthetic minimalism; Upper Midwestern democracy is fundamentally a belief that everyone should act, speak, and look the same in order to merit equal access and representation. The land of ten thousand lakes can't compete with an isle, which etymologically combines land and sea (terra *in salo<insula*=in salt water); Minnesota's *lim*nality doesn't compensate for the borderland and coastal lim*i*nality of California—life in the mainstream is not in a stream at all but stuck in Main Street, the heart deprived of the arts of movement, of the oxygen necessary to circulate, of the ecstasies of heterogenous language and the play of pain, difference, and flamboyant joy. The word *lake* has a direct ancestor that means a "depression filled with water"; a recent NPR interview with the Coen brothers about their film *Fargo,* which was filmed in Minnesota, described the opening scene of the movie as a "shot of pure, flat whiteness."

Unh-hunh. In short, my experience in the stolid Midwest has sharpened my understanding that California (and New York, a city composed of several islands) represents the worldly antithesis of all that is implied by the word *isolation,* and that those connotations could be far more accurately derived from a good long look at the centrum.

Island culture—when rescued from intimations of remoteness and properly retheorized—is in fact a useful paradigm for tracing some of the dynamics of California aesthetics. Californian poetry can and has traveled and become cross-germinal for and with other movements and other locales, rather than allowing its eccentricities or specialnesses to implode and self-devour à la Uroboros.

Islands—Hawaii, the Caribbean, Manhattan, the Philippines, the Cape Verdes—have historically been sites of cross and intercultural traffic, hybridity, mobility, diaspora—all the terms contemporary academic humanists are pleased to deploy to convey a heightened sense of movement and indeterminacy. A famous palindrome—that self-contained island of letters—speaks to the undoing of empire through insularity: able was I ere I saw Elba. Home to unmoored discourses of ecstasy, islands are also vulnerable to natural change through volcanoes, tidal waves, hurricanes—their existence, defined by movement, reflects the global shifts of plate tectonics—they speak to submerged routes of travel such as the Aleutian chain, linking what we have constructed, in our disciplinary desire to compartmentalize and categorize, as different and separated continents that presumably contain entirely unlike peoples, cultures, flora, fauna, terrains. Islands are traces of bridges and continuities, traveling poetic archipelagos, which phrase is meant to realign gently the assumption of out-of-touchness. We are all no doubt familiar with the new ethnographers' (and especially James Clifford's) emphasis on the traveling and mobile nature of cultural production and its producers, and of the many and constantly shifting modes of consumption and distribution as well. Paul Gilroy's conception of the "Black Atlantic" helps us to imagine cultural and countercultural communities and continuities across oceans; the phrase

Pacific Rim similarly evokes the ocean as central rather than peripheral to cultural development; and the converse: that a landmass's centrum—the Midwest, again, forming my most recent experiential reference point—should not necessarily figure centrally in theorizing cultural mobility. The etymologies of words for islands—islands, isles, archipelagos, and so on—reveal the extent to which the ocean determines our understanding of the land we refer to: *archipelago,* for example, used to mean the Aegean Sea itself, then it came to signify the islands in it, then any cluster of islands. *Isle,* as I've pointed out, truncates *in salo,* but the noun *terra* is implied, not stated, while the ocean's salt is explicit. What's important in all of this is that context determines identity—here, the sense of travel over water, nearness to constant rhythm, and immersion in air so rich that just to breathe is to dance with an invisible lover. What's also important in this is the desire to translate social violence into a fertile chaos of cross-cut rhythms and colors, sound and movement that is the heart of poetry.

Of course California is not literally an island, nor is it metaphorically, in the sense of being sequestered from the commerce of culture; but it is a border, with the Pacific on one side, Mexico to the south, and the Sierras forming a dire pioneer zone of mythic cannibalism. As a literally—and littorally—liminal space California shares with literal islands this stopping-point sensibility, this proximity to constant movement and rhythm of the sea, of migrant and diasporic populations, of Peoples of the Sea. This peculiarly wonderful ornate border has produced communities of letters, from George Jackson's prison letters (whose title, *Soledad Brother,* resonates richly with that of Bob Kaufman's first book, *Solitudes Crowded with Loneliness*) to City Lights's pocketbook series designed to travel easily with those who carry no excess baggage.

II. COMMUNITIES

Contrary to what I believed when I started working on this piece, there was no actual household known as the Kozmic Doowop Commune; in Jessica Hagedorn's words, it was a state of mind.

There were, however, many such cooperative households of poets, dancers, musicians, lovers, and collaborators, households born of economic necessity as well as artistic affinity. Halifu Osumare, Nashira Ntosha, Paula Moss, Ntozake Shange, Kitty Tsui, Thulani Davis, Janice Mirikitani, Jessica Hagedorn, Mei-mei Berssenbrugge, Janet Campbell Hale, Carol Lee Sanchez, Nina Serano, Avotcja, and Alta, as well as David Henderson, Norman Jayo, Ishmael Reed, Al Robles, Alejandro Murguia, Roberto Vargas, Victor Hernandez Cruz, Papoleto Melendez, Luis Syquia, Serafin Syquia, Lawson Inada, and countless other artists helped to build an infrastructure of creative expression that was far from parochial. Partly this was because they came from many places— the Philippines, St. Louis, Harlem, Nicaragua, Puerto Rico, China—partly because even when they left California they didn't leave each other, so that that web of verbal and bodily kinesis has continued to expand and become ever more fluid and mature, and partly, of course, because of what Hagedorn refers to as their "rich and complicated ethnicities" and what Shange calls "lotsa body and cultural heritage" (Hagedorn ix; Shange *Nappy Edges* 38). Some, like David Henderson, still maintain dual households; lower Manhattan and Berkeley provide his pieds-à-terre. Ntozake Shange now lives in Philadelphia, after sojourns in New York (as a theater person) and Houston (as a professor of creative writing); she speaks of her Bay Area period as a blessing and a gift, unparalleled in her subsequent experience. Despite the quasi-Columbian "discovery" by Joseph Papp of her choreopoem "For Colored Girls Who Have Considered Suicide When the Rainbow Is Enuf," its production at various women's and bohemian bars in the Bay Area before its triumphant debut in New York City had already ensured its passage into the creative nervous system of the English-speaking world. Hagedorn, who now lives in New York City, continues to invoke her Bay Area period as crucially formative. These artists' names appear in each other's poems and essays, in the litanies that now preface some of the better-known poets' newly collected works.

The nickname Kozmic Doowop Commune itself well articulates the ethos of the milieu. *Kozmicity* gives a playful, streetlike spelling to the union of hybridity and artistic order: the *raza cos-mica* has, since a book of that title appeared in 1925, been a term used to describe the special, avataric intermingling of (native) American, African, and European people in Latin America and the Caribbean into the "race of the future." While this vision aims at harmonious synthesis rather than continued indeterminate heterogeneity, it can easily be re-envisioned as a process rather than a static order at which the social world must arrive. *Cosmos* is also, in similarly dialectical vein, the etymological antonym of "chaos," though we now understand through "chaos theory" that this also is an overly rigid conceptual binary—that the cosmos is shot through with chaos and that chaos is, in turn, not really all that chaotic. The chaos of Benítez-Rojo's island society is intercut with the orders of nature and art, and of human interaction itself (commune). Doowop, the Black popular music of the 1950s and 1960s, owed its distinctiveness to an a cappella feel (if not always an exclusively vocal arrangement in fact), harmonies that had elements of both gospel and vaudeville (voix de ville, the urban people's voice), and characteristic vocables ("nonsense" syllables that nonetheless convey important emotional and stylistic information) such as, of course, "doowah," "oowah," "dit dit dit," and so on. It's considered a relatively light-hearted, youthful music, with permission to play with language in recognizable harmony, less cerebrally outré than bebop or scat but clearly related: bop's kid sister. Commune? The legacy of the 1960s, with its ethos of freewheeling, humane, boho-anarchistic social relations which aimed at equality and fluidity, a direct challenge to the nuclear family and nuclear politics, which had never been espoused by nor had it originated in, minority cultures. Global and local, harmonious and disruptive, familial and unorthodox, the Kozmic Doowop Commune was indeed a state of mind, but it was more than that as well; it was a lived artistic and social creed—not a binding dogma but a shared ethos.

History as well as geography was important in midwifing this scene. Coming on the heels of the Black nationalist movement, which was being decimated by government assassinations, imprisonments, and other repressive mechanisms, and of the related

Black arts movement of New York and Chicago, to which it looked as inspiration, and dovetailing with the growing *raza* consciousness and its concomitant emancipationist interventions in labor practices, especially in California and the Southwest, the kozmic doowop, or, as Ishmael Reed called it, the "dittybop school" aesthetic, was no less political than these—Roberto Vargas and Alejandro Murguia fought in the Sandinista revolution—and some of the African American participants had been active in New York previously. The feminist movement also had its influence; women's presses, women's studies programs (Shange taught women's studies at Sonoma State College while performing, writing, and dancing in Berkeley-Oakland), and women's collectives within the Third World Communications group, as well as the informal but indispensable sisterly support the women artists gave each other in surviving a masculinist scene—these all helped to nurture the movement. Special opportunities were opened if not guaranteed for women in this temporary autonomous contact zone characterized by flux and social destabilization. The emerging feminist consciousness of the 1970s in the culture at large enabled women poets of color—who already supported each other in extended-family-like relationships and communities antedating the terms *consciousness raising* or *feminism*—to receive mainstream recognition and support, the fruits of which can be seen now in the careers of Kozmic Doowop "alumnae" such as Shange, Hagedorn, and Berssenbrugge. I don't want to contrast the Bay Area scene with more nationalist cultural movements to the detriment of the latter; rather, I want to point out the special heterogeneity and fluidity of the San Francisco incarnation of politicized ethnic art. The California scene was eclectic and multicultural, much like its present-day New York counterpart, the NuYorican Poets' Cafe.

III. POEMS

How is the excitement of island ocean border poetry conveyed in the poetry itself? Through thematic and rhythmic invocation of communities, oceans, rivers; through a linguistic trying on of each other's vernaculars and identities, mixing and matching;

through remaking ethnic traditions in present circumstances. Many of these poems practice orthographies of ecstasy and new punctuations, like Dickinson's dashes, conveying unspeakable interruptions in discourse; new collaborative forms evolved— the choreopoem, for example—as did recombinations of traditional styles like blues and doowop rhythms, sea-changed in the time-space of cosmic doowop consciousness. Shange's poem for saxophonist David Murray, "Where the Mississippi Meets the Amazon," describes an erotically and artistically charged love relationship in terms of an aquaspace beyond geography—the poetic, of course, which transcends but preserves difference:

> you fill me up so much
> when you touch me
> i cant stay here
> i haveta go to my space . . .
> . . . .
> a land lovin you gives me . . .
> there's a point where the amazon meets the mississippi
> . . . .
> there's a bistro near the pacific
> & the pyramid of the moon is under my bed
> i can see the ferry from trois islets to rio
> . . . .
> my space is a realm of monuments and water
> language and the ambiance of senegalese cafes
> where the nile flows into the ganges . . .
>
> (Shange, *Nappy Edges* 28–29)

This poem, or a piece with the same title, was performed in New York by Shange, Jessica Hagedorn, and Thulani Davis, the so-called satin sisters of the cosmic doowop scene. In another poem, "several propositions in the middle of the nite when i'm travelling between virginia & nyc & i don't know where you are but i'm working on it," Shange speaks in tongues of French, English, and Spanish to delineate the rapture of her emotions, though her orthography continues to insist on an African American vernacular sensibility (*Nappy Edges* 37). Her poem "Lovin You

Is Ecstasy to Me" blends mythic and actual people; this snapshot of a birthday party in one of the cosmic households achieves the status of mystical communion with vivid human-divine beings in lush domestic rituals—all to the rhythmic intoxicants of the Shirelles, the Blackbirds, and other African American doowop groups:

hey hey hey/the bay bridge becomes dorothy's tornado in kansas and
i fly to a new oz/
moreno y dulce/ . . . laying up w/ de pinoy princess of the avenues . . .
ifa is manifest in furtive greens . . .
the empress singes opium over de stove
norman didn't bring his drums
kapuenda is embroidered with cornelians . . .
sheoli leans upon the kitchen sink/
she is radiant and strawberry almond bread
tastes of her love/
ms jazz-a-belle glistens over boilin pots . . .

(Nappy Edges 31–33)

Thulani Davis invokes liminal outlawry with the phrase that titles her essay on performance poetry, "Known Renegades: Recent Black/Brown/Yellow" (Davis 68); the preface to Hagedorn's Penguin volume, *Danger and Beauty,* refers to her peers and mentors in "the funk mystique of Oakland" as "loup garous, gypsies, sympathetic cowboys, and water buffalo shamans" (ix). The exuberance and euphoria of the times comes through in the breakneck speed of the lines, the extravagance of the language, the love of dangerousness, subversions, and edges of all kinds, the larger-than-life power and charisma attributed to these friends and colleagues.

Jessica Hagedorn, a Filipino writer who came to the United States at age eleven, writes her debt to and alliance with other writers of color by using African American vernacular—"they so fine," she writes about poets so powerful that their beauty is a crime, "they break your heart/by making you dream/of other possibilities" ("Sorcery" 23). Elsewhere she thematically celebrates Latin dance music, and she shows the ways in which prejudice and ignorance at the mainstream level (in her fiction, Filipino characters are repeatedly asked, "What are you," Chicano, Brazilian, or what ["The Blossoming of Bongbong" 44]) translates into complicitous and delicious subversion at the street level of friendships and artistic affinity:

> in new york
> they ask me if i'm puerto rican
> . . . .
> i . . .
> chant to iemaya
> convinced i'm really brazilian . . .
>
> ("Song for My Father" 36)

To read or hear this poetry is to know that one is watching a "scene" but without that left-out voyeuristic feeling that leads to resentful misappropriation. It's a scene that aims at the democratization of poetry; thus it preemptively resists its own co-optation.

IV. SOCIAL VIOLENCE AND THE QUESTION OF POETRY; POETRY AND THE QUESTION OF SOCIAL VIOLENCE; QUESTIONS

The land is a great, sad face. The sea is a huge tear, compassion's twins.
If there is a god beneath the sea, he is drunk and telling fantastic lies.
Poets who drown at sea, themselves become beautiful wet songs . . .
At the ends of the water, the holy marriage of the horizons.

(Kaufman, *The Ancient Rain* 49)

This last section is, though hypothetically the most significant, also the shortest, because the task of theorizing poetry and social violence is one that, properly speaking, would compose an exemplary life, like that of Antonin Artaud, rather than a book chapter. Nonetheless, because I don't want to leave this topic as subtext only, I want to note the politics of that scene, and this one. The puns littering the earlier part of this essay take their cue from the playfulness that typifies the West Coast aesthetic, though, as we so often read and write in book prefaces, any infelicities of style or content are my own and not theirs by whom

I'm inspired. This occidental playfulness, which can be traced in current developments in Language Poetry, the new *mestizaje* writings, and the queer writing scene, all of which vanguards have traditions rooted in the ocean air of the Pacific, should not obscure the serious politics at work in the creative project I've tried to sketch out.

To return to the Benítez-Rojo passage, it is not hard to see that I have been, up to this point and in the interest of creating a celebratory encomium, selectively blind to the many qualifiers and disclaimers embedded in his prose. Here I foreground them:

> . . . the culture of the Peoples of the Sea is a flux interrupted by rhythms which *attempt to* silence the noises with which their own social formation interrupts the discourse of Nature. . . . the cultural discourse of the Peoples of the Sea *attempts . . . to* neutralize violence and to refer society to the transhistorical codes of Nature. . . . (this culture) *expresses the desire to sublimate* social violence through referring itself to a space that can only be intuited through the poetic . . . In this paradoxical space, in which one has the *illusion* of experiencing a totality, there *appear to be* no repressions or contradictions; there is no *desire* other than that of maintaining oneself within the limits of this zone for the longest possible time . . .

These words indicate the degree of strife/striving involved in creating a rhythm of ludic chaos. They do not indicate any degree of success or failure, though the words *illusion* and *appear* suggest that this blissful undulation in the nurturing space of creative community requires an element of active fantasy, which in turn suggests the overwhelming social violence for which it would compensate.

There is (sonically if not etymologically) a resonance between the term *shanty* (derived from the French Canadian *chantier,* and ultimately from a Greek term meaning a "pack ass," or beast of burden), a rough, makeshift worker's dwelling, and the term *chantey* (derived from the French *chanter,* to sing, and ultimately from the Latin *cantere*), a worksong used by nautical laborers to mark the rhythm of the toil. When the material conditions are derelict, one lives in song, poetry, language ("I Live in Music," chants Shange dreamily to jazz accompaniment, "I live on c-# Street . . . " [*I Live in Music*]). Moreover, Bruce Franklin, basing his observation on the research of Hungarian musicologist Janos Marothy, has suggested a connection between sea shanties and North American slave songs (Franklin 95–96). Even without this specific musico-historical link, one could point out that the working conditions of sailors (who were often indentured servants) were comparable to those of unpaid and brutalized workers (slaves); until 1915 sailors were de jure as well as de facto treated as wards of the state deemed incapable of taking intelligent responsibility for themselves (Nelson 20 ff.). And in ports of call, nautical culture made its mark through the transient, tinged-with-scariness allure of Sailortowns, such as the Combat Zone in Boston, which bore some of the same stigmas and stereotypes as other, more stably populated neighborhoods of the urban poor or of racial/ethnic or sexual minorities. San Francisco, in fact, became a "gay mecca" in part because of the large population of men discharged from the area's naval base after World War II (D'Emilio 31).

In addition, as global migrants, sailors often had experiences that taught them cultural relativism (for example, Black seafarers had the opportunity to see how different race relations functioned in Africa, Asia, or Europe); their relative worldliness added to the openness and unpredictability of the mix, the sense of possibility that things could be different *here*, founded on the lived knowledge that things *are* different elsewhere. That this counterculture/subculture was overwhelmingly male in origin makes the place of women, and particularly women of color, charged and volatile: a hot spot within a hot spot—a sun-spot. The Doowop women, at least, flourished, though not without pain (Shange's "wow . . . yr just like a man!" [*Nappy Edges* 13] details the fury and frustration of having to negotiate a legitimate place in a world of male artists); plumes of fiery color, extravagantly wild expressions of creative self-engenderment spiraled out from this decentered center of activity.

To invoke again Antonio Benítez-Rojo's formulation, the culture of the Peoples of the Sea, in this case the Bay Area's multilingual, multiethnic, multiracial arts community, survives in and on the desire to transform—to sublimate—social violence by jumping discursive tracks, as it were, by living in the poetic, the oceanic state of consciousness. This is what Hagedorn means when she valorizes "staying crazy" under the massive pressure of social violence trained on people of color in the United States. To remain in a vast universal polyrhythmicity—kozmic doowop—where rhythms pulsate in eternal but unpredictable flux, not in competition but in concert—commune—is a political strategy for these artists, a means of psychic survival. To be beyond imprisonment or liberty is to encompass both in the same experience, the holy marriage of the horizons, the thin liminal seam of the poetic, the systematic alteration of normative insight. Shange has a poem entitled "This woman thinks we're de beauvoir and jean-paul/ never forget/ i'ma spic and yr a colored girl" (*Nappy Edges* 35). The rending and mind-bending double consciousness of being intellectual comrades and erotic lovers like Sartre and de Beauvoir, on the one hand, and, on the other, being objects of contempt, violence with impunity, and the assumption of subhumanity in a social situation of state racism, can destroy young artists of color. It can also spur them to seek out that horizon, that marriage of land/sea, to dwell in those contradictions with fierce grace and gratitude, and at the risk of sounding banal, community and contact can make the difference between self-destructive implosion and extravagant creative explosion. The poem concludes:

> whatta unlikely wonder is we/
> lovers in a seaport kinda way . . .
> the way we wrap up in the mornin/ is
> all our world
> we're entitled

> (*Nappy Edges* 36)

Poetry can't offer an *alternative* to social violence—that would be insultingly naive and optimistic, and as teachers of literature we surely know better. But poetry—and I hope I've given some examples above—can *intervene* actively in a world of social violence. Shange's lines

> i found god in myself
> & i loved her/i loved her fiercely
>
> (*For Colored Girls* 63)

have become virtually doctrinal to some feminists. "Staying crazy" means cocreating continued active resistance—through making words and taking words in—to normative discourse. This I would say is the key difference between island culture defined as remote and claustrophobic, and island culture defined as contactual, generative, and unbounded. If California's *insularity* is an imperialist trope (that Eden end we can use any means to get to—and they did) California's *liminality* makes it an appropriate launching pad for experiments in cultural politics that have profound repercussions for the rest of the country's social and aesthetic self-understanding.

Finally, we can learn from these artists how to be of use to ourselves. In investigating the depths of these communities of vanguard artists and allowing our soundings to filter into our own academic labor—which we and our students so often experience as alienated, solipsistic, *isolated*—we can enrich and *liminate* our own professional and poetic lives, rewriting literary studies from the ground—at sea level, *in salo*—on up.

WORKS CITED

Artaud, Antonin. *Antonin Artaud, Selected Writings.* Ed. Susan Sontag. New York: Farrar, 1976.

———. *Artaud Anthology.* Ed. Jack Hirschman. San Francisco: City Lights, 1965.

Benítez-Rojo, Antonio. *The Repeating Island: The Caribbean and the Postmodern Perspective.* Durham: Duke UP, 1992.

Bey, Hakim. *Temporary Autonomous Zones.* New York: Autonomedia, 1991.

Clifford, James. "Traveling Culture." *Cultural Studies.* Ed. Lawrence Grossberg, Cary Nelson, and Paula A. Treichler. New York: Routledge, 1992. 96–112.

Coen, Joel and Ethan Coen. Interview with Noah Adams. *All Things Considered*. Natl. Public Radio. 8 March 1996.

Davis, Thulani Nkabinde. "Known Renegades: Recent Black/Brown/Yellow." *The Poetry Reading: A Contemporary Compendium on Language and Performance*. Ed. Stephen Vincent and Ellen Zweig. San Francisco: Momo's, 1981. 68–84.

D'Emilio, John. *Sexual Politics, Sexual Communities: The Making of a Homosexual Minority in the United States, 1940–1970*. Chicago: U of Chicago P, 1983.

Franklin, H. Bruce. *Prison Literature in America: The Victim as Criminal and Artist*. Westport, Conn.: Hill, 1978.

Gilroy, Paul. *The Black Atlantic: Modernity and Double Consciousness*. Cambridge: Harvard UP, 1993.

Hagedorn, Jessica Tarahata. *Danger and Beauty*. Harmondsworth, Eng.: Penguin, 1993.

———. *Dangerous Music*. San Francisco: Momo's, 1975.

Jackson, George. *Soledad Brother: The Prison Letters of George Jackson*. New York: Coward, 1970.

Kaufman, Bob. *The Ancient Rain: Poems 1956–1978*. New York: New Directions, 1981.

———. *Solitudes Crowded with Loneliness*. New York: New Directions, 1965.

Marothy, Janos. *Music and the Bourgeois; Music and the Proletarian*. Budapest: Akademiai Kiado, 1974.

Nelson, Bruce. *Workers on the Waterfront: Seamen, Longshoremen and Unionism in the 1930s*. Urbana: U of Illinois P, 1988.

Pratt, Mary Louise. *Imperial Eyes: Travel Writing and Colonialism*. New York: Routledge, 1993.

Rosenbaum, Fred. *Free to Choose: The Making of a Jewish Community in the American West (the Jews of Oakland, California)*. Berkeley: Judah L. Magnes Memorial Museum, 1976.

Shange, Ntozake. *For Colored Girls Who Have Considered Suicide When the Rainbow Is Enuf: A Choreopoem in Three Acts*. New York: St. Martin's, 1974.

———. *I Live in Music*. Audio cassette. Watershed Intermedia, 1984.

———. *Nappy Edges*. New York: St. Martin's, 1978.

Stierle, Karlheinz. "Identité du Discours et Transgression Lyrique." Trans. Jean-Paul Colin. *Poétique* 32 (Nov. 1977): 422–41.

Third World Communications Publishing Collective, eds. *Time to Greez!*

An Anthology of Third World Writing. San Francisco: Third World Publishing Collective, 1974.

Watanabe, Sylvia, ed. *Into the Fire: Asian American Prose.* Greenfield, N.Y.: Greenfield Review Press, 1997.

Wilson, Rob, and Wimal Dissenyake. *Global/Local: Cultural Production and the Imaginary.* Durham: Duke UP, 1996.

CONTRIBUTORS

CHARLES ALTIERI, author of *Enlarging the Temple, Art and Quality, Self and Sensibility in Contemporary American Poetry, Painterly Abstraction and Modernist American Poetry,* and *Subjective Agency,* teaches modern literature and literary theory at the University of California, Berkeley. He has just finished a book called *Postmodernism Now* and is working on ways to adapt philosophical treatments of the emotions to the study of modern poetry.

MARÍA BOLÍVAR has a Ph.D. in Spanish literature from the University of California, San Diego, and she is an assistant professor at Arizona State University, Tempe. She is the author of the poetry collections *Ciudad que se me escapa,* published by the Universidad Autónoma de Sinaloa, and *La palabra (H)era,* awarded first prize at the Sixteenth Chicano Literary Competition, 1989–90, University of California, Irvine. Other poems and short stories have been published by Blanc O Móvil, Mester, Sahuaro and the Institute for Regional Studies of the Californias. Her essays on cultural criticism entitled "Los reflejos del tiempo en el lenguaje" and "Huérfanas, abandonadas y bastardas: Las historias que emergen del silencio" were included in the book *Sin imágenes falsas, sin falsos espejos,* published in 1996 by El Colegio de México. "Terra incógnita" appears in the collection *Mujeres latinoamericanas: Historia y cultura. Siglos XVI–XIX,* published by Casa de las Américas in 1997. She is the author of *Topografías, tipografías y subjetividades,* on the fictitious role of history in Mexico at the turn of the century. She has just finished the book *Mapping Terrains, Forging Voices,* a culturist approach to noncanonical texts and voices in contemporary Mexico.

JACQUELINE VAUGHT BROGAN, professor of English at the University of Notre Dame, is herself a poet, critic, and theorist. Among her published works are *Stevens and Simile: A Theory of Language* and *Part of the Climate: American Cubist Poetry,* as well as numerous articles on such writers as Gertrude Stein, Elizabeth Bishop, June Jordan, Adrienne Rich, and Alice Walker. Her own poetry has appeared in numerous journals around the country, from *Kalliope* to *The Wallace Stevens Journal,* from the experimental *HOW(ever)* to *The Formalist.*

MARTINE WATSON BROWNLEY is Goodrich C. White Professor of English at Emory University and former director of the Emory Institute for Women's Studies. Among her publications in English literature are two books on Clarendon and articles on Johnson, Gibbon, and others; in women's studies she has co-edited *Mothering the Mind* and published on Behn, Piozzi, and Atwood.

CORDELIA CANDELARIA is professor of American literature at Arizona State University in the Departments of English and Chicana and Chicano Studies. She is the author of *Arroyos to the Heart* (poetry, Santa Monica College Press, 1993); *Seeking the Perfect Game: Baseball in American Literature* (Greenwood Press, 1989); *Chicano Poetry, a Critical Introduction* (Greenwood Press, 1986); *Ojo de la Cueva/ Cave Spring* (poetry, Maize Press, 1984), and many other titles. Her most recent publications include essays in Warhol and Herndl's *Feminisms: An Anthology of Literary Theory and Criticism* (rev. ed. 1997) and in Hernandez-Gutierrez and Foster's *Literatura Chicana, 1965–1995* (1997), as well as new poetry in Wright and Cervantes's *Fever Dreams, Arizona Poets* (1997).

MARIA DAMON teaches poetry and poetics at the University of Minnesota. She is the author of *The Dark End of the Street: Margins in American Vanguard Poetry* (Minnesota University Press, 1993), as well as numerous articles on poetry, cultural studies, and ethnic identity. She is a member of the National Writers' Union.

MARGARET DICKIE, Helen S. Lanier Distinguished Professor of English, University of Georgia, has written books on Hart Crane, Sylvia Plath and Ted Hughes, the modernist long poem, Emily Dickinson and Wallace Stevens, and Gertrude Stein, Elizabeth Bishop, and Adrienne Rich.

CELESTE GOODRIDGE, professor of English at Bowdoin College, is the author of *Hints and Disguises: Marianne Moore and Her Contemporaries,* and coeditor, with Bonnie Costello and Cristanne Miller, of *The Selected Letters of Marianne Moore.* She is currently working on a book entitled *Consuming Lives: Biographers, Subjects and Readers.*

LAURA HINTON, assistant professor of English at the City College of New York, is the author of *The Perverse Gaze of Sympathy: Sadomasochistic Sentiments from* Clarissa *to* Rescue 911 (SUNY Press, 1999). She also has published articles in *Women's Studies, Eighteenth-Century Studies,* and *Film Criticism,* as well as an interview with Leslie Scalapino and Lyn Hejinian in *Private Arts.* She is currently working on a book on contemporary women's fiction and theories of fetishism.

CYNTHIA HOGUE directs the Stadler Center for Poetry at Bucknell University, where she is associate professor of English. She has published two collections of poetry, most recently *The Woman in Red* (1990), and a critical study of American women's poetry, *Scheming Women: Poetry, Privilege, and the Politics of Subjectivity* (1995). She has been awarded NEA, NEH, and Fulbright-Hayes Fellowships for her work. Her third collection of poems is *Three Streets from Desire.* She is at work on a fourth collection of poems, entitled *The Incognito Body.*

JANET MCADAMS, assistant professor of English at the University of Oklahoma, is presently writing a critical study of contemporary Native American poetry. Her poetry, fiction, and reviews have appeared in *TriQuarterly, Poetry, North American Review, Indiana*

Review, Lullwater Review, Black Warrior Review, American Indian Quarterly, and other journals.

SUSAN MCCABE is an assistant professor at Arizona State University. Her book *Elizabeth Bishop: Her Poetics of Loss* appeared in 1994, published by Penn State Press. She is currently working on a book on H.D., Mina Loy, and Stein which examines the relationships between modernist poetics and early cinematic method.

CRISTANNE MILLER, W. M. Keck Distinguished Service Professor and professor of English at Pomona College, is author or editor of several books and essays on Emily Dickinson. In addition, her recent publications include *Feminist Measures: Soundings in Poetry and Theory*, coedited with Lynn Keller (University of Michigan, 1994), *Marianne Moore: Questions of Authority* (Harvard, 1995), and *The Selected Letters of Marianne Moore*, coedited with Bonnie Costello and Celeste Goodridge (Knopf, 1997).

SANFORD PINSKER is Shadek Professor of Humanities at Franklin and Marshall College. He writes widely about American literature and culture and is the author of several collections of poetry, including, most recently, *Oedipus Meets the Press and Other Tragi-Comedies of the Time.*

SUSAN R. VAN DYNE is professor of women's studies and English and is director of the Women's Studies Program at Smith College. She is working on a book, *In-siting Poetry: Contemporary American Women Poets and Their Traditions,* which explores the politics of representation and the construction of literary traditions. With Marilyn Schuster, she edited *Women's Place in the Academy: Transforming the Liberal Arts* (1985). *Revising Life: Sylvia Plath's Ariel Poems* (1993) analyzes the interrelationships of gender and the creative process, especially the ways Plath reworked autobiography in composing and revising her late poems.

ANNA WILSON has published three novels, *Cactus, Altogether Elsewhere,* and *Hatching Stones.* She has recently completed a study of feminist interventions in the public sphere, *Persuasive Fictions and Perceived Changes: Feminist Narrative and Critical Myth,* which argues for a reassessment of the received notion that (feminist) books change lives. She currently teaches American literature, women's studies, and lesbian and gay studies at Bowdoin College.

INDEX

279

Index

Index

Index